if You find this Letter

this

Letter

My Journey to Find Purpose Through
Hundreds of Letters to Strangers

a memoir

Hannah Brencher

HOWARD BOOKS
A Division of Simon & Schuster, Inc.
New York   Nashville   London   Toronto   Sydney   New Delhi

Howard Books
A Division of Simon & Schuster, Inc.
1230 Avenue of the Americas
New York, NY 10020

Copyright © 2015 by Hannah Brencher
Certain names and identifying characteristics have been changed.

First Howard Books hardcover edition March 2015

HOWARD and colophon are trademarks of Simon & Schuster, Inc.

For information about special discounts for bulk purchases, please contact Simon & Schuster Special Sales at 1-866-506-1949 or business@simonandschuster.com.

The Simon & Schuster Speakers Bureau can bring authors to your live event. For more information or to book an event contact the Simon & Schuster Speakers Bureau at 1-866-248-3049 or visit our website at www.simonspeakers.com.

Interior design by Davina Mock-Maniscalco

Manufactured in the United States of America

10   9   8   7   6   5   4   3   2   1

Library of Congress Cataloging-in-Publication Data

Brencher, Hannah.
  If you find this letter : my journey to find purpose through hundreds of letters to strangers / Hannah Brencher.
     pages cm
1. Brencher, Hannah. 2. Letter writing—Biography. 3. Love-letters. I. Title.
  PN6140.L7B73 2015
  808.86'93543—dc23
  [B]
                                    2014028453

ISBN 978-1-4767-7360-5
ISBN 978-1-4767-7362-9 (ebook)

To Nate—
For the stuff of angels, movements, and things bigger than this.

Interviewer: What is something you always carry with you?

Maya Angelou: I'm a child of God. I carry that with me.

Note from the Author

The names and identifying characteristics of the characters in the book have been changed, except for a few, to protect the guilty and the innocent. While all the actions within the book have happened, there are particular events that have been combined and reordered to maintain the book's continuity. I tried my best to piece together events through research, conversations, digital evidence, and journals. There are undoubtedly things I've gotten wrong but all the situations remain true, to the best of my memory.

Dear Reader

$\mathcal{E}$verything about your narrator is unreliable except for her heart.

I needed to say that first and get it out in the open before we go any further. Before you bunch up your hands into fists and strap on your extra-loud clomping boots so you can clomp-clomp-clomp all the way back to the bookstore and roar into the ear of the manager, "Youuuu solddddd meeee a boooookkkk with annnn unreliablleeeee narrattttorrrrr! Rarrrr!" No, he didn't, I told you first that I am unreliable.

I'm unpredictable. I write poems in my head as I roll through Target. I live life in the clouds. And I will let you down. Because I am human. And that's what humans do. More often than we would like.

I built stories in my brain all throughout my childhood and I think it's followed me well into adulthood. My mother is probably still clutching her face, aghast over the thought of people reading this, wondering if I will think to bust out the tale of the time she sent my brother down the river in a basket when he was just a newborn. I shared that story with my second-grade class. That was actually Moses, not my brother.

But my heart is good and golden. We won't be steered wrong as long as my heart leads.

I'm going to be reliable in my writing to you. Faithful, in a way I never learned how to be when I had seventeen pen pals to my name from a single subscription of Girls' Life magazine yet never thought to write to a single one of them. They wrote to me for a little while. They sent me glossy photos and I took them to school to show them off as "sisters" but I never picked up the pen to write back. I guess I felt I only had time in my life to receive the mail and pat myself on the back for collecting pretty friends from Kansas and Kentucky like trading cards.

But this time will be different. I am going to sit down and write to you in a start-to-finish kind of way, as if this whole thing were a love letter that I am hoping you will find. And I am praying, if you find this letter, it will be words you've needed for a long while. Whether you've struggled with loneliness. Or worthlessness. Or connection in a disconnected world. This story is for you. It's written for anyone who's been afraid to turn off their phone at night or say goodbye come morning. To the winners. And the losers. And above all, the dreamers. For the ones with yellow roses on their countertops and strong caffeinated drinks in their hands. For the ones who still miss Whitney Houston or struggle at night over the reasons why they're here. This book is for anyone who has ever believed their smallness could not serve others. For anyone who grapples to fit within a world that doesn't always hold them so dearly.

Truth be told, I never imagined you and I would meet like this. Not a fold or crook of this story was ever one I imagined others would find or retell to their friends. I only envisioned myself with swooping hands, one day telling babies with the same sunshine red ringlets as me, "One day in New York City, your mama started writing love letters to strangers. She would leave them behind wherever she went. She liked it so much that she decided never to stop. Others joined her and they, too, liked it so much that they decided never to stop."

I thought this would only be a story to show those children of mine how much human hands do matter. Within a world that is always talking too loudly about what it means to "matter," I wanted this entire story to tell them the truth of it: that they will matter when the sun is up and when it is down. When there is sunburn on their shoulders or when their shoes no longer fit. Or their luggage never arrives. Or they come back from Paris with a ramshackle heart and one less body beside them. I wanted this story to convince them that they matter, always, and that the point has never been to know it but just to accept it.

Yes, this was supposed to be the story they could carry with them when they could hold me no longer. But now you're here. You picked me up somewhere. Somehow, you've found me. I have to believe there's a reason for that.

Tying you closer than most,
hb

Section 1

Make Me Come Undone

Sticky Love

The day I moved to New York City is way more poetic in my memory than it actually was. My mother would tell you the air was dry that morning and we didn't talk the whole car ride to the train station. I tend to exaggerate the whole thing and say I witnessed the birds chirping and the mailboxes waving good-bye with their little red flags as we rolled through New Haven, Connecticut, to get to the station. She would tell you I left stray bobby pins in the corners of my bedroom. I would say I packed everything I needed that day—dreams tucked beside cardigans and wishes packed up against rain boots.

That's always been my downfall, the thing my mother always calls me out on. I romanticize things. I insert heartbreak where there shouldn't be any. I feel things too deeply. I hold on much longer than I should. All of life has always been one big book of poems to me. I think every person is a living poem—from their hopeful heart to their ugly habits. Life is just too busy to ever stop and dwell on one thing for too long.

In actuality, the back wheel to one of my suitcases broke and everything was off balance after that. The wheelless luggage taunted me from the backseat as my mother and I took exit 1 off the highway and approached the New Haven train station.

I refused to tell my mother about the broken wheel. She's never been the anxious type, but she would have worried. And she would have tried—with every last motherly shred in her—to help her baby out.

That was me—the baby of the family. There was my older half brother, my real brother who I used to claim was my Irish twin (he isn't), and then me. I always tell people I am a balance between my mother's whimsy and my father's dirt-beneath-the-fingernails work ethic. I'm drawn to deep conversations with people and good-looking Spanish men because of my mother. I'm sucked into collecting things because of my father. The two of them make a good team. My father has been bringing things into our house for years, hoarder-style, and my mother has been waiting for him to fall asleep on the couch to cart all of it off to Goodwill. I'm somewhere in the middle—always wanting to hold on to everything that comes into my orbit and let it go all at the same time.

For the longest time growing up, a lot of people didn't even know I existed. People were surprised to learn the gangly, redheaded child who was silently weaving friendship bracelets beside the fences at baseball games was the sister of these boys who were town legends when it came to diamonds, or courts, or any kind of arena that was competitive. I lived in their shadows a lot. It wasn't anything I did on purpose. I just kept to myself. And I liked constructing my own little worlds where I could control all the elements and pretend I was best friends with all the good-looking men and women in the JC Penney catalog, models I cut out and pasted into my little-kid diaries.

I was the last one of the family to leave the house with the turquoise shutters and morph my parents into empty-nesters. My oldest brother had gone off to college and then moved in with his girlfriend. He and I were different in the sense that he's always known just what he wanted and gone after it. And me? I'm more of the type to have an existential crisis over selecting a coffee flavor for the morning. My other brother struggled with addiction at the time, so he lived in the house when he was sober and out of the house when he was not.

* * *

As we waited for the train, I watched my mother wedge something into the belly of my suitcase, with the hope I wasn't looking. I tried to force myself to forget it was there. I fidgeted and folded my ticket, waiting to leave. I knew it was a letter. It was always a letter.

My mother is a nostalgic creature. There are three things you should know about my mother: The first is that she is always, somehow, the life of every party. The second is that any person my mother has ever loved could tell you the exact way a kazoo sounds when it's left in a voice mail on your birthday. It's nailed tight to my memories of growing up—watching her flip through the pages of her address book and find the name of whoever it was she'd marked on her calendar. I remember hearing the dialing of the cordless phone. My mother would wait. And then the sound of a kazoo being played to the tune of "Happy Birthday" would stream throughout the house.

The third thing to know about my mother is that she's a nostalgic creature and I have to believe she made me into one too. She's hidden love letters for me to find all my life. There was a note tucked on top of a piece of chocolate cake when heartbreak visited my freshman dorm room for the first time. There was a card left on my dashboard the day after Whitney Houston died. Confetti fell out from the inside. Musical notes skittered across the front. She wrote six words to me in red Sharpie: *And I will always love you.* I am the product of my mother's bread crumb trails of love letters.

Every coming and going we've ever shared has been built up with letters, notes, trinkets, and the like, as if tiny wedges of paper and confetti could keep a person always coming back. She'd trailed tiny clues four years earlier as we moved me into my first dorm room. I found letters tucked in plastic Tupperware bins and notes within books I hadn't even opened yet. Pieces of my mother would pop up and appear throughout the semester. In random classes. At staff meetings. On retreats. My mother is an expert at leaving evidence she was here in the lives of everyone around her.

One of the notes she mailed to me in my first week of college included a long quote she'd copied from *O, The Oprah Magazine* while sitting in a waiting room of a doctor's office. The quote was about a mother and a daughter. The final point of release. The girl was leaving, marching into adulthood without her mother's steady hand to hold. The girl turned at the door and the mother went to reach out, wanting to tell her daughter one last thing, but she pulled back instead. It was that moment when the mother finally had to say, "I've given everything I can and I have to trust it is enough. She must go out there and see and feel and understand the rest on her own."

The breath fell out of me when I read that quote for the first time. I kept reading it out loud. I felt bare and exposed through my mother's scratchy handwriting whenever I read it. The card with the quote inside of it somehow got lost and my mother couldn't remember what issue of O she found it within. I spent the next summer going through every O magazine at the town library, looking for any last evidence the paragraph ever existed, but I never found it. I'm still looking.

The letters from my mother kept coming throughout college. I was one of the only students who had a reason to go to their PO box at the end of the day, and that was mainly because my mother didn't have a cell phone or text messaging or any kind of social network to check into. I'd told her a bunch of times she should get a cell phone but she only ever said the same thing back to me: "I've gone over fifty years without anyone needing to find me. Why start now?"

I guess I never understood the power in her letters, or the reason why she sent them, until my grandmother died. I was a college freshman when she passed. It was September. The air was changing. My grandmother had spent that whole summer sitting in a hospital bed, delirious. She was like a stranger who borrowed the eyes of someone I loved. I knew my mother and all her siblings were just waiting for the release, a way to tell one another she was finally gone and in a better place.

I moved into my first dorm room with the assurance I would get the phone call about my grandmother soon. You know the kind of phone call. I remember sitting in my orientation program on the first night of college while leaders clad in matching outfits pranced around, strumming guitars and rapping like only white people can, initiating icebreakers that made us reveal the layers of our summer vacation like an onion. When it came time to share about my summer, I fought the urge to say, "This summer I learned how death unbuilds a house. Brick by brick. Shingle by shingle. Death shows up like a worker who rises to beat the sun and spends his days undoing a person you learned to love with your whole body. He unchisels and unscrews until nothing is left but the skinny frame and eye sockets of someone you used to know. That's what I learned. Do you want to sing a song about it?"

The call came three weeks into the semester. In the span of a weekend, I heard my father deliver the news, packed a duffel bag full of all the black clothing I owned, traveled home, tried to apply mascara to swollen eyes, laughed until I couldn't help but cry, swapped stupid memories with cousins, watched my grandmother get closed in a casket, and learned that missing someone is just the beginning of grief. Then I traveled back to college to push forward into my fall semester. It happened quickly, like ripping off the Band-Aid, trying to pretend there was no sting. Death is like that—it can teach you more in forty-eight hours than you've learned in a lifetime.

The letter from my mother came in a golden envelope just a few days later. The envelopes never matched the cards but they were always the brightest colors she could find in the card aisle. Silver. Indigo. Lilac. A small sun—gold and stenciled—was on the front of the card. I stood there, in the middle of my college's post office, sucking in my mother's words:

It's beautiful outside. We took Scarlett and Chloe for a hike the other day. I've started crying. Finally. I find myself going into the bathroom, shutting the door, and spitting on the bathroom floor. Something feels freeing about that.

I pictured my mother hocking wads of saliva onto the tile floor. Spitting and crying. Spitting and crying. Trying, through the spitting, to let her sadness release. Letting loose on the linoleum. The image in my mind looked pitiful. Desperate. Too hard to watch for a girl who'd only ever allowed her mother to be strong in her eyes. It was one of the first times I realized you can tell a completely different story to someone when you've got all the vulnerable space of a page to back you up. You can say things you might not have the courage to say elsewhere. You can let honesty loose on the page and then fold it up and drop it in the mailbox. Away, away the release of your troubles could fly.

That letter is still the most treasured chunk of my mother I hold. Like a secret only I know. I kept the card on my wall all four years of college. I packed it with me on the day I moved to New York City.

"Do you need any help?" she asked as I bustled the suitcase with the broken wheel onto the platform.

"No," I told her. "I have this."

She tried to reach for the handle but I snapped at her. "I need to do this on my own. You need to learn to let me go."

She got real quiet. I wasn't being nice. I get snappy when I know a good-bye is coming. I sort of shut down and close off. The last thing I wanted my mother to know was that all of this was hard for me.

Realistically, I would only be a couple hours away from her. But somehow we both knew something different was happening this time. It wasn't like the kind of good-bye you said before college or summer camp. It sat in the throat for a very long time and made you hope you'd learned enough from the other person to be okay on your own.

"You have everything you need?" she asked. I nodded. "I made this for you. For the train. If you get hungry." She pulled out a thick wedge of tinfoil from her red pocketbook and placed it into the side pocket of my carry-on bag. Without unfolding the square mess of silver, I knew it was two peanut butter and jelly sandwiches. Four slices of whole wheat bread. Peanut butter from Trader Joe's. Raspberry jelly.

She'd handed me those wads of tinfoil for the last fifteen years. They were the first form of religion I ever knew, before a Bible or a pew. Just several sandwiches she carried with her always to pass out to hungry people she would see along the way in New York City. She never took a train into the city without them. She taught me to be a brave little child who walked up to bums and handed them peanut butter and banana sandwiches. No matter how many sandwiches she packed to hand out, there was always one left for me. It was her way to tell me, "You've got this. You've got this day, but you'll grow hungry along the way." All those years, we called it Sticky Love.

And that's just what my mother always told me to aim for—Sticky Love. It's different than a skinny kind of love. It is a love so much rarer than the kind your eighth-grade boyfriend could give you. It's big. It's loud. It makes you into the kind of person who leaves something behind when they finally turn to walk away. And though no one can quite touch it or understand the DNA of it, everyone can still tell, by the way the atmosphere has shifted in the room, something was left behind.

As the train pulled into the station, she reached in for a hug. "I love you. Be good. Be safe," she whispered. It felt like we'd been on that train platform for hours.

"I love you too," I whispered back. We pulled away and I walked toward the train.

I hoped the engine would start and pull away quickly. I needed her to go home. Like I said, good-byes have never really been my thing. I'd rather go in the night. Leave a note. Walk away quickly and not linger in a hug. I don't want to be the one left standing there. It's the hardest part about making new friends and giving them rent space in your heart; you have to be okay when they tell you it's time to go away.

I tried to focus on the passengers around me. They were staring down at their newspapers. There were businessmen wearing suits that looked stifling in the August heat. I noticed a woman two rows up standing outside the train. She was putting her hands up against the window and leaning her forehead against the tinted glass. It was my mother. Trying to find me. One last time.

She looked crazy enough to scare the people sitting in the seats ahead of me, with her head of gray hair and plain desperation painted across her face. She didn't look like poetry in that moment. She looked like someone who didn't know how to say good-bye.

She went window after window until she came up next to mine. I sat back as far as I could in the seat and sank down low so she wouldn't see me. If she found me, she would see the tears dribbling down my cheeks. She would know I was afraid of everything ahead of me. Of never finding significance. Of missing the point. It was like I packed each emotion up the second I felt it, not wanting to look it in the face. That sort of stuff becomes baggage if you don't take the time to unpack it.

She peered for a few moments and then walked back to the middle of the platform, her red satchel at her side and matching red flip-flops on her feet. I put my hand up against the window and scripted a letter to her silently in my mind.

Mama,

Life is looking brighter than it ever has before. Even with you looking a bit pathetic with your face smashed up against the train window, we both know that life is looking bright for me.

This is my chance to make you prouder than you've ever been before. I know you'd tell me you're proud already, that no motive in life should ever be about making someone proud, but I can't help but want it.

Now is my chance to show you that I can find my place in the world. Maybe find God too. (I know that you and I haven't always agreed on Him—how He looks or how He smells—but I still thank you for at least giving me something to believe in that's bigger than my own body, even if I don't fully understand it. I'll keep my eyes open for Him in Manhattan.)

I know you're worried about me. Not because you think I am incapable but because you secretly have always worried that life would go by without my ever learning how to stomp in the puddles or fall in love. I can promise you I'll learn. If anyone is a teacher for that kind of stuff, it has got to be New York.

Thank you for letting go. Even if we both could have held on longer, thank you for letting me go.

Love,
Your girl

I never did say those things to her. So many of the things you think and want to say to a person never spill out in real life. They stay locked in secret rooms inside of you. They live for tiny lifetimes inside the hearts of people who don't have the courage to say what they meant this whole time. Some people leave, and go, and die, and change, without your ever getting to tell them how you truly feel about them.

My mother began to wander away from the platform. The train started pulling away slowly. I watched her body get smaller and smaller on the platform. I made quiet promises beneath my breath I hoped would float out from the windows of the southbound train and get stuck in her hair. "I'm going to try to make you proud. So proud."

Dotted Lines and Destinations

There's a common story that gets told about girls who move to New York City to follow their dreams. Their days are detailed by long work hours squeezed down to the second by fascist fashion editors, sweeping racks of the fall's runway trends, and dozens of errands to master—all while balancing a cardboard tray of piping-hot lattes on pencil-thin heels. The protagonist is beautiful in a way that is hard to lay a finger on. She's known to be awkward and clumsy but roars into every conversation with striking ambition. She knows what she wants. She's the underdog in a lot of ways. And there's a dream that's heavy and twinkling in her eyes.

I memorized that story line. Swallowed it whole. Spent years consuming it as if it were a dessert plate I couldn't quite lick clean. The day *The Devil Wears Prada* came out and we all got our hands on some sort of Holy Grail insight into the fashion magazine world, I got even hungrier. I wanted the long to-do lists, the longer days, and a role that would bring me to the top of my field with a lot of hustle and hard work. I wanted to be the New York City girl who could hail a cab with a slight flick of the wrist, walk across the street with reckless abandonment, and parade around in clothes from every notable collection while being chic enough to know black comes in more than one shade.

But there was something about those stories that always pricked me. They always left this deep, unsettled feeling in my stomach. Right at the end, the girl—no matter her ambition—would always fall in love. She fell in love or her love fell apart and then came back together, but the closing scenes were never just of her. I'd followed her all the way there, clutching my pillow, thinking, *That's me, that's me.* But I always felt abandoned at the end of those movies.

In a world that has always made me feel like I need to constantly be looking for "the one"—to find my missing puzzle piece of the sky in a sea of blue cardboard cutouts—I wanted something else. It's no one's fault we operate like this. There are enough movies and books and advertisements out there to convince all single people that we are missing pieces. That we haven't arrived yet. That we must hurry to meet someone, even if we are floundering to just figure out who we are in all of this. I wanted the kind of love story that made me stop and count the wrinkles in the hands of the saxophone player in Central Park. To say thank-you and really mean it. To know in my gut there was a reason to hurdle suitcases in the middle of Grand Central to just catch that train in time. To wake up believing there might be magic for me. I wanted to find something in this lifetime to make me know it's all worth it.

I wanted to learn to live inside of a life that said, "Girl, this whole dang thing is your love story. It's not a tragedy. It ain't a victim song or a blank notebook waiting for a pen to scribble inside of it. It's a love story, ready to climb on up those silly castle walls you've built. So, baby, let down your hair."

There was a guy at the beginning, though. And the reality is pretty simple: I fell for a guy who never chose me. It's not the prettiest story. It isn't really the thing you bring up over Thanksgiving dinner or while dyeing Easter eggs with your relatives. But that was the story I carried at this point in my life.

I met him in my last semester of college. Chaotic and messy, the tail end of senior year is like a war zone. It's like the Hunger Games with résumés and career fairs and good-bye dinners. Everyone starts clawing to just stretch out the semester. People act all sorts of irrational. They start professing their love to each other because either (a) they don't think they'll get another chance to, or (b) they're just so desperate to hang on to someone they think might hold them longer than the flimsy few days left on the calendar before the "real world" comes stomping through.

The "real world." That's what we called it up until graduation. They were taboo words no one was really allowed to say out loud. It was like talking about Voldemort square in the middle of Hogwarts. We bought suits for job interviews. We prepared résumés and learned how to balance cheese plates and wineglasses while passing out business cards so we could look really prepared and at ease when we attended cheesy networking events. We tiptoed around the subject of "what's next" over Natty Ice and Barefoot wine until someone got too drunk and started crying. As graduation loomed in the near distance, someone always took it upon themselves to quiet the circle.

"Shhhh . . . We can't talk about it anymore," they'd say. "We need to stop talking about the 'real world' and just enjoy this moment."

We were all just trying to avoid the inevitable: What's next?

His name was Ryan. I met him in an English class. He asked me for a spare sheet of notebook paper. That single sheet of loose-leaf paper was like a bridge between us. It spurred the occasional walking out of class together, talking about assignments and other surface-level things. I liked the way he laughed and his whole face would get red. And half the time I hadn't even planned to walk in the direction he was walking in but I made up all sorts of excuses just to talk to him for a little while longer. Without even trying, the ten minutes between 10:20 and 10:30 in the morning—when we would walk and talk on the way to all the places I never needed to go—became the best part of my day.

We were sitting in my car one night after I'd offered him a ride up to his apartment. It was pouring outside. The drive was only two minutes but the conversation kept going. The engine sat idle. I turned the car off. The connection was effortless. The rain didn't stop. My cheeks were burning. I was afraid to even move, afraid whatever this thing was would be gone. His lips kept moving but I felt like I'd disappeared from the car. *Like, can it really happen that way? Can you really just meet someone—get sucked into a conversation that feels like both a second and a decade all in one breath—and never be the same again? Can a connection to a stranger be that powerful?*

I felt my stomach flipping. And when I write *stomach*, I really mean *heart*, but I am not so sure why people say you feel something in your heart when, really, you just feel nervous enough to vomit all over the other person. My stomach was in knots the entire conversation. And it was my stomach that flipped when he said her name.

She had a name. He already had someone. They had a history. And as he told me more and more about his girlfriend, I didn't find myself angry or even jealous. I just kept thinking to myself, *She's a lucky girl. She's a really lucky girl to have you.*

Listening to him talk about her stirred a tiny hope inside of me that one day someone out there would talk about me the same way. His cheeks would glow, and his eyes would get real big. I knew I wanted that.

Hope. I kept thinking it was hope at one day finding that as I watched him get out of my car and run for the door that night. I thought it was hope that carried me to the door of my apartment, not even caring if the rain sloshed all over my face. I thought it was hope—just hope—but then this unexpected sense of sadness swept through me as I slipped into my bed that night and tried to fall asleep. It was this empty, hollow feeling. Part of me wished I had gotten there first. Like I wished history could rewrite itself while you were sleeping at night and maybe you'd wake up to a different plotline in the morning beneath your pillow, like a dollar bill replacing a front tooth.

I never meant to be the other girl. It wasn't exactly the heroic agenda I plotted for myself. And I learned really quickly how unendearing the whole mess of it is. To your friends. To your family. It's easy enough to surround yourself with the kinds of people who tell you to hold out, you might win in the end. They'll be the ones to sit beside you and dissect all the Facebook photos to see if the two are standing closer together or farther apart than the picture before. I look back and think it's kind of crazy we live in the kind of culture that glamorizes stealing another person's "someone." Nothing feels glamorous when you're inside of it. It feels really empty, especially when you're forced to try sleeping with the truth spooning you: It's not you, girl. It's just not you.

No matter how you stared at the thing, it was a blaring train wreck between two people who didn't know how to let it go for good. I thought, with almost every brain cell in attendance at the time, he would leave her. And so I unlocked doors for him I had sworn I would never open. And I laid down insecurities like playing cards. And I pretended like I was the only one. But no, I never planned to be the other girl.

I planned to be a world changer, if you can believe that. A difference maker. I was going to be all the things I used to believe you could tell someone about without their looking at you strangely when they asked you, "What do you plan to do after you graduate from college?"

Turns out, "Change the world" isn't a good enough answer for most people. So I just started getting comfortable with telling people I would do a year of service after college instead.

They have these sorts of programs all over the world. Some people call the year of service a "gap year" but I never really liked that name because it makes you think of a person just pressing the big "pause" button on their life, when really, during a service year, many people find their life. You voluntarily forgo a salary for the year and step into an underserved community. You live with other volunteers for the year and build a life together out of things only the group of you will probably ever understand.

People would still look at me funny when I'd tell them about the service year, as if they could see the little green alien antennae sprouting out from my head. Who would ever want to do a thing like that?

"It's like the Peace Corps," I'd be forced to say. And then I'd reference an article from the *New York Times* about the rise in "gap years" and they'd let the hot air out from their cheeks. "Oh! The Peace Corps! You're such a good person." The conversation would fizzle shortly after.

I thought I'd do international work at first. I fell in love with this one little school in Port-au-Prince, Haiti, where the kids frolicked around the grounds in blue uniforms the color of berries turned ripe in the sun. I'd be a schoolteacher for an entire year, living with the kids at the boarding school.

The night before one of the last interviews for the school in Haiti, I was talking a mile a minute about the opportunity with one of my friends, Jen from high school. It was two days before Christmas and we were sitting in the middle of the town's Starbucks. And, as it always goes with old friendships, we cradled lattes between our hands and built bridges back into the lives of each other with all the stories that happened between September of the school year and now.

A man at the table across from us kept trying to get our attention and bring us into conversation. I am pretty sure he was crazy. And drunk. He was trying to show us a wedding ring he bought or something. Jen was pretty certain we were going to get abducted. The man wouldn't stop harassing us. Out of nowhere, two people from across the coffee shop started waving at us.

"Sam! Veronica!" the woman at the table said as she kept waving. Jen must have been Sam. I must have been Veronica. "Girls! It's been too long! Get over here!"

"Sam!" I squealed, playing along with the woman's ploy to rescue us. I nudged Jen and we both picked up our drinks and moved over to the woman's table, where the crazy man with the wedding ring couldn't wedge himself into our conversation any longer.

"That was a good call," I said to the woman as we both sat down.

"You got it," she said back. And, as if they'd never saved us, she and the man went right back into their conversation. Jen and I continued rattling on about my service year. When the word *Haiti* fell off my lips, the woman's eyes narrowed in on me.

"You?" she asked. "*You* are thinking about teaching in Haiti?" Her whole demeanor changed. Her eyes darted straight through me.

"Yeah! It's a ten-month program in Port-au-Prince. You live and work with the kids on the school grounds—"

"Oh, no, no, no," she interjected. "Pretty little girl like you? You are gonna get snatched up, killed, and sold on the black market. Your parents are never going to see you or your organs again." The guy across from her just kept staring down at his cup, twirling it in his hands as she went on to tell us that her uncle owned plantations in Haiti and she had seen the very worst. I tried to defend myself but she grew more and more persistent.

"No," she said again to me. "You get off that plane and no one is ever gonna see you again."

Regardless of the bad omen in the middle of Starbucks, I moved forward into the last interview clutching my kidneys close. I learned there would be no leaving the school grounds. Exercise would come mainly from digging holes outside or running around the perimeter of the grounds (if you had the energy in the sweat-dripping weather). Fuel would come in the form of carbs, and lots o' them. Spaghetti for breakfast. Possibly lunch. Definitely dinner. Spaghetti here. Spaghetti there. Spaghetti ev-er-y-where. I felt like something kept punching me in the stomach repeatedly as I answered the interview questions, knowing this wasn't it.

I ended up pulling my application from the pile and watched the city of Port-au-Prince be ravaged on my TV screen by an earthquake just a few days later. I'll never know if that was a sign of something, if that was the confirmation that was bigger than the bowls of spaghetti. And I went back to searching for the place that would fit me when college pushed me out.

*   *   *

A few days after Christmas, I met up with a friend who was midway through her volunteer year, living in Chicago teaching schoolchildren in the city how to work computers. She'd never been a computer kind of gal but I could tell by the way her eyes lit up when she talked about the work that she was soaring. It was electric, really. I could see her spirit shifting as she spoke.

"It's hard," she said, pushing her empty coffee cup around the table and tearing at the edges of it. We were sitting in that same Starbucks, which held too many of my memories, surrounded by work-from-homes who burrowed little territorial holes into designated spaces at the coffee shop and businessmen shuffling through the *New York Times* before heading to work. "You'll struggle with the sacrifice. Community is a tough thing. But it's worth it. I can feel myself changing."

"There is a service site in the Bronx?" I asked her. "In your program, right?"

"Yeah, one of my friends works at the preschool there. Two of them were teachers and then the other one is at the UN."

"As in the United Nations?"

"That's the one. The group has a small NGO there and one person in the program gets to be the New York representative. He's it. He goes to meetings for them. He sits in on presentations. All this cool stuff that he has to report back to the mission."

I would live in the Bronx, New York. I would work in Manhattan as a liaison for a human rights organization at the United Nations. When I heard those two letters, sitting side by side—*UN*—it was like everything else stopped moving.

"So . . . so you mean I could apply for this position?" I asked her.

"You could try," she said. "It's definitely worth the shot."

In a lot of ways, I wanted to go after what I loved but I was more concerned with slipping into a job that felt concrete and legitimate sounding so when all the college award ceremonies before graduation happened, people would be able to nod their head and say, "That one, she'll be okay." At the time, that was reason enough to chase those two letters—*UN*. I wanted to make people proud. I didn't want to get lost in the crowd.

* * *

When the e-mail came accepting me into the UN position, I told Ryan first.

The small e-mail informed me I would move to the Bronx, New York, in August. I'd spend the week before the move in Philadelphia for a weeklong orientation. I'd meet twenty-six other volunteers. Four of those volunteers would end up being my roommates. The rest would move off to Chicago, Massachusetts, San Diego, Peru, and South Africa. Our mission would be the same, no matter what pockets of the map would keep us: serve people and figure out how to love them harder than you thought humanly possible.

As a community of five in the Bronx, my roommates and I would learn to budget together, have meals together, and serve the community together. We'd each get a $25 weekly stipend as we all worked in our separate jobs—two of my roommates would teach English-as-a-second-language (ESL) classes. Another roommate would work at a women's shelter for single mothers. I would be the only one going in and out of Manhattan to work for our organization at the UN. It wasn't the typical New York City life but I was willing to do anything to get myself into the city.

When I texted Ryan the news, he came immediately and found me in the campus dining hall. I still remember his swallowing me up into a hug in the middle of the line for stir-fry. And I remember it mostly because I could see my best friend standing straight ahead of me when he mouthed those words, "I'm so proud of you." And I hadn't told her yet. He'd been the only one I thought to tell. Regret ripped through me with the strength of an Alabama Roll Tide.

Later that night, he and I were standing side by side before a window that overlooked the entire college campus. I still remember his eyes being on me as I got up from the desk where all our papers and textbooks lay open, still jarred by the excitement of the day. Weeks ago, the campus had felt big enough that maybe I would never need to leave it. I suddenly felt like Goldilocks, surprised to say, "It's too small," as I looked out and traced the roadways I knew by heart.

"I can't believe I got it," I said to him.

"I can believe it," he said. "You're already too big for this place. I see you talking to people and I always think, *She's already gone.*"

I glanced back at him. When I was younger, I thought I always wanted the kind of guy who watches you when you aren't looking and commits part of you to memory. I thought about the quirks and the habits he might know about me without ever admitting it. How they might still jingle like pocket change when we went our separate ways.

"I've wanted this for so long. The city, the job . . . all of it. I know it will be tough, challenging. But I want this more than anything."

"Well you have it now. And you're going to do great." He grinned at me. "I want to know how your story turns out."

I want to know how your story turns out.

I tried to act like he hadn't said it.

I want to know how your story turns out.

I could pin down that moment instantly. It was there—in the center of that moment—that I realized he would never be a part of my story. I see it better now than I did standing by the window that night just praying time would make an exception and stand still: Some people are dotted lines and other people are destinations. Some people get you somewhere and some people are just a place to be, all in themselves. But you cannot force those dotted lines into destinations. It doesn't really work that way.

Still, we went on like this. For probably too long. I rationalized to all my friends why I was fine to stand in the void: There's a chance. No chance. There's a chance. No chance. And so now I never wonder why people go on for so long thinking a gray sort-of love story could fit them just fine—we sometimes just want whatever scraps will be given to us of someone else. I wanted to be chosen. I wanted to win. Love isn't even the kind of thing you can win, but I wanted to win so bad.

It felt like every time we would meet up and talk for another pocket of two or three hours, we were looking for some sort of solution. Some way to keep each other in orbit. I'm not sure what we had would have ended up being love even if all the barriers were removed or if it was just human nature to want to hold tight to the people who move all the parts of you around like furniture. That isn't always enough to make a thing last though. We would graduate. We'd move. We'd let go.

"You're gonna have to show me around the city," he said to me one night the week before graduation. I remember the sound of highlighters scraping across the page as we sat side by side in the library at one a.m. I could peer out from the window of the tutoring center we were taking refuge inside of to see students passed out over their books.

We were laughing over something. We were laughing so hard we were crying. He put his head down on the computer desk and he said it, that thing about coming to see me when he was in the city.

I let the strands of his tired laughter fall to the ground. I stopped. I pushed my chair out.

"You know that isn't going to happen, right?"

"What?" He looked at me, confused.

"You and me. We aren't the type to 'meet up and have coffee.' It could never work that way." I snapped my textbook closed and started gathering up all the stray pieces of paper around me, all the evidence that I'd once written term papers on the topic of postcolonialism. "After tonight, you and I are never going to see each other again." I hoped it would sting when I said it.

I didn't even stay to see the look on his face. I just turned and walked out of the library. I trudged up the hill to my apartment. He followed close behind me.

"We can talk about this," he said. "We don't have to leave it this way."

But there was nothing left to talk about. I'd already asked him to let me go. This was good-bye. And so I held back, even though I wanted to scream. I wanted to crawl back to a starting point we both could agree upon. The starting point for him and me was obvious: some things should never start. Some people should never know each other's names. They should never stop, and talk, and laugh in empty hallways that carry an echo. No matter how much their friendship looks like poetry or fits like puzzle pieces, some people are better off staying as just a glance from across the room that never leads to an introduction.

We tumbled into an argument at the crossroads between my apartment and his. It was nearly two a.m. and we were fighting in the middle of the street, standing on the two yellow lines that weaved parallel, never touching, all around the campus. We kept arguing over good-bye and what that looked like and what that would feel like, to finally mean it.

"It wouldn't work," he finally interjected. "You're supposed to go out there and do big things, Hannah. But you were meant to do them alone. You need to go to New York alone."

Alone.

The word crashed into me. I was left with nothing more to say. He was telling me something I already knew. And finally saying good-bye was releasing the fears that lived behind the word, tipping over and pouring out: *I am afraid to leave. I am afraid to change. I am afraid to go alone. I am afraid you will forget me. I am afraid to find out I am the forgettable type.*

But maybe that is why some people walk into your life—to tip you over and pour you out. Maybe some people storm into your life just to tell you they're not supposed to be there. That you can't take them or anyone with you wherever you're going next. Maybe not every person we encounter is a love story. Maybe some are wake-up calls.

"Alone." His words trailed back to me as my new roommates and I drove over I-95 into the Bronx. We'd spent the week in Philadelphia for orientation and just met one another for the first time, so the conversation the whole car ride to our new home was full of new things—favorite foods, best memories from college, commonalities, and

ways we took our coffee. But the car slowly became silent as we saw all the buildings and skyscrapers come into view.

We crossed over into the Bronx. It would have been the perfect time to cue Frank Sinatra, all of us huddled close in the car packed tight with our own forms of baggage. Our new home was coming into view. Things would change. We would change. Life would fly at us from every angle. There was not much we could actually predict. But life would start all over again, like hitting a "reset" button. I'd carry most of the things I'd brought up until this point, but the rest of it would be new. *New, new, new.*

We Need a New "After"

There's a secret that stays pursed behind the lips of New York City but you have to hang around her for a little while before she'll spill the beans to you. She'll let you go on thinking she's unlike any other place because of her lights and her buildings, the concrete jungle she has become in the last few decades.

But if you spend enough time in New York City's grip, she'll entrust her secret to you. She'll get closer to your ear and cup her hands around her mouth to say, "Psst . . . It's the people. That's what makes me who I am. It's the way everyone in this place carries stories: stories of love and loss and grief and discovery. Stories sit in the way they fold their arms on the subways and stories tuck and roll down my avenues when the commuters come charging up out of the station on a Monday morning."

It's most certainly the people who make her, and that's probably because New York City is no accidental place. People get here on purpose. They make an entrance. They leave with a strange sense of loss in their bones. I've yet to meet a New Yorker without a story. It isn't really the place you close your eyes and pick out on a map saying, "Let's find a place with cheap rent and neighbors who want to bring us housewarming casseroles. Oh, this place looks nice."

And New York City is details too. All little details. Yes, if you really pay attention, New York City will shower you at nearly every corner with those kinds of compact moments that shock you, and change you, and convince you to believe in elements of surprise again. It's full of people who have no idea they're really just art to other passersby. There are probably thousands of them who head home feeling worthless, like failures, never fully knowing the impact they made on a complete stranger just by walking out to face the world that day. Never fully knowing they were the beautiful spot in someone else's ordinary day.

I like to imagine the details of New York—wide open for you to witness—are just her way of saying, "This life thing you've got is a gift. I'm not concrete. I'm really just a holding spot for all the lives you might just touch."

My roommates and I didn't have the typical hurdles of New Yorkers, so that was a blessing. There was no scramble to figure out which borough to live in or the trial and error of terrifying Craigslist roommates with strange fetishes. There wasn't that internal thought process I've witnessed my friends endure. The one that goes sort of like: *Okay . . . I live in a shoe box. Indeed, it is a shoe box with no windows. And I will just have to decorate this shoe box with adorable succulents I purchase from Whole Foods.*

Our apartment was waiting for us when we arrived. And our rent was covered. That was a good and golden part of our service year, in particular—living expenses were paid for and we were just asked to spend no more money than $25 a week. Which comes across as much easier when you set the whole thing up like some *Survivor* challenge. You can get really crafty with only $25.

I did much better with spending no money than I anticipated in these first few weeks, but I can only really give credit to the book I was reading at the time. At the orientation, the directors of the program handed out copies of the book *The Irresistible Revolution*. The book was recommended reading for our volunteer year. I'd picked up a copy of the book early and devoured it over the summer break. While someone else might have been fine to just read the book and then put it down, I got all mangled by the book and basically made a plan to give away all my clothes and stop wearing shoes and move to Uganda to cuddle orphans. I was legitimately sure I needed to burn all my belongings when I stepped inside of the Bronx.

Come to think of it—the book started mangling me even before I moved, specifically at one of my going-away parties. (I say "one of" because there were maybe three or four, due to the fact that every time my girlfriends and I would go to our favorite dueling-pianos bar, I'd request "Empire State of Mind" and sit on top of a piano as the men on the pianos would sing out, "Hannah is moving to New York! Everyone say good-bye to her!" And so that's basically a going-away party.) I'd spent the earlier part of the day reading the book. And I'd come across a story about Mother Teresa and the fact she had pretty decrepit feet. And in all those years of having the imaginary version of her at my tea parties, I never once thought to look at her feet.

The story goes that she used to wait on the shipments of shoes that came into Calcutta for the street children. She—being a saint and all—would spend the next day passing out the shoes to all the shoeless little children. She waited wordlessly for all the pairs to run out before she wedged her own feet into whatever stray shoes were left. Whether they were size 6 or size 8, she took comfort in their soles all the same. Years spent parading around Calcutta in too-tiny shoes left that woman with deformed feet.

The story grabbed me and held me so tightly it became the only thing I wanted to talk about for a while. I was standing in the center of the piano bar, watching other people hit on one another mercilessly, and all I could do was think of all the things I would have asked Mother Teresa if she were still alive. A guy bought me a drink that night and told me he liked my legs. I used his bringing up the topic of body parts as a gateway to bring up Mother Teresa's feet. Needless to say, he didn't buy me another drink. But for the time I listened to him talk, before I brought up her feet, I couldn't rid my mind of the idea of sliding a chai tea latte into Mother Teresa's hands and just coming out with all of my questions: "How did you do it? How, oh, how did you keep a broken world spinning off your love? How did you love on the lepers, Mama T? And how did you squeeze the outcasts into your arms so tightly?"

Sometimes I thought she might shake her head at me, saying something along the lines of, "How can you expect to love this whole world when you don't know how to look outside yourself? You don't even know how to love other people right."

Other times, I thought maybe she'd be sweet and touch my wrist and smile at me through her wrinkles, saying, "Darling, darling, you've got to learn how to be a light. Not a flicker. Not a generic kind of lightbulb. But one of those lanterns they place on the tops of hills to guide other people home. That's the kind of light you need to learn to be."

That's the good and golden part about doing a service year. The goal—or at least one of the many goals—is to get from a Me perspective to a We perspective. To turn that big ol' capital *M* upside down and make it look more like a *W. We.* A life about others and not yourself. During orientation they told us when you take on the We perspective, everything else naturally finds its place on the back burner.

Living a life where you and what you want fall to the back burner for other people sounds really romantic and selfless and good, but there is a very big difference between saying you've always wanted to help others and be a better person and then actually giving stuff up to try to become that. The back burner is a gritty, hard, intense spot to be in, especially in a culture that teaches us how to be front and center and always on fire.

Given where we lived, though, it was easier to find the back burner than it would have been in most places. The bottom floor of our apartment building was actually an immigration center, where two of my roommates would teach their ESL courses.

Saint Rita's Immigration Center stood to serve newcomers to the Bronx—mainly Vietnamese and Cambodian populations. A lot of the immigrants who came in and out of the center had arrived in America with the hope that there'd be promise waiting for them. At the center of it all was Sister Jean Marshall—a woman who'd arguably cleared out all the clutter in her heart to make room for other people, specifically the ones of this neighborhood. A picture of her and Bill Clinton hung on one of the walls in the center, taken when she was one out of five Americans to receive the Eleanor Roosevelt Award for Human Rights. A lot of mornings, I would slip from my white comforter and take the three flights of stairs down to the center to sit in the middle of the hallway and journal before the day would begin. I liked the quietness of it. I liked sitting square in the middle of the space and imagining the center filling with people in just a few hours. It's like I could gather strength for the day from the walls of that place. Not many people can say that the bottom floor of their home doubles as a heartbeat to hundreds of people within the inner city.

On that first day we carted our suitcases up the three flights of stairs to our apartment and slowly but surely began unpacking our lives into the bedrooms that jutted out from the long hallway. I wish I could tell you about the color of our carpets or the textures of the walls, but that's where memory—or the part of me that likes finding significance in every detail—fails me. You see, if there isn't what I presume to be some sort of earth-shattering revelation inside of something, I forget about it altogether. It never can just be a pantry to me. It's never just a crawl space. You could show me the blue tiling on your kitchen floor and there is the slimmest chance I might remember it. But if you told me how cool the tiles felt against your forehead when you curled into a ball and just lay there on the floor for a while, the blue of those tiles would be burned into my brain forever.

My bedroom had bright red curtains that didn't match anything else in the room. But I called it the room with the red curtains because that was the one distinct thing about the room. When my mother visited the Bronx for the first time, she stood waiting for me on the subway platform at Fordham Road with her bright red digital camera around her wrist. I asked her what she planned to take pictures of.

"Your neighborhood," she answered so nonchalantly. I let her see on her walk to the apartment that my neighborhood wasn't exactly the sort of place that offers many photo opportunities. She only ever took one photo during that whole trip. It was of the red curtains.

The first thing I ever did in the room with the red curtains was hang letters on the wall. It's the only way I can turn the four walls I live inside of me into an actual home. I have always needed words to be sitting all around me, cloaking me like a shawl, full of wisdom and hope.

The letters took up nearly three bedroom walls. People would ask where the letters came from and I could tell them some came from my best friends, some from my mother. But the majority of those letters were the result of one word: *mandare*.

Mandare was a tradition on the senior retreat at my college. It's an Italian word that means "to send out." At the end of a weekend full of reflection for seniors ready to graduate and be sent out into the world, a half dozen volunteers would emerge from the back of the room holding big, brown paper bags. In chunky black Sharpie marker, the name of each attendee would be written on a separate bag. Inside of each one was a heaping stack of letters collected in the weeks prior from family members, close friends, and relatives. They'd all gotten a letter in the mail that basically said, "Hey, this person in your life is graduating, please write them something that will make them ugly-cry." It was probably more formal than that but people had the chance to spill their guts on paper and wish you well in your new endeavors in a way that felt like it lasted much longer than a Facebook wall post. I spent a solid hour of that retreat crying my eyes out, reading letters from my parents and aunts and best friends and people I didn't even know beyond a wave on campus. And I spent pockets of time looking around the room at people who each had a slim bundle of letters in their lap. Or no letters at all beyond ones written by people who were forced to say, "I met you once. You were wearing a blue sweater. I'm sure you're nice. Good luck with your loans!" I couldn't help but think about them as I sat in my own puddle of snot and cursive. Even after I packed up the letters and took them home, I always wondered what it might be like to give something like that—a bulging package of love letters—to someone I didn't know. To someone who might never get that sort of thing otherwise. Stranger or not, we all need the same kinds of reminders sometimes: You're worthy. You're golden. You've got this.

* * *

The first thing we noticed about our apartment was that no one was kidding when they told us at orientation that we would be living in a building attached to a church. A very, very large church. The Cathedral of the Bronx if you want to get precise. It was as close to us as other people's patios. Like, "Yeah, no big deal, there's just a massive Catholic church in my backyard."

One of the priests from the rectory our building was attached to waited for us by the gates to take us on a tour of the grounds after we settled in. Our first stop was that church.

"We had P. Diddy come here once to shoot a music video," he told us as we walked up closer to the front entrance of the church. "Everyone was pretty excited about that." I looked it up that night and, sure enough, there was P. Diddy in his "Angels" music video. If you skip to 2:16 in the music video, you'll find Diddy walking like a boss into the church where we lived, right before he rides off through the streets of our neighborhood on a motorcycle.

The front entryway of the church was boarded up and under construction. We walked through a temporary door to get into the chapel. The priest told us that a few months earlier someone had set fire to the front of the church, but I don't think they ever found out who did it. People were praying inside when it happened. They didn't even know there was a fire until one of the parishioners pushed them out of the church. Even with the heavy construction, mass still look place every Sunday—in Spanish and English.

We stood in silence for a few minutes as we reached the doorway of the church. My shoulders tensed up. My palms started sweating. And honestly? My palms are sweating now. My heart is beating fast. I can't help it; that's just always been my body's natural reaction when I have to bring up the topic of God—more specifically, religion.

I write the word *religion* even though I don't actually use the word anymore. I write it because I used to think it was the only word out there until I heard a pastor on television say it was about a relationship with God. I like that better. Relationships are something I understand, most of the time, and so it puts me at ease, like maybe there is a hope I could understand God too.

Either way, I just find religion to be a sticky topic, and you often find yourself circling around people who only want to win an argument. As if finding a name for what fills you at the end of the day is the sort of thing you can win. When it comes to my own relationship with God, all I can say is it started as a craving for something bigger than my own body. And, at the time, I didn't know if that was God or unconditional love or a savior or just someone who could give me all the things humans couldn't seem to.

But it was a faith-based year of service I was walking into. Specifically, it was a Catholic program with a specific focus on the life of Saint Augustine. There was this one line on a bunch of the program's materials, *Our hearts are restless until they rest in you*. I loved that. I loved knowing a restless heart wasn't an accident. I loved the idea of finding the sort of God who would just let you rest in Him. But when people found out I was going to do a year of Catholic service, they sort of looked at me like I was crazy, because I wasn't confirmed and I wouldn't classify myself as a Catholic. To that, I would just say, "God is God, right? And if God is who people make Him out to be, then He shows up regardless, no matter what denomination we think is so important."

I actually didn't say those things. But I would have liked to. Instead I told people it seemed like the perfect fit because I did grow up with a fascination with nuns and Ash Wednesday. If you can picture a girl in elementary school, legs as skinny as two yardsticks, anxiously rubbing pencil shavings onto her forehead in the girls' bathroom, that was me. I was resentful of (downright spiteful toward) my Catholic classmates for having a religion that let them wear pretty white communion dresses and get a second middle name when all I was getting was a confirmation that I'd either need to get braces or live a long existence as a fanged child. All that existed in my own nondenominational bubble were flannelgraphs of Jesus and the chance to be dunked into a cold pool of water. Hence my decision to lie about my faith and rub the lead from my unicorn pencils on my forehead every Ash Wednesday to blend in with my soot-headed peers.

I wanted to fit in. And I guess when you're growing up, everything seems to get funneled into that. I wanted to be cool. I wanted to be accepted. Come to think of it, maybe those feelings never leave us. Maybe we never stop funneling all the things we do, and say, and believe into that one statement: *I want to belong.*

I definitely never felt like I belonged in my own church growing up. My peers always looked so tame and put together wearing their Sunday best, and I wouldn't even let my mother invest in a hairbrush for me. They wore little suits and lavender dresses with flowers lining the collars while I was this little scrawny thing—appropriately given the nickname *Boneyard*, because I looked emaciated up until the age of twelve—who paraded around in cowboy boots and white Michael Jackson gloves. My friends always seemed so into the felt storyboards about Jesus and his disciples, and I just didn't understand where all the fascination came from. Jesus seemed like a bit of a show-off to me. He was like the dude everyone ended up hating in high school because he was such a goody two-shoes. He wasn't even that cute. I always thought he would have been more of a stud if he cut his hair. That would have upped his chances of getting a girlfriend and he could have used all his cool miracles on her instead of fostering so many bromances. I would have absolutely dated a guy who could turn my water into wine.

All my peers had a mom and a dad who sat in the pews like bookends. My mom was doing the faith thing solo while my dad was at home, never wanting to come. I didn't like watching the young father slide the baby's car seat into the pew beside him. I didn't like watching the wife tuck her head on his shoulder and watching him make tiny circles with his fingers on her back. I didn't like how this scoffing little voice barreled into my head: "You? You think you will ever have that? You're cray, girl. You. Are. Just. Plain. Cray." That voice never left me, even as I got older. I would still sit in the pews—looking more like a hooker in my crop tops and skintight jeans than I care to admit—and wonder if I would ever get to marry someone who would take my hand before dinner and pray with me about all the things I already knew human hands were never equipped to fix.

I guess I just stopped wanting those things after a while. Or I stopped acting like I really wanted them. And the second my mother stopped forcing us to sit in the pews beside her, and I realized I was only ever doing it out of obligation toward her, I stopped going to church. Only once did I ever track down one of my megacrushes from Sunday school, thinking maybe he had waited for me all this time. *Maybe I could be holy after all*, were my exact thoughts when I found him on Facebook, friended him, and waited for the confirmation. I waited that whole night for some message that maybe read, *My little lamb, the Lord toldeth me to waiteth for you and I am like a deer panting for water over your profile picture*. He never said anything though. He just accepted the friend request. And then I stumbled onto photos of him with barely any clothes on and I am pretty sure he likes guys now, so I guess I'm not his type after all. Our love story died hard.

At the orientation for the service year the week earlier, they'd asked us to write out our "faith journeys" and share them with the group of twenty-six. A faith journey is basically all the left- and right-hand turns a person took to find God and how it changed the way they were after that first encounter. We all came into the program for our own reasons, but I think we all probably wanted a lot of the same things, just in different orders. Some wanted to get away. Others wanted another year to figure things out. Most of us wanted dirt beneath our fingernails, to know we were doing good work that really mattered. A lot of us wanted to know the face and the callused hands of a God we'd heard of for so many years.

Whether we'd found him pent up in children's Bible stories or modern-day religion, it was time to take it a step further and ask our questions upward: *How do you move, God? And how do you dance? And tell me about those angels. And what were you thinking when you knitted a thing like me?*

God took on so many shapes and forms in that room as people took turns sharing their stories throughout the week. To some, He seemed to be standing at every street corner and intersection. Others compartmentalized Him and only let Him into some areas of their lives. In some testimonies, He whispered and stayed a bit quiet. In other stories He boomed with a vengeance. Mind you, the God of my mind always resembled Mr. Clean, so as much as I tried to block out the image, this God with bushy white eyebrows, blaring blue eyes, and a clean white tee showed up in every story that was shared within that circle.

When someone new stood up to read their story, I pictured the Mr. Clean version of God lounging back in His heavenly lawn chair, knocking back pink lemonade and snorting over who we painted Him to be with our words. I pictured Him shaking His head and fist-pumping when the stories got good and He got to play all the right hero parts. I imagined Him jotting notes and highlighting sections about things He'd need to fix in some of us. I saw Him shedding egg-size tears when His own creations damaged one another. I pictured Him blushing a bit when we said lovely things, and used constant kinds words, the day we asked Him to stick around. The day when we really, really meant it.

Some of the stories were pretty and compact. Some you could barely pay attention to because you dwelled on the teller's shaky voice and fidgeting hands. I was drawn to the ones that didn't resolve well, that still had holes and threads left unknotted, because maybe that is how I felt about my own faith. Like it was half-finished. Like it was just beginning.

The Bronx community was the last to share our stories, so while other people from the program would go off to bed after a long day or congregate in hotel rooms to get to know one another better, I kept finding myself down at the hotel lobby computers beside businessmen checking their e-mails while I tried to wrestle God down onto the page. I wanted people to believe what I was saying. I wanted to believe the words myself. But I just kept laying my hands against the keys every time I went to type and thinking, *What if I don't really know You? What if I am just writing a bunch of lies so that these strangers will think I've actually found You?*

Found is a funny word. What I actually "found" when I sat down to write out my story was memories of myself swirling in the middle of the Christian-based mind-control cult I had gotten involved with in college. One that is banned across different cities and college campuses. It's been cracked open by dozens of news stations that have gone undercover to produce exposés. Apparently the structure of the church and the severity of it has morphed in the last few years, but, at the time, it was still listed in those encyclopedias that get down to the bones of cults across the world.

Mind you, I would have laughed if anyone told me I could be sucked into this sort of thing. I had always associated the word *cult* with a series of other associated things: Kool-Aid, Charles Manson, people who abandon their families overnight, brainwashing, Shawn Hunter. I thought about that one episode of *Boy Meets World* where Shawn joins a cult and no one can seem to break him out of it. I give a lot of kudos to those directors for jamming so much into a thirty-minute episode. If anyone reading this knows those directors, please pat them on the back for me and relay the message that I walked away from the TV after that particular TGIF night and thought, *It just got really real up in here. That was too real for my liking. What if Shawn and Topanga and Cory are gonna keep doing this deep stuff until they fully grow up and leave me?*

It was my junior year of college. In my first few years of college, I'd watched my mother learn how to live without her mother and do this cyclical dance with my brother—her own baby, who was addicted to painkillers with long and drawn-out names I never really could pronounce. I'd watch my mother stand in the kitchen after my brother and I screamed words at each other we couldn't take back and I always wondered what kept her so strong. To watch her beautiful boy morph into some sort of stranger when he would take little tablets. I want to be clear and truthful: my brother never became someone mean; his heart has never deviated from the solid and sweet thing it always has been. He is unarguably one of the nicest people you will ever meet. I just found it really hard to stand in the same room as him and not wish better things could be delivered to the front door for him, like delivering pizza.

Maybe my mom cried for him more than I'll ever know, but I watched her—every college break—act out the same morning routine regardless. Seven a.m.: Drip coffee on the stove. A splash of half-and-half. A flipped-open Bible with the same leather case it'd been tucked inside for years, the side pockets spilling over with old church bulletins. She'd copy down the scriptures of that Bible until the second pot of coffee ran dry. She kept my brother's sickness like a secret. It was like any sort of darkness didn't even stand a chance against all the joy she surrounded herself with. She worshipped by the sink. She planted verses into all my letters—not because she felt any urgency to help me find God. I just think she knew I'd feel fuller if I admitted He was already there.

So, in the fall of my junior year of college, I decided I wanted to find God too. For myself, but mostly for her. To show her I'd really found Him. Almost like Elizabeth Gilbert, minus India and Bali and hot Italians, I went on a quest to find God. I was nineteen years old and barreling around a Catholic campus looking for Him, as if He were the Waldo with the wiry glasses I looked for all those years.

I'd been asked by someone a year earlier if I wanted to come and study the Bible with her. She asked me a lot, actually. The answer was always no. Until it was yes. And I started studying one-on-one with her and attending her church. Another woman was always in the room with us, taking notes for me. I guess it was sort of strange she would be in the dorms so late with us when she had a family at home. I remember one study where the girl and woman asked me to turn to a new page in my notebook. On the page, I needed to write all the sins I could recall committing. I remember thinking, *Like, last week? Or last year?* But she said I needed to write down everything. Every sin I could remember from the past.

Memories of lies and pain and addiction and lust filled the pages of that notebook. I remember thinking I would get a new notebook when this Bible study was over. I didn't want this one anymore. And when the writing was done, I had to speak them out loud and explain the sins in detail. My hands were so hot. I felt so embarrassed talking about nights where I drank too much or nights with random, empty-feeling hookups. I hated going into the details of exactly what happened. It's not like that sort of stuff doesn't make a person feel empty enough already. Talking about it with people who are practically strangers, feeling like this umbrella of shame was hanging over me, made me feel absolutely worthless.

Looking back, it's all a little sad to me because even in those shameful moments I still wanted whatever those people had so bad. Everyone was so nice. And everyone so genuinely wanted to get to know me. I felt really loved and included. Even if I didn't agree with everything those people were telling me, nothing could top those feelings of belonging—*You are loved. You are whole. You are okay.* It wasn't until I got a text from one of the guys at the church saying, "I can't wait to call you my sister in Christ," that I realized there was probably a hurdle I didn't know about. A divider between us. There was that feeling again. That feeling of not fully fitting in.

That's when I learned I wasn't in the light yet. More specifically, I was led through a study to prove I was not in the light. As we read scripture after scripture, it became evident to me that only those who got baptized into this church were in the light. Only then would God want something to do with me. The road to salvation was through this church alone. My friends would go to hell—I needed to save them. My family would go to hell—I needed to save them. The whole of my campus, "all wolves in sheep's clothing," was going to hell. And me, if I stepped away from this path . . . I would be damned too.

So I made a decision to be baptized into the church, and I was flooded with rules in the days leading up to the baptism about what I could and could not do once I became a member. I could not attend parties. I could not consume alcohol. I could not date boys outside of the church. My point in life would be to disciple others. My purpose was getting more people into the water and more people into the pews. I just remember thinking, *God, I don't want a rule book. I just want to feel something.*

It wasn't until the night before my baptism that the older woman I'd been meeting with decided to bring up one last issue with me before I was saved. My mother. She told me that my mother would go to hell if I did not get her into this church. I needed to save her.

That was it for me. I thought that was the breaking point. I wanted to scream in her face, "You have no idea the woman of God my mother is. Over and over again, my mother has saved me. You do not get to damn her to hell."

I know I should have left the room right there. But instead, I agreed to try to save my mother just so I could have my salvation. I was tired of the endless hurdles. I just wanted to be saved.

Twenty minutes before my baptism, for reasons I will probably never understand, I told my roommate what I was walking into. I don't remember the exact words I used but I know I stood at the doorway where her bedroom connected to mine and I told her I would come home changed that night, like a new person. She told me she didn't want me going. Wherever I was planning to go, she didn't want me going. The next few hours were a jumble of panic and screaming and crying. My mother still says she's never been more afraid for me than that moment when she picked up the phone to hear me crying out, "I don't want to go to hell. Please help me. I think I am going to hell." I hadn't told her or anyone what I was doing, where I'd been studying, or my plans to get baptized into the church. I wanted it to be a surprise. I wanted her to be proud of me for the holiness I'd found.

I didn't get baptized that night. Instead, I spent two hours on the phone with the wife of one of the elders of the church I'd grown up with. My hands pressed into the floor as I listened to her repeat to me on speakerphone, "You aren't going to hell. You aren't."

And it wasn't until the next day, sitting next to my academic adviser, who identified proudly as an atheist, that I began to understand what was really going on. I told him I needed to be in the light. Right in the middle of picking classes for the next semester, I told him I wanted to be in the light. He immediately sent me to the campus ministry. That was smart of him to do. After all, there really is no correlation between "being in the light" and what level of creative writing you want to take in the semester ahead. I came back to his office a half hour later with the name of a group I needed to Google, given to me by someone working at the desk at the campus ministry. She said a lot of what I was telling her sounded familiar. I should look up this specific group. My advisor offered up his computer to me and stood behind me as I dropped the name of the group in the Google search bar. The word CULT came back at us, plastered all over the screen. I read the words beside him: "This group has all the traits necessary to classify it as a mind control cult, including the teaching that it is the one true church, love bombing, deceptive recruiting, time control, relationship control, and the rest."

I was one of the last people to leave the academic support center that night. I found myself in the corner of the room where a group of four computers was kept, sobbing as I read stories of women who left their husbands and boyfriends who left their girlfriends—gradually or suddenly—to find salvation through this cult. I wrote down everything that had happened to me and delivered it to the campus ministry the next morning.

If you can believe it, I tried to wedge that entire story into two sentences and slip it into my faith journey so it would go unnoticed. It didn't. The other volunteers had all kinds of questions. The story came out again the night before all of us left for our separate service locations. We'd spent the last day cruising the boardwalk of Atlantic City and coming out red as lobsters. We washed the sand and salt from our bodies and put on our best khakis and sundresses for dinner. As we waited for the tables to be set inside of the Italian restaurant on the water, someone asked if I could tell more of the story. So I told the group the story of what really happened. Like a special-edition Blu-ray, I included all the deleted scenes. And, when it was done, someone asked what happened after. Someone always asks about the after. What happened after you'd been gutted and plastered "most selfish sinner of the century" to your chest like a name tag? What happened after the administration sent out campus-wide e-mails about the presence of a religious cult on school grounds? *Where did you fall, Hannah?*

* * *

Well, shortly after it happened, I learned how to turn my "cult story" into a really good crowd-pleaser at parties and gatherings. And it was a guaranteed way to blow a guy's mind on the first date because not many people can start a sentence with, "This one time I was almost in a cult." I got really good at telling the tale, joking about it, never getting into the real pain of it all. I think if you searched down deep enough, you'd see the real hurt that lived inside of me when all my prayers were birthed out of this desire to grab God by the shoulders and scream, "How come when I searched for you, you led me into this mess? How come you let your religion be so ugly when it gets into the hands of some people?"

I remember a few days after things settled on campus, I called my mother at work to report to her my latest discoveries on the psychological tactics of the group. That's the way I always get—I become obsessed with researching the stuff I can't understand. This time I had pages and file folders full of highlighted testimonies and articles on the group.

"You won't believe what I found today. Remember when I told you about how they—"

"Hannah," she said, stopping me midsentence. "I know you want to figure all of this out. I get that. But I know you don't care about the answers as much as you care about where God is in all of this."

She paused. "You maybe have to think that God was the one who got you out of this. That He stepped in when He needed to. And now you're out."

And with that mind-set—that little bit of wisdom from my mother—that maybe God rescued me from the cult, I packed up my stubborn heart and a change of clothing and went on a weekend-long retreat for my college. And in the hills of Massachusetts—at some random retreat center that made the best comfort food known to man—I let go of my bitterness for the first time. I just laid it down for a little while. I took walks all over the grounds enveloped by these gorgeous hills that were too far off in the distance to actually get to the place where the land meets the sky. And there was so much laughter up in this one tiny yellow room where a group of five girls and I sat together in between sessions and bonded over some picture of Jesus hanging in the room that made him look like a *GQ* model. We all forged this kind of friendship up in that room with the yellow walls that's really hard to define beyond just that: *GQ* Jesus. And I met my best friend, Celia, in that room. If it wasn't for that experience, I'd never have really gotten to know Celia. And if you have ever had a best friend who gets you better than you've ever gotten yourself, you'll know automatically how important of a thing it was to meet her in that yellow room.

That was the version of "after" I'd always stood by. It was solid and sturdy and it never wavered. At least not until that day in the Cathedral of the Bronx, the day I moved to New York. Suddenly, that version of the "after" felt shaken. I could feel the wave of nausea spreading through my insides as we stood silently in the center of the church. Like I was looking for a place to run but there was nowhere else to go.

I felt like I was standing in the middle of the apartment of an ex-boyfriend. Except there were pews. And lit candles. And a massive crucifix at the front of the room. God isn't my ex-boyfriend (just to be clear) but it stirred the same kind of frothy emotions. It was like remembering all the little things that made you miss someone, someone where the good-bye didn't go quite the way you planned. It was familiar in a way that almost hurt me, to stand there in the middle of something that belonged to God and know we weren't quite fixed yet.

It was as if God and I were finally setting the Facebook status of our relationship in that church. And the status was clear: "It's complicated." And it was exactly what "It's complicated" actually means—we were a bit broken and estranged; we could not fully let the dance go so we still called from time to time but neither one of us was ever bold enough to look the real issues in the face long enough to ask the defining question: Are you staying or are you leaving? Pick one.

I didn't say anything, not when the priest told us the history of the church and not when he said we could go there anytime. Day or night, we had keys to get inside. I thought I would go. I pictured myself showing up there late at night, while the rest of the world slept, sitting in those pews and soaking in the beauty of that church. Finding all those two a.m. hours to just watch the stained glass windows and ask the bigger questions.

But if I had gone, what would be left to say? What would be left to whisper into the bigness of that church to a God I hoped might hear me beyond, "We need a new after. If You're here, I think we need to find a new after."

You Are Here

From the moment we stepped into the Bronx, it was like we were wrapped into something bigger than ourselves. It was this feeling like you could walk away for a little while, come on back, and everything would still look the same. The people might be different, their stories might have grown more glowing or grim throughout the dragging months of August and October, but everything around would still pulse with familiarity.

We became neighbors without even trying. It wasn't like the striving I felt in the fourth grade when I created a wardrobe of only neon colors—I mean like harsh, burn-your-eyes highlighter colors—because I thought it would make the popular girls want to sit with me at lunch. Or college, where it felt like I had to get dinner at the dining hall eighteen times with the girls in my dorm before easing off from the fear that they'd forget about me. It wasn't any of that. It was just, "You're here, and so you are one of us. You are a part of us now."

It wasn't like that in all parts of the neighborhood, but it was easy to feel wanted where we lived, and I've come to miss that feeling. I took being seen for granted while I was there, and now I miss the way people I didn't even know greeted me as they walked by. They simply loved on us. In a way I didn't know was possible because I'd never encountered that kind of love before. It was almost like I wanted to whisper,

"How could you possibly love me? Sit with me? Talk to me? Dare to know me? You know nothing of me. Could it really be this easy?"

One of my roommates called it "agape." I'd never heard the word before, but it was her favorite word, and I was instantly enamored because the definition of *agape* is loving a person for exactly who they are—not who we hope they'll become with enough fixing. It's this idea that every person has their layers, so you can never confine a person to only what you know about them from first glance. It's stacked on the premise that to love anyone is to hope in them always.

And so I tried my hardest to practice agape in those first few days and I quickly fell in love with everything about our neighborhood—our stoop (yes, we had a stoop, like a legitimate *Hey Arnold!*–type stoop). And we would sit on our stoop clasping a cup of Moty's coffee. At only sixty cents, that's still the best cup of coffee I've ever had.

Moty's was the bodega across the street from our apartment with aisles so narrow they birthed new forms of claustrophobia. You'd go right up to the counter and ask the man with the gray hair who always stood off to the side of the register for a cup of coffee.

"Light and sweet, please."

"Like you." He'd smile and disappear behind the counter and reappear sliding a small Anthora paper cup with two napkins placed on top over to you. One sip. You're hooked. All bets are off.

And then there was Juan.

Juan, you could say, was basically the prodigy of the barbershop situated directly across the street from us. The shop was always packed, at all hours of the day and night, and there'd be groups of people lounging outside it in plastic lawn chairs throughout the day. I'd see all the kids in the swivel chairs right after school let out, getting stars and zigzags shaven into their tiny heads. The chairs in that place were always full. People were always laughing.

I saw Juan when we first parked our car inside the gate of our apartment and began pulling our suitcases out of the backseat and hauling them from the trunk. He looked at me with this smile that pulled me in. I instantly felt stupid for wearing a volunteer-program T-shirt, as if I were showing up to the Bronx as a summer camper. My cheeks flooded with red. I watched him go on cutting hair and shaking his head at me. I saw his smile, even when his head was down.

In the first few weeks, I strategically sat on the stoop with my nose buried in books while he cut hair. We'd eye each other like fourth graders but I was all talk and very little game. Change that—I had no game at all. It was like a repeat, every single afternoon, of how Jimmy Thompson made me feel in the eighth grade. Palms sweating. Heart racing. I was a goner when it came to Juan and his beautiful beard.

One of my roommates and I were sitting out on the stoop one morning in what became "our spots." Hers was tucked in the right corner. Mine was up on the top stair where I could see Juan.

Across the street, a man stepped out from the crowd of men talking by the window of the barbershop. He looked us both dead-on, put two fingers into his mouth, and let out this shrill whistle from his lips. He pushed his feet together abruptly and went into full salute.

"He's saluting us," I mouthed to my roommate.

"Yes, he is," she whispered back.

Not even looking to see if cars were passing down the one-way street, the man started charging toward us. Full-on charging. It was one of those moments where you swear your life is flashing before your eyes. You think about the wedding you haven't had yet. The grandbabies you've yet to swaddle. He was gaining momentum. But then he stopped, halted right at the foot of the steps up to our apartment, and went back into his salute position.

"*Capitana! Sargenta!*" he said loudly. He was waiting for us to salute him back, and then his demeanor softened and he took off his baseball hat to reveal a bald, shining head and he took both of our hands to shake them.

His name was Sargento. That was about all I understood. The rest of the things he said needed to be translated from Spanish, but even my roommate struggled to figure out what he was really talking about. He told her he was in the military (though we think that was years prior). He rambled intensely about the neighborhood being under attack. We needed to be ready to fight. Hence the nicknames he gave us: Sargenta and Capitana.

While he talked, I could not help but notice the dirt all over his face and cap. His military jacket was filthy. His eyes were two different colors. One was blue, the other a strange sort of silverish-white. He was easily distracted by the business of the neighborhood. But there was a gentle spirit about him.

In the weeks to follow, we'd try to coax more answers out of him—about who he was—but he didn't go much further than the battle orders. We knew he was homeless. I think he might have been a bit drunk most of the times we talked. He'd occasionally sweep the floors of the barbershop and then use the extra couple dollars to try to buy us things. I asked him where he slept one day. I winced when his finger was drawn right to a bench in the park across the street. I tried to pretend it was the kind of thing I could forget. Thinking about him, balled up on a park bench as the numbers shimmied down the thermometer into single digits, made everything about our interactions that much harder for me. I wanted to give him a bed and all these things I didn't even have to give.

As strange as it was, standing there and listening to the ways we needed to save the neighborhood, I felt seen by Sargento. That's the word I've wanted to use for a while: *seen*. Picked out from a crowd. Noticed. The second he spotted me, from that day forward, he'd turn straight around, give that sharp militarylike streak of attention that cut into the air, and go into full salute. Then he'd plow across the street to get to me.

I wrote down everything I felt in those first few weeks in a dark red journal with a magnetic clasp on the front of it. The pages quickly stacked. After several weeks of writing, I packaged up the journal and mailed it off to Celia. She'd find the journal waiting for her in her campus PO box in Massachusetts. She'd take the journal, fill up the next two or three dozen pages, and mail it back to me.

Those journals became our space to save our thoughts. Even if you couldn't have that person sitting right beside you to see life from your view, you still felt like you could hold them and take them from sight to sight every time you cracked open the journal and placed the pen on the page.

We started sending journals back and forth the semester after we met. I was a year ahead of her in school. Celia went off to Prague for the semester and I stayed to finish out my senior year and graduate. She was twenty and I was twenty-one. We were both gathering proof, and all sorts of evidence, to back a truth that no one ever warned us about: life is a series of letting-go moments. You just start to get comfortable with a place, or a person, or a job, and then everything shifts and you have to find new balance again. It happens over and over again in your twenties. And probably in your thirties. And I would bet it happens all the time as people get older and friends start to slip away without ever saying "Good-bye" or "I love you" or "I'll miss you."

It almost feels like at some point life whacks you on top of the head and hands you a list of all the things you can keep. The list is surprisingly long. You can keep letters. You can keep trying. You can keep secrets and you can try your hardest to keep promises. You can keep your eyes on the road. You can keep his sweatshirt, the one he left on the living room floor. You can keep photos and you can keep the memories. But you cannot keep people. People are not things—you can't keep them.

"Sometimes I think I don't want to go," Celia said to me on that last night before she left for Prague. The white lights sprawled like ivy across the room. We were sitting on the floor of my apartment nursing cups of Lipton tea. That was our thing.

"I know," I whispered, wanting to keep her in one place. "But you have to go out there. You have to see what is out there for you. And you have to choose to be all there. We're all gonna be here when you get back."

In my mind, I wasn't all that certain, though. I knew she would leave and I would change and things would move in different directions and we might never know anything but long distance from that point forward. It was hard not to let my mind wander into all the compartments of the future—travels, graduation, new jobs, romance, families. It could all happen too fast if we even thought to blink. Still, I told her she couldn't live in two places at once. She had to choose. And be invested in that one place for a little while, however long that little while could afford her.

A few weeks into that last semester, the first journal showed up from Prague. She wrote inside the front cover, "Promise me you'll never forget me because if I thought you would I'd never leave." We'd found that quote carved into an old bunk bed once. It definitely lost some of its value to us when we realized the quote was originally something Piglet said to Pooh Bear.

There was something about being able to carry Celia with me or reading about her adventures on a page instead of a screen. The tangibility of the journals conquered all our other forms of communication. It felt different from a text message, different from just telling the other person everything, instantly. There was no immediacy. There was no need to get to the root of the mysteries surrounding us. I think if ever some great historian gets a grip on our pretty little journals, he'll probably conclude this: The two had very little figured out. They were trying though. They fell in love. They looked for God. They loved constructing miracles out of the mundane. Above all things, they cheered for each other. And they made each other stronger. And that meant everything.

I spent so much time writing to Celia from the stoop of our apartment those first few weeks of September. And Celia was the first person I wrote to when I learned my job in Manhattan would not turn out exactly how I expected it to.

The year before, the position as the UN representative had been a part-time one. Whoever served as the liaison at the UN also worked doubly as an ESL teacher in the immigration center downstairs from our apartment. It'd become a full-time job the year I stepped into the role and while it looked as though I would spend my days attending meetings at the UN and writing summaries and preparing articles and serving on committees, the job wouldn't provide me with nearly enough work for a full forty-hour week.

The overseer of my position worked to secure office space for me by the UN headquarters. I bought supplies. I had a complete *Devil Wears Prada* moment in trying to haul a printer down Lexington Avenue in heels. But there wasn't much to do beyond a few hours of work every week. While my roommates settled into jobs in the Bronx, I would take the train into Manhattan and try to make work for myself.

"You have to appreciate baby steps to work in this place," one woman told me at the orientation to the UN I attended in my first two weeks on the job. "Things move slowly sometimes but there will be little victories."

I clung tighter than she'll ever know to the idea of little victories as I learned how having your hands full with work fuels your sense of purpose. Without work, you just feel helpless. I needed to find another way to supplement the hours.

"Can you tell me again who this is?" The voice on the other end of the line was coated in a thick Irish accent.

"My name is Hannah. I am one of the volunteers this year living over at the immigration center. Is this Sister Margaret?"

"Yes, this is Sister Margaret here." Things clattered and echoed in the background.

Sister Margaret was the executive director of a community life center serving the Fordham neighborhood. The center offered every service imaginable, from a universal pre-kindergarten to a residential home for single mothers. When I Googled her name, all that was spat back at me was a phone number and a blog site that had not been updated since 2008. It didn't do justice to the work Sister Margaret had done in the Fordham Road neighborhood for the last thirty years. If you ever get her to sit down long enough to tell you the story, she'll tell you the whole thing started with a cup of soup and a sandwich roll. Those humble beginnings stretched far beyond a line for a soup kitchen in the next thirty years and became an umbrella organization to serve several demographics within the Bronx community—including children, homeless men and women, single mothers, immigrants, and persons with AIDS/HIV.

"I was looking for some additional volunteer work," I told Sister Margaret over the phone. "Someone recommended that I—"

"Oh, come on over! Come on over! We would love to have you here."

"When should I—"

"You can come over today. Come over now. If you just take a right from your building and turn right where the road forks by C-Town, you'll see our building on the right. There's a banner! I'll see ya soon!" The line went dead.

There were no hurdles. No debating. No "we will call you back if we think you might be a fit for us." It was just come. Come right now. Come as you are. In a matter of minutes, I was out the front door, turning by the grocery store C-Town, and walking down a long hallway, classrooms full of preschoolers from the Fordham Road neighborhood on both sides; the hallway walls were covered in foliage-inspired artwork made by babies.

"Can you get us into that book everyone is talking about?" It was one of the first things she ever asked me. I followed Sister Margaret as she took me through several of the classrooms, where snacks were being pulled out from brightly colored lunch boxes and sandwiches shimmied out from the wrappings of tinfoil on the table.

"The book?" I asked her.

"Yes, that book. The one on the computer. You are good with computers, right?"

"Do you mean Facebook?" I asked.

"Yes! That's the one! Everyone keeps saying we need that."

"Yes," I answered back confidently. "I can definitely do that."

And with that, she was rushing me into her office to meet the two other women who worked in the back office of the pre-K.

"Sandra! Shelley! You have to meet our new volunteer. She's gonna be with us for a little while!"

They cleared a space. They gave me a desk. It was that same sort of feeling again—that feeling of belonging. The feeling of being wanted just as you are.

Small Hands

New York will always and never be the city for me. I think I shall live in that chasm until my hair turns gray and falls out. Always—because I know I'll never get tired of the people-watching that goes down in that city. Never—because I am never just content enough to sit still during a commute. I'm a do-something sort of person and that doesn't really mix well with the commuters of New York City. That was my problem though: for the whole time I lived in New York City I wanted to strike up conversations. I wanted to shatter the word *stranger* with a sledgehammer. That's the thing the people who rode the subways with me all those times will never know; I found ways to carry them long after we parted. I thought about them as they were sitting there. I wrote them into letters.

I've always been that way. I'm a people watcher. Or I care too much. I don't know which one it is but I would watch the homeless man giving his speech for the thirty-second time that morning as he walked through the subway car. I would keep my eyes glued to the clearly disheveled, half-clothed woman who was belligerent and incoherent, and I always wondered why no one would look up from their books to just see her.

My eyes darted around the train, circling all the things that were subtle and easily missed. Two people fighting off in the corner of the train, trying to keep their voices down to a hushed whisper. Him looking distant. Her looking defeated. A woman wrapping her arms tight around her child, pulling him in closer with every stop along the way. Closer and closer, the child in the poufy black North Face coat came into her chest. She was so careful. So quiet. Yet she kept kissing the top of her little one's forehead and pulling him in, as if to say, *Don't grow up on me just yet*. A girl across from me, trying absolutely everything just to keep herself awake. I couldn't help but watch her cross her legs, left and then right.

There was nothing so interesting about her, or the mother, or the two people fighting, but my eyes fixated on all three story lines, wondering what I would say to them if I had the chance. I pocketed strangers in my memory, one by one, and tied them closer for all the ways in which they looked completely normal, all the ways they looked like me. And I could somehow think we were all together on this 4 train riding uptown. As the train kept pulling and pulling, I'd pick several people out and I would imagine what it would be like to talk to them, to know their fears, and to ask them three simple words: *How are you?*

"How are you today? Really. Tell me, tell me. Is your heart good? Was it easy to roll out of bed this morning? Did you feel anticipation in your lungs or has this whole thing looked a little gray for too long of a while?" Maybe we're all a *how are you* away from not feeling so alone in all of this today.

I wanted a way to say to someone I would never meet, "Hey, maybe our knees will never touch, and maybe we will never dig deep into politics at a dive bar in Brooklyn, but maybe you need to know someone else is out there. They too have struggles. They want the best for you. They're cheering for you loudly, even if you can't see them with their fists in the air."

I wanted to do anything beyond what I really did every time I would get on the train and surround myself with other strangers headed in the same direction: pull out my phone and pretend to be somewhere else.

My phone became a way to pull away from the people who surrounded me and just stand in my own space with my own conversation and my own noise. And truthfully, it made me lonelier. It made me lonelier to know I was standing somewhere, surrounded by people whom I could have very easily learned the names of, and I was just another person in the thousands who would rather focus on whatever was happening on the screen of a sleek, white rectangular box with a half-eaten apple plastered in silver on the back of it. I pulled it out constantly to scroll and scroll—not really looking at anything—just hoping I would look important or needed or wanted in that moment.

I would pretend to dial someone's number and put the phone up to my ear.

"Hello."

The silence would hold on the other line.

"Oh hey! How is your day going?"

Silence.

"Great! Yes! Let's do that!"

More silence.

"Perfect! Six thirty sounds fantastic. I love that little wine bar . . . Yup . . . See you then!"

I was inviting myself to places. I was laughing to nobody. I was pretending that somebody, somewhere, was waiting for me.

I spent a good amount of my days on the train as my life became an even split down the middle. I spent one half of my week amid preschoolers, becoming an expert in storytelling and deciphering the cries of four-year-olds. I gave the rest of my week to my position as the NGO's liaison at the United Nations, a place where stories are still told and cries are still deciphered, but in a completely different manner.

During the days I spent at the preschool, I found myself floating around to wherever Sister Margaret needed me. One morning, I subbed in for a teacher's aide who was out sick. After shuffling the kids into circle time, I sat off at the back of the room watching all of them learn to hiss out the Ss that slithered like snakes slurping smoothies. Another teacher sat beside me. She didn't say a word. Her arms were crossed over her chest. I'm naturally the kind of person who flounders during awkward silences when you are standing right beside someone, so I tried to find a way to break the ice and make conversation.

"I am so tired," I said. It was the only thing I could think of that might start a conversation with the woman.

She turned her head to face me. She looked me up and down. Up and down again. "Honey, you would not even begin to know what tired looks like." Her eyes stayed on me for several seconds before she re-crossed her arms and resumed staring straight ahead. The hisses continued dancing around the room.

Ssss . . . Ssss . . . Ssss . . .

I stared down at my shoes and shoved my hands into the deep billowy pockets of my dress, immediately regretting my decision to say anything at all. I wasn't trying to offend her. I was only trying to find some common ground. I didn't say anything for the rest of that class. When it was time to herd the kids into a straight line and take them to the bathroom, I tried to make as little noise as possible.

That woman was right, though—I didn't know anything about tired. Tired, to me, was not getting the full eight hours. Tired, to me, was a busy weekend packed with parties and coffee dates. I didn't know anything about the world I was standing inside of, the people I was greeting daily, where they'd been and what they'd seen and how all of that added up to just how tired they really were.

I write this, knowing still that I will never be able to claim to understand the poverty I saw snaking through my own neighborhood. I never want to try to act like I was some expert on that. I was standing in the middle of a borough that held one of the poorest congressional districts in the US and yet it was just subway stops away from the richest district. I walked into the volunteer year at a time when the newspapers would say the Bronx was a battleground in which people were rallying for a living wage.

Even though our stipends were only $25 a week, I quickly became aware there was a difference between us and our neighbors, even if we tried to ignore it. I could see it every Wednesday morning as a line would begin forming just past the door to the immigration center. The line of people waiting with carts would be robust and winding by seven thirty a.m. as it roped past our apartment door. The people of the neighborhood would line up every Wednesday to get a box of food from the food pantry that was run out of the basement of the church. No matter how cold it became outside, you could always count on the line being there on a Wednesday. I couldn't look at the faces in the line as I walked by. I kept my head down and I plugged my earbuds in. They weren't just people. And they weren't strangers. They were my neighbors. And I didn't know how to help them.

I wanted to pretend like there wasn't a difference between us. But it was there. In the economic sense and in the sense that I'd been afforded a life with different opportunities. I'd been in the best school systems. Growing up, I operated within a calendar that included gymnastics and dance classes and student council. I had the privilege of attending a private Catholic institution. And although I had over $50,000 in student loans hanging over my head, I had made the decision to take on those loans. My parents had the economic stability to cosign for those loans. I was very lucky and figured out "lucky" didn't fix things.

Up until that point, I guess I'd been mainly surrounded by things I could fix. Circumstances I could change. The planner in me, the fixer in me, always thought I could just make things better. That's the only way I ever knew how to cure all wounds. Sad? Make a checklist. Overwhelmed? Create a system. I thought for every problem and heartbreak, there was some sort of system waiting in the corner to be discovered.

My mother is always quick to tell me, for that reason, that she doesn't know where I came from. Where I got all the rules and need to fix things from. That is our main separating point. While I shove my whole body into being everything, to everyone, always, she just lives. She doesn't restrict herself. She often looks at me like I'm a feral cat because she is afraid of me and how I doctor the world with systems.

I remember after my first heartbreak when I was a freshman in college she drove three hours to rescue me from my college dorm room. He and I, we'd been together for nearly four years. To an eighteen-year-old, it felt like the world was ending. My mother and I sat like classy little humans in the middle of an Applebee's in Auburn, Massachusetts, and I told her I would make a list, a system of sorts, dedicated to all the ways I would get over this and be stronger.

"Or you could just be sad . . . and not make a system," she said quietly. "Maybe just eat a little cake and cry if you need to."

My mother lay on the floor that night and listened to me whimper and check my phone to see if he'd called. She didn't go to sleep. There's really no point in typing that last line but I think it's too beautiful to leave out.

No system would work this time. I just felt inadequate.

If I am being completely honest, that's the one word I would use to describe how I felt when I would arrive at my desk in Manhattan most mornings. Inadequate.

I'd only be sitting at that desk for five minutes—enough time for the computer to fully load and my e-mail to open—before all the ugly thoughts came tumbling out of their hiding spots. It was like that part in *The Wizard of Oz* where Glinda coaxes all the munchkins to come out from behind the trees and little munchkin huts. Except these munchkins might as well have been holding spears and wearing Hannibal Lecter face masks, because not a single one of those ugly thoughts was trying to push me forward down any sort of yellow brick road. Those were the kind of thoughts that, if you entertained them for too long, would put your whole day into a headlock.

What do you think you are doing? It always began with that thought. *You actually think you can make a difference? Look around, girl; you're not doing a single thing that matters.*

The cannibalistic munchkins kept huddling closer, the pack of them growing thicker, and I would try to distract myself with busy work. *You want to actually do something that counts? Oh . . . how cute.*

Any progress yet? Didn't think so. You should probably just give up. You're stupid. You're not good enough.

Those thoughts were merciless. And they were always there. If there was a way to shoo them off or push them into a corner, I didn't know the remedy. From spending just one hour at that desk, I could have told you that the reason a lot of people never do anything, or go anywhere, or move to the place they've always wanted to move to or go after the things they always talked about, rarely boils down to other people's not believing in them. I believe now that we're the enemy to the things we really want for our lives. We get really good at telling ourselves ugly lies on repeat every day. *You're unworthy. You're ugly. You're inadequate.*

Back to that word for a minute. *Inadequate.* I don't think I ever anticipated I would feel that particular emotion so strongly. No one really walks into a new chapter of life thinking, *This might just be the one where I feel totally and completely inadequate.* It's not even that common of a word. But everything surrounding me—the issues happening at the UN, the budget cuts happening all across the life center—all these big problems, global and national and everything in between, left me standing in the middle of a room feeling like I couldn't help anyone.

I don't know if they told us there would be a honeymoon period to the service year or if I just made that up to reassure myself once the honeymoon period was evidently gone. Either way, it came and went. Quickly. With very little mercy. New York was still New York—hauntingly beautiful. Cute guys still rode the subway. Beggars still begged. Nothing about the world really shifted except my own perspective— that got chipped away. And I think I lost a good deal of hope because the world was so broken and I couldn't turn away.

My roommates and I tried out a church one morning in the Bronx. This was after I exhausted all my efforts in pillaging all the self-help sections I could find in the Bronx.

Libraries are like a winning lottery ticket when you can't spend any money or get on a plane to go find yourself. I borrowed nearly a dozen self-help books. The woman at the circulation desk slid them through the security gate with a look of dismay spread across her face, but I guess I would have done the same if I saw some girl checking out nine books that all contained *Change Your Life* in the title. Red flags. Big, blaring ones.

I was really thankful Juan the barber never approached me from a distance on the day I dropped the pile of *Change Your Attitude* and *Change the World* and *Change Your Life Now* books all over the stoop. I would have been forced to tell him I was on a quest to learn how to be full and whole, while laughing with my inner child, while learning how to clutch my love handles with thick infatuation and be my own source of light. He probably would have looked at me sideways and asked why I was trying to learn how to fix my life by reading a book.

The books were anticlimactic. In case you were wondering. I wanted some secret, a step-by-step process that might actually stick. I am sure it works for some people but self-help just always made me feel terribly alone. Every time I opened another book, I didn't know how to rally with the universe. And the universe felt so impersonal— not the kind of thing you could jam your forehead up against to peer through the glass of it and see where you fall in the midst of all the chaos.

I guess I was too young to realize we don't always get that kind of control in steering life. Sometimes, to learn how to be a better version of yourself, you have to trudge through some serious mud. It's not pretty. It's not rhythmic. It's not step-by-step or in any recipelike fashion. It's just mud.

It was my idea to try this church. I had made the promise to my mother that I would, at least, lift up a rock or something while in the Bronx and try to find God. The church was only about a half a mile away from our apartment. Small and plain sitting beside its brick siblings, it looked like a classic white-steepled church—the kind you see in movies.

We walked quietly into the building. People already filled the room, hugging one another like they hadn't seen each other in years. There were gasps. And exchanges. And people you just knew had touched someone's shoulder last week and said, "I'll be praying for you," and really, really meant it. They had really, really pinned that person down to their nighttime whispers that week.

It was what I like to call a "church that doesn't just happen on Sunday." It was about some real belief that God wasn't just going to show up on Sunday and cop out by Tuesday morning. The way they talked about God, and brought Him into their conversations, made me wonder what I was missing out on. They sounded like they were sitting down to talk to God every morning. I'd only ever known how to script a bunch of wants—long, like a Christmas list—and then whine all week when God wasn't "showing up" to give me everything I asked for.

At random points before the church service began, people came by and shook our hands and asked what brought us to their little church. Their little community. There were a few who skipped the handshakes and went right for the hugs, spreading their arms out wide and challenging us to come at them. It felt as if their arms swallowed me up for tiny eternities. I winced when they drew me in. I winced when they released me and went back to their conversations with other people. I couldn't help but be jealous as they let go and walked away. As strange as it sounds, I wanted to be one of the people they missed from the week before.

People sang. Feet stomped. Hands clapped in ripples. There was shouting up to the ceilings, "Jesus Christ! Hallelujah!" as if Jesus himself were hosting a private party in the steeple. Everyone was swept up and singing in unison. It felt like the walls of the tiny building might give out from all the rejoicing. If joy could break windows and hallelujahs could break the floorboards, this church would have been broken down by noon.

A woman waved a yellow flag violently through the air, coming up and down the aisles. Another woman fell down onto her knees, lifting her hands up while tears stampeded out of her eyes. People yelled upward in different languages. The scene was intoxicating.

I was swept into the celebration. Every kind of emotion crashed into me. I gripped the pew, feeling nearly drunk and dizzy from all the joy that was nose-tailing me from every direction. *God doesn't feel this way,* I thought. *God is a boss. An authority. A dictator.*

He was a conditional lover. He was a gossip who always had something to say about what I had done wrong. He struck tallies against me on His chalkboard in the sky. He ripped the winged petals of daisies off, "I love you, *I love you not . . .*" I dumbed Him down. I dressed Him in doubt. I cloaked God's shoulders with an accent of judgment and always thought He was some angry being perched up in the clouds, throwing down thunderbolts and clomping all over the bar scene yelling, "SINNNNERRRRSSSSSSS." He was the dude who ruined the party, not the one who started it.

What kind of God had these people met and mingled with? What different chunk of heaven were they all partying hard in? I wanted a piece of their heaven. If this was heaven, I wanted a piece of it.

The music trailed throughout the church. I touched my cheeks and noticed I was crying. Emotions I could not categorize were scampering all around my insides. I was hungry. This was a different kind of hunger. I was lonely. I was envious of the people all around me, of what they had. How they all held hands so easily. They leaned on one another so completely. Here I was—always wanting to stop the poverty or touch the poverty or know the poverty—and I didn't even know how to acknowledge my own. I didn't know how to admit that I was missing something.

You know that moment where you've gotten all the goop and slime out from the inside of the pumpkin, just before you're about to carve that sucker and morph it into a jack-o'-lantern? That's what it felt like—just the guts and truth of me in place of the pulp. But even in the pulp, there are always seeds just waiting. Waiting to be noticed for what they could become if you grow them right.

I was the stubborn one who walked into the year thinking I was going to "help" someone. But in that church, as something was ripping on the inside of me, I realized I was the one who needed help. I was the one who was going to be helped as the year unfolded. Like I said, there were hopeful seeds.

One afternoon, a few weeks into working with Sister Margaret, she took me along with her to attend an informational meeting across town for a grant application process. She had some grants she wanted the life center to start applying for, so I offered to help in filling out applications and trying to get some extra funding. Truthfully, I didn't have any idea how to apply for grants but I was ready to get my hands on any sort of work. My answer to everything in those days was yes. Yes, I will attend the meeting. Yes, I will figure this out. Yes, I will do anything if you just promise to keep my hands full.

I tried to stay focused at the meeting but I didn't know half the terminology the woman at the front of the room was firing at us. I only picked at the company-catered cookies in the center of the table, carving the little chocolate chips out from the middle and stacking them into a pile on the napkin before me. My eyes kept darting from person to person, all applying for the same loans, and then back to Sister Margaret as she rifled through the massive stack of papers they handed out when we arrived at the front door. If she was worried in that moment, she kept it unseen like a secret.

I can't possibly help this situation, I just kept thinking. *I don't know how to help her. I really don't.* I wished I had a solution to all the budget cuts and decreased funding. I wished there was a better system. All I could really do was stare down into my lap at the smallness of my hands. I felt helpless. I felt like there was so much I didn't understand.

Looking back, I wish that everyone could have that sort of moment: a moment where you realize that your hands are so impossibly small and this world is so impossibly big. And the two don't seem to add up. Maybe recognizing the smallness of your own hands is just the very first step to changing anything at all.

Speaking of small hands, I found myself falling in love with twenty-six little pairs of them. Instead of continuing to float from classroom to classroom, helping out where there were spaces needing to be filled, I ended up mostly staying in one of the classrooms beside an aide named Ms. Cheryl. I was pretty certain from the beginning of working with her that she didn't like me. She was stern and no-nonsense with the kids. I tried not to get in her way, weaving around her and trying to act like I knew the way the classroom operated. But she let me start reading with the kids in the morning. And then I found a place beside her when we'd take the kids to the park every afternoon.

Through the patterns of serving breakfast and laying Superman and princess sheets across bright blue cots on the floor at naptime, a relationship formed. For the first few weeks she called me "punk," and "punk" slowly morphed into "girl" and "girl" frayed into "mama." And I loved that she called me "mama" because I know that I called myself all sorts of ugly names when I got ready to fall asleep at night and I'd come back every morning and she'd still call me "mama." I didn't know it at the time, but that was grace. "Mama" is the best definition of grace I've got.

Our relationship unraveled into something not quite replaceable, just like that. It unraveled and we became something while we sat in tiny-human chairs and made friendship bracelets out of brightly colored beads and black pipe cleaners. I slowly learned that Ms. Cheryl is soft more than she is no-nonsense. She's soft but she has a voice. And she was the first to point out I didn't have one.

"You're a mouse," she told me. "I'm gonna wait for the day when you're not a mouse anymore." She was honest like that.

I kept going back to Ms. Cheryl and the kids. I found ways to spend more and more time with them. Sometimes, when I knew my NGO meetings were in the afternoon, I would go into the life center early to have breakfast with the kids. Even just the familiar task of ripping the lids off the Malt-O-Meal cereals beside Cheryl was a routine I looked forward to. Maybe it sounds too simple but I liked being needed. I liked having a role where if you left for a little while, there'd be pictures and little trinkets waiting on your return. I'm not even trying to say that selfishly. I just want to be wanted. I want to be the kind of person you'd think to miss if something happened, and life shifted, and I wasn't here anymore.

I like to think my heart endured the same kind of transformation the Grinch's did at the point where he hears all the Whos belting their brains out. It swelled. And it grew. And I started harboring all these weird maternal feelings every time another tiny human with a bright blue T-shirt and leopard tights would call me "Miss Hannah." I was a goner for each one of them—Joel, the heartbreaker. Yarelis, the troublemaker. Isis, the sassy one. Even at such a small size, they were little firecrackers and optimists and tattletales and bosses. And even though it was frustrating that their peanut brains would forget everything you taught them the day before, I liked getting to watch them remember the sounds of the alphabet. I liked the way manners were slowly stitched into their conversations and they learned to say *thank you* and *please*. I liked how they would cry over the strangest things and you'd try to hold them through their sobbing but their words were so muffled and breathy you never got down to the root of what made them start crying in the first place. And I liked that five minutes later, the crying would be gone. It wouldn't stick. It wouldn't hold. It wouldn't follow the babes throughout the day. They bounced right back, and I admired them for it.

And so some days the best part of my day would be attending a really great meeting on hunger or girls' education in one of the pockets of the UN. But most days, the best part of the day would be right after I squirted twenty-six individual pumps of hand sanitizer into the tiniest of hands and scooted the kids into the classroom after bathroom break. We would turn on the music and we would dance. The sounds of Justin Bieber would flood the classroom. A chorus of "Baby, baby, baby," sung by babies, easily became the soundtrack of my life.

"We gonna make a sandwich," the little girl said, bringing over a bin full of plastic shapes of all different colors. She wore lime-green, thick-framed glasses. Her eyes stuck out like bug eyes beneath those frames. Little braids adorned her entire head. She was the smallest of the class but she had this robust laugh that spilled into every tiny thing she said and touched.

She sank her baby brown hands into the bin and began plucking out shapes. Red ovals. Blue hexagons. Green circles.

"We gots cheese," she said, handing me a square of what we imagined would be baby-blue American cheese. And then yellow triangular ham. Rectangular green chicken the color of grass come spring.

"Thank you!" I shouted with every layer she put on my sandwich. My hands were cupping a colossal sandwich full of colors and shapes. She giggled furiously every time I said the word and pretended to devour the entire thing.

"Thank you! Thank you! Thank you!" Her laughter exploded and I know it got stuck in random parts of me, like shrapnel.

It was in those simple moments that asked for no attention and didn't flaunt themselves as big and flashy that I genuinely wanted to be able to say those two words: *Thank. You. Thank. You. Thank you.* I wanted to believe them. I wanted to be grateful. I wanted to remember I had the kinds of blessings I should think to count more.

So I counted. I counted because it made me feel closer to Celia and the lists we used to write back and forth to each other on scraps of paper in college and leave inside of each other's mailboxes. We called those lists "thirty reasons" and it became our tradition.

When one of us was complaining or having an off day, the typical response from the other became, "Make a list . . . get a piece of paper out and make a list of thirty reasons to be thankful. And don't stop at thirty if you don't have to." Instantly, gratitude would flood back in by the handful. We made lists and lists to ward off any feelings that the blessings we had might not be good enough. They were plenty. And a simple list could show us that.

Sitting on the stoop, after work was done for the day, I counted my blessings in the red journal that went sailing back to Celia in the mail, trying to just focus on the good things all around me.

1. *Being alive and well*
2. *Moty's 60¢ coffee*
3. *My stoop*
4. *Yellow ribbons (a little girl just walked by with one in her hair)*
5. *Cute barbers*

I counted as a way to try to release the worry. I counted to convince myself the loneliness wasn't real and the disconnect wasn't there and it was okay to have small hands and no idea what to do with them.

Fitting Rooms

In the middle of September, I met up with Jessica, a friend from college. We graduated the same year. She was living in Brooklyn now and working for a theater company. She proposed we go to a football game at Fordham University, just a mile down the road from where I lived. Our alma mater was playing against the Rams that weekend and friends from college would more than likely be in the area.

"Is it crazy that I miss it?" I asked her.

"College?"

"Yeah, I keep feeling like we'll just go back or something," I said.

We only made it up to halftime before we decided to ditch the game completely and just take a walk around the campus. The air smelled fresh that day. Septembers just seem to carry a scent of newness that makes me feel like I've been granted a do-over.

I wondered if she felt the same way I did. Like college had broken up with me. Like I was somebody, until I didn't feel like somebody anymore. I guess it's like any other breakup in that sense—you either live in the past of old sweaters and questions you can't possibly answer or you refuse to be defined by something you outgrew.

We made our way into Fordham's library. We took the stairs up to the second floor and moved toward the big glass windows overlooking the campus.

"Is it what you thought it would be?" she asked as we plunked down in two armchairs facing the window. I swung my legs over the side of the arm.

I knew the answer immediately: it wasn't. It felt like my whole life was on pause sometimes. While other friends were out there getting salaries and starting to make a dent in their student loans, I felt like I was playing pretend in the middle of the Bronx.

"Yes and no," I told her. "I mean, it's not like I actually thought I would move to New York City and everything would be perfect. Like I don't actually think I thought I would come here and instantly fall in love in a coffee shop or something."

"I read that blog post of yours," she said.

"My blog post?"

"The one you wrote about falling in love in a coffee shop."

I'd nearly forgotten that even as I was experiencing New York City for the first time, people were following the journey from their own computer screens.

I'd started blogging nine months earlier, during my senior year of college. I thought I was being really clever when I created a blog and called it As Simple as That. As Simple as That was birthed out of the twenty-year-old version of me who thought you could tie up everything in life into a big white bow. That's the main beef I used to have with the girl who started that blog. I used to think that if I could, I'd sit the younger version of myself down and ask, "Yo, girl, what's the deal? Why so happy? Why must everything end so poetically?"

She probably would have just shrugged at me and given me a really simple answer: "Because you don't let me go deeper than that. You don't let me write anything but pretty stories that make people feel like they're tromping through unicorn vomit while holding baskets of cup-cakes in their arms."

She would have been right. I was used to editing. I was good at fil-tering. It wasn't until I published a piece about my relationship with my father that I realized the truth: life isn't really simple.

I wrote about the shame I felt over his occupation as a town gar-bageman growing up. How I would spend years carrying that shame and shutting him out of my life because I wished he would just do a worthy job. My hands were trembling as I wrote about the most distinct feature of my father: his callused hands. I grew up thinking they were just dirty hands, but now I know they were a symbol of sacrifice. The post was my way of trying to reconcile the day my mother came to me in the kitchen as I was unloading things out of the dishwasher and said, "You're breaking his heart. You're breaking the heart of the best man you'll ever know." It was a peace offering to make up for a war zone he didn't even know I'd created during all those years when I lied about who my father was and what he did for a living.

I published the piece. And the dean of my college e-mailed me to let me know he had sat at his kitchen table after reading it, crying into his hands and telling his wife all these things he'd never actually said about his own blue-collar father. And my father, he was never more proud of anything than he was of that piece. He printed out copies and shared them everywhere. He and I, we've tried harder since.

I changed the name of the blog shortly after that piece. And I stopped hiding behind the pretty words. I learned vulnerability is a bit like those Russian nesting dolls, the ones that get smaller and smaller in size when you twist the top off and pull another one out. In the end, you're left with the tiniest doll, that one nugget. No more layers to take off. Nothing left but a surprise, the surprise of finding out the littlest doll is the most solid of them all. It doesn't hide inside of itself.

And once I was vulnerable, I started to form this community with my blog readers. It was sort of like we were all traveling together on the Oregon Trail, except none of my blog readers ever died of dysentery. I started blabbering on about Emily and Stephen Ko and Chase and all these other people I'd never actually met in real life but who were my blog homies. And I learned the Internet is really just a thin veil between us. Sometimes you're only a blog comment away from meeting a best friend or falling in love.

*   *   *

Back to Jessica and falling in love in a coffee shop.

"You know," she said, her voice quiet, "I think you are going to fall in love in that coffee shop." She paused. "But I don't think it will happen in the way you expect. I think there is going to be an idea, some sort of idea you will have. You're going to fall in love with it in that coffee shop. And your life will change right there."

I thought I'd be the girl who always wore a red hat and stood off on her own waiting for the train, smiling for no reason at all and making everyone around her think she was full of mystery. Sort of like Delilah—the girl in New York City with a boyfriend who had a guitar who wrote lines like, "Times Square can't shine as bright as you." I always thought New York City would be romantic, like a boyfriend who would kiss my hand or throw rocks at my window to get my attention.

In actuality, the closest I ever came to rocks getting thrown at my window was the barber Juan, standing three floors down below me on the ground, with his arms crossed in front of him. It was ten p.m. We'd continued to exchange glances from across the street until the day he came over and introduced himself and gave me a business card. I didn't ever call the number on the card. I just hid it beneath my mattress until the night he showed up outside my window. My roommates forced me out the door.

"Why didn't you call me?" he asked me when I met him on the stoop.

"It's complicated," I answered.

"With me?"

I didn't know what to say on the spot so I blurted out, "I have a boyfriend. And it's complicated."

I was lying to Juan. Right to his beautiful, bearded face, I was blatantly lying about a boyfriend who didn't exist back home.

"What's complicated?" he asked. "Doesn't he see what he has?"

His answer punched me in the gut. I was a bad person. This was one of those moments where God smacks you in the face for lying through other people's sweetness.

"Distance is a hard thing," I said back. That much wasn't a lie at least. He didn't ask me what I missed or if he could do anything to make it better. He just changed the subject.

"What will you do when this is done?" he asked. I'm sure he was used to seeing volunteers go in and out of this apartment, year after year.

I hesitated to answer him. I wanted to say I would like to be a writer, but nothing about saying it ever felt practical. It was like you were just gearing up for people to put their worried eyes on you and answer back, "Oh, so you want to live in your parents' basement and eat ramen noodles until you conjure up the next Harry Potter? Sounds really responsible." I'm just the product of my grandmother telling me for years she would see my name on the spines of books. That's why I wanted to be a writer—because someone I loved told me I could be one. And I would do anything it took in this world to be able to tell that one person she was right to believe in me.

"I want to be a writer," I said. I waited for him to flinch. I should have known he wouldn't. He just smiled and told me that sounded good to him.

"How about you? Has this always been the dream? You're pretty good at what you do." He was the one everyone always talked about.

"This is just something I do," he said. "I've always wanted to be a cop. That would be pretty cool."

"So be a cop then!" My voice screeched with excitement. "Go out there and be a cop!"

"Eh, maybe." He shrugged. And then he smiled.

"You're too skinny," he said after a few seconds. "You need to eat more chicken." And just like that, the moment of chasing after dreams on the stoop was gone.

We talked for a little longer. He apologized again for my boyfriend (the one I made up) being a dud. I walked inside a few moments later and bolted the door behind me. I put my head up against it and let my back slide all the way down to the floor, where I sat in the dark for a few minutes before going upstairs to my roommates.

I wondered why I wanted so much. Juan could cut hair and cut more hair and his dreams of being a cop might never actually turn into something more than that. And then there was me. I'd gotten the dream I always said I wanted so badly: the chance to live in New York City. And yet I was unhappy. And I rarely said thank-you for it. And I was looking for escape routes all the time. Ways to not fully be there, to be distracted by other lives, the lives of people I knew from high school and college that were happening in different states and cities. I would waste hours comparing my life to theirs, sitting the two of them side by side and circling the things that seemed out of place in my own life, like the "What's Wrong?" pictures in the back of the *Highlights* magazines.

I don't exactly know what happened that night after I went upstairs. What I did or what I said. But the routine every single night seemed to be the same. It meshed into a slow, unbreakable cycle. I'd keep the phone clutched in my hand as I tried to fall asleep. I would scroll and scroll and scroll through the thoughts and images other people posted online, absorbing their fragmented glimpses of daily life, like old hymns you read with the hope you'll find yourself known through them.

I'd wake up the next morning and I wouldn't even push the white down comforter off me before I was checking in and seeing where I'd been missed or mentioned the night before. Being seen somewhere at two a.m. through a "like" or a retweet didn't actually fill me. It was about as filling as the massive muffins, the ones the size of your head, they sell at the gas station. You take one look at that rock of a thing with blueberries sticking out of it and you swear it's going to keep you full for the next three hours. Alas, the sugars and indigestible ingredients only hold you over for about five minutes before the rumbling ensues. This time, louder.

There was a hollow space inside of me. So I looked for things to fill that space, and social media was there. I would crawl into bed at night and I would let social media spoon me and try to soothe the parts of me that whispered, *I want to be seen. I want to be known. I want to be more than just a face in the crowd.*

The deep, stinging loneliness only throbbed more by the glow of the screen. The disconnect grew.

In one of my sociology classes in college I had read a book that identified America as an overdiagnosed society. We were depressed. We were anxious. We were paranoid. And then a cluster of pharmaceutical companies swept in to medicate us and make their billions. The book didn't necessarily make an evil out of antidepressants, but it was frightening to read interview after interview of people who'd only sat down for twenty-minute appointments with therapists before they walked out of the office with a prescription for Zoloft. The book terrified me. I made silent vows to myself I would never be someone to sit in a therapist's office, cross my legs back and forth, and wait for the diagnosis of depression to drop off the therapist's tongue like an anvil.

When that time came, I learned I actually sit real still in those kinds of situations. That first visit to see a therapist, I kept two feet planted firmly on the ground. I sat up straight as a rail, even when the therapist told me I could relax. That's what the pillows were for.

He wasn't really a therapist so much as some sort of angel I found on Google. It was fate or destiny or something that I chose him after a search engine spit back hundreds of therapists waiting in the skyscrapers all around my Manhattan office. I coaxed myself to make the appointment for one p.m. on a Thursday. And I further coaxed myself to show up for the appointment and not vomit all over his rug.

We were building a relationship, I told myself as I walked into his office for the first time. That's what this would be. Me and him. We would be an "us." I felt this overwhelming urge to make him like me, to make him think I was completely fine. Which is probably a jacked-up idea: let me not say what I really feel because I want to seem put together in front of a person who earns a living trying to help me get all the pieces back together. I didn't want to be a mess in front of him. I wanted him to chuckle to himself and say, "Darling, you don't need therapy."

I was really reserved. And he told me he'd started reading my blog after I e-mailed him. When he'd bring up a post I had recently written I'd want to say, "*Yo, dude, I'm a steel trap.* Nothing you read on that blog page is going to give you a lens into how I am feeling now. These tears in my eyes are the only real thing you've got of me."

But only two sessions into "us"—only two hour-long sessions into our relationship—he told me in the sweetest, most angelic voice that I didn't have the right insurance. He'd been slow on processing the paperwork but it turned out I wasn't covered. Just one of the sessions would be five weeks' worth of my stipend. I sat on his couch, clutching his throw pillow, knowing I had to leave. We were over. I couldn't pay over $100 to weep for an hour when I managed to do that just fine, and daily, for free. I could get a real boyfriend for that.

"You're doing good in this world," he told me. His hands wrapped around his notepad as he talked. "I used to be able to do the same, and I miss that. So I want to help you. And I want to take you on pro bono."

And so formed our unspoken agreement that he would listen and I would cry and we'd keep our lips zipped when it came to payment. I liked that he had this look on his face that never changed and he never seemed fazed by me, and I became the puddle, the crazy one in the relationship who always felt like the sky was falling down around her. And I just let the therapy work the way it was supposed to work. And, in a short time, therapy could have gradually been renamed "Dribble snot into throw pillows. Then pull yourself together. Breathe through your nose. And get real resolved on what is actually happening below the surface." Because that's just what we did every week for an hour on Thursdays. I stayed. I waded through messes. Even when he said it.

"You have depression," he said to me. "It seems to be situational, but I would say it's depression."

I stared at him blankly, like I suddenly wasn't understanding him. I wanted to tell him he was wrong to even say it. "My life is good. My life is blessed. I have two parents. They love each other a lot. They show it in little ways. There are no broken dishes. I went to college. I have great friends. The heartbreaks of my life are minor. I am only twenty-two. It would make very little sense for me to be depressed." I opened my mouth to say something but he cut me off.

"I just don't want you to think that crying every afternoon at two p.m. is a normal thing. And I also don't want you to think it has to last forever." He paused. "But most of all, I don't want you to think this is just a matter of 'get stronger.'"

I went home that night with the word *depression* scribbled on a piece of square paper. It sat on my desk at the other side of the room. But surprisingly, nothing about the word changed anything. The *D* and the *P* and the *S* didn't leap off the paper and bully me. The diagnosis didn't change anything inside of me. I just thought: *I guess it fits. Just like walking into a fitting room, I guess it fits for right now.*

"You've got this," I *whispered* to the stretch material of the dress as I pulled it down around my legs on both sides and turned sideways in the mirror. I kept saying it over and over again. "You've got this. You've got this."

It was the first of what would turn out to be dozens of fitting rooms for me and the girl in the mirror. I needed a dress. I'd been invited to a gala at the Time Warner Center by a friend I'd met when I was a sophomore in college. A week after we met he'd called me up on Valentine's Day and told me the guard at the front gate of my campus gave him five minutes to come and find me. I met him in the middle of the parking lot outside one of the dorms. He handed me a yellow rose. Yellow is the color of friendship. I don't know if we were ever supposed to push for more than that. He'd graduated two years before me and took a job on Wall Street. And now we were here—the same city.

After a morning at the Guggenheim, we wrapped up our reunion at Sarabeth's, for the usual chaos and clinking of coffee cups that was New York City's beau on a Saturday afternoon: brunch. Sweet-syrup-trickling, goat-cheese-smearing, whole-wheat-pancakes-nomming brunch. A church of its own in the already-worshipped city. Over the most mammoth of pumpkin waffles that Manhattan could stomach, globbed with honey and sour cream (an unlikely couple that turn out to win prom king and queen), he asked me to attend the benefit with him.

I would need to get a dress. Me and said dress would have a prenup before I ever slipped her on. We would have one night together. Nothing more. Nothing less. And then, at the end of the night, when the train took me back to the Bronx, I would slip her off and leave her at my ankles until it was time to stuff her back into her black shopping bag and bring her back to the store, all the tags intact.

Just to be clear: I wanted the dress. And I wanted to act with more integrity. And I totally respect store clerks. But a stipend of $25 doesn't really afford you much and everything inside of me felt guilty every time I swiped my credit card.

We were here. She and I. Me and the girl wearing my clothes. The one with the wild hair. Eyes that always looked prettier when she cried. The green would soak up the brown and yellow like a sponge and it looked like something electric was finger-painting around her pupils. And that girl wanted to be someone different.

I don't know if you've ever wanted that. If not, I am fine to stand alone as the only person ever—in the history of ever—who wished she could trade lives with someone else. Someone who didn't think so much or care so much or act as if her whole existence were a twelve-track CD of apologies on repeat. Someone who got kissed in the rain often and had too many awesome plans to remember to buy groceries and would bring home flowers randomly, just because they were beautiful and she liked the way they looked in her gold vases.

It's surprisingly not as simple as the days when I was five years old and my best friend and I would pretend to swap hair, as if they were helmets we kept on our heads, every day before plowing out onto the blacktop for recess. She'd swap her ropy braids with me for my orphan-Annie haircut and we thought nothing was more brilliant than getting to be somebody else for a solid thirty-five minutes. Turns out, that kind of mobility and imagination peaks and fades around the age of thirteen.

Still, in that fitting room, I wanted to be someone else. Someone in the rooms surrounding me.

"Why am I here?" The question churned and flipped as I whispered it beneath my breath. I was just hoping I might be heard in that fitting room.

"Use me," I whispered. "Please, use me."

It was those two words, repeated over and over again, that hummed deep inside of me those days. Some mornings I called them a song. Other mornings they were an anthem. That day—in the middle of another random fitting room tucked inside Manhattan—they were a prayer.

"Use me. Use me."

If you're real, if you're good or not good, if you care or don't care, just use me. Just do something with me. Just give me some sort of purpose for standing on this earth.

"Use me, use me."

You don't have to love me, you don't even have to look at me, but if you have something for me, please show me. If you made me—if you really, really made me—then you know about this heart of mine and how badly it is breaking to just do something that matters.

"Use me, use me." The prayer spread itself wide like a Chinese fan. *Use me. Find me. Show me. Meet me. Please, just don't forget me.*

Section 2

Lost and Found

Dear You

"This is a Bronx-bound express Four train," the woman over the intercom said as I settled into a seat and placed my bag on my lap. "The next stop is Grand Central. Forty-Second Street."

"Stand clear of the closing doors, please."

The two prerecorded voices—announcing every stop along the way—had somehow morphed into my faithful travel companions throughout the last two months. When no one would talk on the subway, those two automated voices were reliable and truthful. I made up stories for the two of them. I liked to imagine they were real people who met each other at the MTA subway voice auditions and both nailed the roles as Subway Voice #1 and Subway Voice #2. They'd been virtually inseparable after that day. I wrote their wedding vows to each other in my head—how the woman always promised to let the man know where they were headed and how he always promised to warn her of the closing doors right in front of her. Together, they lived a long and happy life tangled in white sheets in their apartment overlooking the Hudson River. And, of course, they started a family. And they taught their babies how to speak in robust and authoritative voices so they could one day carry on the family business of being subway voices for the MTA.

It was on the brink of October. October is just a month you naturally remember in a calendar year. October is a ruler. She captivates the Northeast like a dictator and pulls people in with her crisp air and the way she makes something truly beautiful out of summer dying. I was on my way home from work. As the train pulled into Grand Central, I braced myself for the rush of commuters waiting just beyond the glass to squeeze into the subway car, taking up every inch of extra space. It was that hour of the evening when everyone is trying to get away from the day and get home to dinner tables and cocktail hours and lovers and dogs. The end of the workday feels almost tangible in New York City, as if you can latch on to it like a rung of a ladder.

I looked down at my shoes as the people filled the train, and then I saw her. I saw her shoes. She wore those beat-up unlaced construction boots. I followed the shoes, laceless hole by laceless hole, all the way up to the face of an old woman. She was tiny. She had a slight slump in her shoulders. She was short in stature and wore a bright red cap. Wisps of gray poked out from beneath it.

As she came toward me, I swear she looked me in the eyes. It was maybe only for half of a second, but I know it happened. Her whole demeanor was flooded with exhaustion. From the second I saw her eyes—the color of mud—I tucked her and her eye color into a concordance in my mind. *Brown, brown, brown.*

She reminded me of the morning my mother brought a friend to church whom I hadn't seen in years. When I saw her, I didn't even recognize her. Her eyes looked hollowed out, leftover remnants of eyeliner from the night before still stuck on her lids. My mother blinked twice at me in the middle of the lobby, and when her friend walked away to get some coffee she said, "She doesn't normally look like this. She had a late night, I think. I don't really know what happened." All I could see was emptiness though.

The dirt on the woman in the red hat was traceable. I watched her make her way to my side of the train. She sat down across from me, settling into a narrow seat wedged against the wall. Her eyes darted around the train quickly. Her hat covered parts of her face but I could still see the wrinkles whispered deep into her skin. She folded her hands in her lap, clasped them together like she was ready to pray, and put her head against the wall. She didn't move. She didn't flinch. Her feet stayed planted on the ground. I kept looking back at her construction boots, perfectly lace-less. No way to tie bows or make rabbit ears out of long leather laces.

I can't explain it. I wish I could. I have no real explanation for why she, out of all the people who pushed into that subway at Grand Central Terminal, would catch my attention. But I couldn't shake it.

I'm crazy. This is it. I'm going insane. They'll come for me soon with their pretty white jackets with sleeves that tie in bows in the back so your arms can't move, I thought. I felt crazy for staring at her. For being unable to look away. For wanting to say anything that would break the silence of the train as it pushed uptown. I was secretly praying she'd open up her eyes, look me straight in the face, and say something along the lines of, "Yeah, girl, I'm lonely too. Just look around, we all are."

I could get down on my knees, my black tights kissing the dirty subway floor, and scoot over to clasp her hands and ask her about her day. My mother would have done that. My mother has this gift that's hard to pin to a page with words because she is always thinking about everyone else first. She just wants everyone around her to feel known.

I thought of my mother as I watched the woman, her head still down, and I could trace the dirt on her hat. Her fists were clenched tight in her lap. I thought about all the measures and the might and energy my mother took out of herself to make me strong. How when my body lost fuel or my mind started to wander into dark places where I shut love out, she'd always been the one to bring me back to center. How, during college, the visit to the post office was the best chunk of my day when I found a letter waiting for me with her scribbles etched on the envelope.

I was watching the old woman, pulling at the curls in my hair, and thinking about the love letters my mother wrote and how she must have known an ordinary piece of loose-leaf paper morphs into a love letter when a person puts their self into it. Suddenly, the words steam off the page. Suddenly, your hands are caked with the remnants of someone else's understanding and compassion and goodness.

Words, I thought, remembering the notebook in the belly of my bag. I could write the woman a note and give it to her as I exited the train. I could drop it at her feet.

I pulled the notebook out from my bag. It was my favorite notebook, a bright blue and green peacock feather sprawling across the front of it with speckled dots of gold playing in the veins of each feather wisp. I turned to a new page and began writing a letter. The words spilled out of me. There wasn't a gap of silence or question of what to write as the words clattered out and onto the page. It was syllables spilling like gushing water. They were the kinds of words you read back and every lettered limb surprises you because you never knew you really felt those things the whole time.

> *Dear you,*
>
> *You and I have never met so we should probably just start here. Before any other words get placed on this page, you should know that our time together is limited. We probably won't ever meet beyond this one encounter. You won't know me apart from the creases in this paper and swooping of my cursive. We won't ever sit down over coffee or laugh like we're plucking old jokes from our memory. We may never have this kind of thing and I want to learn to be okay with that . . .*
>
> *I'm struggling. Struggling in a way that I don't know how to admit to anyone around me. I moved to New York City just two months ago and still haven't found myself at home among the clamor. I feel like I should have sunk more easily into this role as a New Yorker, as a Somebody who doesn't speak and doesn't smile and sits in coffee shops alone and is just fine with the solitude. But I'm not. It's driving me crazy. I'm falling apart. I see a girl and a guy meet up in the center of Grand Central, after they've both said good-bye to the longer part of their day, and something inside of me starts to ache. Because I want that familiar face. I want someone, anyone, to tell me I am not alone in all of this.*
>
> *I don't know your story and I guess that doesn't really matter now, at least it doesn't stop me from wanting the very best for you. You deserve that, don't you know it?*
>
> *It's a little funny. That's the thing we never say to one another—that we all deserve goodness. That we deserve the best stories. That our lives are something to be in awe of and we are*

*just so lucky to be alive and breathing today. It is the first thing I
forget. It will probably be the first truth I discard when I fold up
this love letter and walk away. I will continue bustling around
like crazy, thinking I might find another moment to tell someone
how much they truly matter to me. And then I will forget to look
up. And the day will suddenly be over.*

*I don't want you to slip through my fingers like that so do me
a favor and know the truth: You're worth it. You are absolutely,
unbelievably worth it and you were made for mighty things.
Keep pushing on. Keep pressing. Don't let anyone in this wide,
wide world ever try to snuff out the light you bring. You have
to know that it matters. The world is going to try to convince
you otherwise but don't listen. Please. Don't. Listen. You are a
marvel. It matters that you are here. If ever you start to forget
these things, come find me.*

I looked up without signing the letter. I hadn't even heard my MTA
subway voice buddies announce all the stops up to 161st Street, Yankee
Stadium. The train had shifted. People had moved from their original
places and we were already crawling up close to the stop where I'd get
off and walk the quarter mile home past all the dress shops and fast-
food restaurants that led up to our apartment.

The shoes. The laceless construction boots. I went to look up at
them and they were gone. The woman was gone. It was like she'd never
even been there to begin with. It didn't make any sense that I could become so swept up with the letter writing that I hadn't even noticed her
clomping away from me. A boy with a fauxhawk replaced her now. His
eyes were closed. He had more room to breathe since the congestion of
the train had cleared out. His legs were stretched out in front of him,
one crossed over the other. All of his laces were intact.

After I wrote the letter, I wasn't sure what to do with it. It was
done, but she was gone, and she'd never know it was for her. I stared
down at the unsigned letter, wondering if I should write my name or
leave it unsigned. I didn't know what to write.

I couldn't let the woman go. Despite my best efforts to push her from my thoughts, the image of her followed me home that night. And into the next morning. And I looked for her on the train during the busy commute the next day. I never found her. I still look closely at people wearing bright red caps and I check their eye color to see if it is the same muddy brown as the eyes of the woman on the train.

The letter stayed tucked inside my notebook until I figured out how to sign it with a name that felt genuine and true. Eventually the right signature came:

> *Sending light and love,*
> *A girl just trying to find her way.*

A girl just trying to find her way. The description fit me the instant I scribbled it down on the page. The title felt solid, like the way it feels to put on a good pair of shoes and get a little giddy over the realization the backs of your feet won't blister if you walk around in them for extended periods of distance. I'd listened for too long to the rumor, which somehow morphed into a truth, that I had to have everything figured out, I had to know where I was going. The next turn. The five-year plan. The big "What's next?" I was sitting there on the train with a brand-new signature before me. I knew close to nothing about what would happen next at any given moment, and surprisingly, that was okay.

This was me, lost in the way that makes you say to yourself, "Okay . . . I don't know exactly where I am going, or where I will be led, but I'm just going to follow this letter writing and hope. Just follow this and hope."

Hope can be a mighty powerful thing when you decide to tangle it into a journey. Hope can shake things up a bit. It'll convince you that even if you don't know what direction you're headed in, something will meet you at the end.

Something broke inside of me when I wrote that first letter. Maybe it was the silence, maybe it was the need to make everything look perfect from the outside, but the truth was staring back at me from the page. I could have slabbed honesty thick onto everything that day because it made me remember how it felt to let things out instead of holding them inside of me until something exploded.

Those same kinds of honest letters came marching out of me one by one until soon I filled up the notebook. I couldn't end it. I stopped choosing words when I started writing the letters. The words chose me. They were waking me up at two a.m., begging to be written down. They were etched into the rhythms of the street vendors on the way to work. They pummeled one another, stampeded to get out of me and find a resting spot on the page. Like a light switch going off inside me, it went from "Let me write a letter to someone" to "Either these words are going to come out of me or they are going to haunt me until I let them go."

I began picking people randomly, all along the avenues. Short people. Tall people. People who were evidently tourists. And, though they will never know it, they became my pen pals for the afternoon. I would take them through my life and together we would grapple in tiny coffee shops and on the benches lining the roadways in Central Park with the things we never understood. I would talk to them about life and love and the things I always wanted and the things I was afraid to say I wanted out loud because it made them seem more real.

I wrote with an honesty that I didn't have at any other time, even when I went to write in my diary at night. These letters were different. They were big, blaring chunks of my heart, but they were stories. Each one made me realize so much was happening all around me, even when I wanted to chalk it all up to normalcy. Or nothing so special that you would pluck it out of a day and hold it up to the light. I stopped feeling so alone within a city that, for some people, echoed more than she sang.

I filled an entire notebook. And it was back on the train, just a few days later, that I decided to flip through them. I'd written dozens in such a small pocket of time. They never felt like they were my own. They always felt like they were meant for other people.

I don't know where the idea came from first. I wish I could pin it down to the page, but I realized in that moment the words would never serve me again. I didn't need them. So I went to the first letter and I ripped it from the binding of the peacock notebook. I looked around to see if anyone noticed what I was doing. No one looked up from their Kindles and their phones.

The plan was so clear. Clearer than anything I'd felt inside of me for a long time. I was going to scatter these love letters all over New York City. And once I set each one in its place, I would write even more. And you want to know why? Because it made me feel something. I didn't understand it, but I thought I could fall in love with this thing. And it felt like I was just supposed to follow after something I could love. For once, I didn't even want to know the root of it or try to figure it out. I just wanted to see where it would lead me if I followed.

After all, the notebook was full. What other choice was there than to rip and tear and leave the letters in places where other people would find them?

I tried to imagine what would make me pick up a letter, thinking it might have been for me all along, if I found it on a random subway train or in a coffee shop. I traced through the options in my head: *Open me. Pick me up. Take me home.*

I settled on something simple: *If you find this letter . . . then it's for you.* If I found those kinds of words scrawled onto a piece of paper, I might pick it up. I might see what was inside. And I honestly didn't know what I would think upon finding a love letter sitting inside of the creased sheet, written for me.

I wrote those words on the first letter.

I folded the letter and placed it behind me, my lower back holding it in place up until my subway stop would come and I could let the letter slip down onto the seat as I walked away. I kept looking around the train to be sure that no one noticed the letter hidden behind me. I tried to look unsuspicious. I reminded myself several times that I was not a criminal and I had not done anything wrong.

At Grand Central, I waited for the doors to open, and then busted out of my seat quickly. Darting through the doors, I kept walking faster and faster once my feet hit the platform. Away from the letter. My nerves surged. There was a whiff of adrenaline as I got farther away from the train, disappearing inside of New York City. *Gone, gone, gone.*

A while back, there was this love letter floating around the Internet a man wrote about his wife. In the letter, he described how her weight plummeted and how she found herself worrying about everything—work, failures, and problems with the children. Bags collected beneath her eyes and he eventually grew hopeless, figuring they would soon get divorced, because, really, what else was there for him to do as his wife left her body? But the man turned an unexpected corner and he did something that seems a little radical for the world today: he started to care for her more than ever before. He loved on her extravagantly. He met her in every moment with compliments. He flooded her sunken body with love. And she started to get better.

There's this last line in the letter, and it gets stuck in my throat every time I try to read it out loud: *If you love her to the point of madness, she will become it.*

That letter was out there, spiraling anonymously through the Internet, until somehow Brad Pitt's name got pinned to it. For a while, people thought he had written the letter about Angelina. The myth died hard though. People still don't know who wrote the letter. But when I read that last line, *If you love her to the point of madness, she will become it,* I decided to let go of my need to know the writer. It wasn't important anymore. No matter who wrote the words, they found a way to carry me somewhere else. And maybe that was the point of the letter all along—not to be known, but to carry people away for a little while.

I didn't need to sign the letters. I didn't have to hitch an e-mail or a phone number to the note. The point wasn't to be known. The point wasn't to be found. I was just so in love with the things of this world that take you elsewhere—out from your own shoes—I thought maybe if I could put a few of those things out there in the world, it might be enough for that day.

If You Find This Letter

I don't know if anyone has ever told you this or not but on Craigslist there is a section of the site that I like to call the "Secret Garden of Craigslist." It's called "Missed Connections"—though they really should rename it "watch the next few hours of your life get sucked away for good the second you click inside."

It's a virtual message board for all the people who see someone in a coffee shop, a dive bar, the grocery store, wherever, and wish they had the courage to say hello.

It's a booming collection of people who missed out and are grabbing for another chance. I saw a "missed connection" once from a boy who posted a picture of a note left on his lap while he was sleeping in one of the libraries of NYU, nearly two years ago. The note said something like *Hello, sleepy boy, I wonder what you are dreaming of.—The girl who sat across from you on the couch.* For two years he could not shake the girl who left him the note while he was dozing on piles of textbooks.

I think that boy is just one of the millions of us who keep wondering about a person we've never met or known or shared so much as a coffee with. A site like "Missed Connections" works because (a) we're human, (b) we crave connection, and (c) there is something dually haunting and beautiful about the idea of what might have been. The what-ifs. The maybes and the "Perhaps, one day"s.

I would read "Missed Connections" that year more than I care to admit. A few times a week I would scroll through the hopeful messages. One day I was sitting across from a guy on the subway, riding back up to the Bronx. He had these blue eyes that stick with me still. I've only ever dated boys with blue eyes. And he wore work boots, really dirty ones that made me think of my father. I thought for a second we might fall in love, because people always say you'll fall in love with someone who is just like your father or your mother. He looked my way a couple of times. I looked his way too. But at 125th Street, he stood to leave and didn't look back. It was nothing like those cell phone commercials where the girl shoves her phone number against the train window and suddenly you're touring through the flickering scenes of their falling in love and starting a family and raising the next great political leader. None of that happened.

I checked "Missed Connections" that night for the blue eyes. I thought about posting a note—*I saw you on the train. We had only ten minutes together. There was a mariachi band playing off to the side of us. The train was crowded. Thanks for making me feel like I was the only one there.*

I didn't post the note. There's a chance I might one day. I think it's just nice to know there is a message board that keeps all the hope—false hope or not—and that all the places we are standing in and the people we make eye contact with and the letters we leave for others to find aren't all for naught.

I kept Tucking and leaving, tucking and leaving. It became a pattern to my life. Tucking and leaving was basically my religion that October. I left the letters everywhere I could. I propped them on bathroom sinks. I slid them into coat pockets in department stores. I left them in fitting rooms. I would stick them into the seats at the UN when I would attend meetings. I was playing Juliet to the city.

I wrote stories. I brought people with me. And then I found stories I liked to tell and I kept telling over and over again. In a few of the letters, I wrote, *PS3563.08749.* A collection of numbers and letters I knew by heart. They still hang on the inside of me like bunting that drapes from memory to memory. That line of letters and numbers will only ever mean something to me. In the library on my college campus, there was a book on the third floor, right at the spot where *PS* and *PR* met.

It was a ritual in college that happened every single time I was having an off day. I created it for myself. In the middle of the chaos, on one of those days when nothing could seem to go right, I would close up my books, turn off my phone, and make the journey over to the library to pull the copy of Toni Morrison's *Beloved* out from the stacks. The language in that book is devastatingly beautiful.

One of my professors assigned the book to my class during a course on African-American literature. The professor taught with the confidence that books change you. They mess up your insides. They make you drool over the prospect of being a better human and a better lover and a better friend. They pull at your stomach and leave you raw and open and naked. Books can straight up mangle you and sometimes it's just better if you let them do their work.

She recommended we read the book by candlelight so we would be forced to scrunch up our eyes to focus on the words. It's a really thick book in the sense the language is as rich as molasses and it demands that you be slow, slow, slow with it if you want to get anything out of it.

I sat curled up in the coat closet of my apartment beside wellies and raincoats reading the text. The language, the plots, the character flaws—all of it just grips you tighter when you keep the phone turned off, when there is only candlelight to guide your eyes across the page. The words greet you slowly. You learn how to appreciate them more.

I know it sounds romantic, but I could only sit with the book for fifteen minutes at a time before needing to take a walk or go on a drive somewhere. Something nested inside of my stomach every time I picked up the book and I melted quickly into a pool of tears and snot, cross-legged in the middle of a closet.

"Hatred. You are feeling the wrath of hatred. Of the way humans have learned to hate one another," the professor said to me after class one afternoon when the rest of the students had packed up their things and left. I just sat there until the room emptied out, tears streaming down my face.

"Read on," she told me. "There has to be love somewhere." And so began my quest to look for love in most things. In piles of fear and hatred and worry and greed—I tried my best to wait on love instead.

After that class ended, I started going to the library to read it. After taking the copy of the book from the rack, I'd meander through the stacks until I found a small stool. There, I would sit, open the book, and turn to the very last page.

> He wants to put his story next to hers.
>
> "Sethe," he says, "me and you, we got more yesterday than anybody. We need some kind of tomorrow."
>
> He leans over and takes her hand. With the other he touches her face. "You your best thing, Sethe. You are." His holding fingers are holding hers.
>
> "Me? Me?"

That last page never changed. It never left me. It never walked away. It was always there, no matter how many times I made the journey back to those stacks. *You your best thing.* It was a reminder. A confirmation. A thing I could very easily go an entire day or week without remembering: be your own best thing.

It wasn't just the words though. It was everything about that routine. The secret spot in the library that only I knew about. The act of shutting down when everything got too crazed around me. Taking the break. Going for the walk. Breathing the whole way through. Deep breaths, deep breaths. Getting there. Holding something. Reading those words. Closing the book. Walking away. The whole of it added up to something I could always rely on when the world spun me off balance.

That same professor who ripped a hole into my life with that book, I can still see her holding the tattered copy of the text we were reading high in the air, as if she were trying to give the pages a glimpse of the sky. She brought the book down again to hold at her chest and came around the front of her desk. Sat down on top of it, slid her thighs back on the surface, and her feet dangled as she continued to talk.

"I spent the first two years of college trying to become what someone wanted me to be," she told us. Her tone was personal, as if there were cups of foaming brew between our hands as she spoke and this was an ease we'd found with one another after years of conversations like this one.

She spent so much time molding and shifting and pushing herself to be someone different from who she really was, and it only ever led to a breakup and a resolution inside of herself: never again would she change for someone else, get smaller for someone else, be sorry because of someone else. She resented the process of trying to fit into the box of someone else so much that she decided she would never date and never marry. So when one of her friends from college told her, at the beginning of summer vacation, that he would write, she shrugged it off. She figured he wasn't being serious. He wouldn't actually write.

I propped my hands up on my desk and listened. I still have not unlatched my fingers from her love story. The year was 1971. They couldn't text. They couldn't e-mail. There wasn't any sort of social network to dig up information on each other. No way to dress their feelings in emoticons or fragmented chunks of letters just to let the other person know they were laughing out loud. They couldn't walk into the conversation already knowing the other person liked country music, running marathons, and *The Catcher in the Rye*.

Three days into her summer break—the time it would take for a letter to sail from Oklahoma to Pennsylvania—the first piece of mail showed up. And then another. And then another. He wrote her a letter every single day for that entire summer break. When the mail would not arrive on Wednesday, there'd be two letters waiting for her on Thursday. And at some point her heart shifted.

While some people might have used the distance as an excuse, distance became their resolution. They went up against the hours and the time zones to prove sometimes distance is just fear dressed in a poorly made ghost costume when you use it as an excuse to not be with someone. They entrusted their love to the United States Postal Service, to the reliable men and women in blue who dutifully dropped answers and aches, songs and starting points, into mailboxes that lined the sidewalks. And maybe those postmen knew, or maybe they will never know, the weight of what they carried all those years when they delivered envelopes to lovers whose hearts surrendered to Cupid's arrows.

"There was nothing to do but just talk the whole time," she told the class. "We weren't face-to-face so all there was was talking. I'd be writing him letters in my head all throughout the day and then I could take my typewriter downstairs at the end of the day and just talk to him." I pictured her putting it all out there, with no hope of getting it back—the quirks, the odd habits and old childhood stories—funneling them through ink and stamps and stationery spritzed with scents of home and new beginnings. She told him everything. Sealed up the letter. Dropped it into the mailbox. And then waited. Not because patience was a virtue but because waiting was all there was to do. Waiting was all they had.

"You never did know what the other person was going to think or say or do," she said. "You just had to put it all out there and then wait. You didn't know when the person got the letter. You didn't know how they were going to react. You never knew if you'd get a letter back."

It was there, in the waiting time, the two fell in love. Eventually, she just knew in the thick of her heart he was it.

"Your generation is never going to have that," the professor said to us, scanning the room. I remember her saying that more than anything else.

Her words fell flat into a room full of millennials who were texting their friends beneath the desks. It wasn't a question. It was a statement. She was right. It was nearly impossible to even think of sitting down and writing someone a letter. It was incredibly intimidating to think of what I would say to someone without the filter of a 140-character limit. But I never thought it meant we actually would miss something.

There was something to be said about the scratchy forms of cursive and the feeling it stirred when someone wrote the words *I love you*. There was something about barely legible handwriting and just the thought of someone pulling out a piece of paper and thinking about you the whole way through with an intention that is so much harder to unearth when the browser is up and the iPhone is pinging and we've got six conversations rolling in at once. I wanted that presence so bad. I wanted someone, somewhere in the world, who thought I could be the center of their universe even if for only five minutes.

I decided to blog about leaving the love letters all over New York City, and when I got to the blank white space of the page, the story about my professor and the love letters came out naturally. And then the truth came out too. It was maybe one of the first honest truths I'd written in my blog during my time in the city: I felt like I was missing something. I was missing conversations. I was missing connection.

I was missing the nights I had taken for granted where it would just be you and one other person and a phone would never ring, and a text would never come buzzing through. I missed knowing it would take so much more than a status and a retweet to get someone to take their eyes off you. I missed the way it used to be just me and him or her or them—and the mountain of things we could finally face when we pulled ourselves away from the screen.

I guess I was the foolish one to think nothing would ever change or shift from the way it was in college, surrounded by people. We were probably naive to think that wrinkles and stretch marks would never reach us but we didn't talk too loudly about distance or obligations or rent checks or RSVPs while we had one another in arm's reach. We just acted like the early twenties were a mystery and we swallowed hot chocolate without worrying about the calorie count and took diner trips at two a.m. knowing it might never be this way again. And there's nothing you can really do about that. You can't put the moments in a box. You can't keep people forever. Those moments are meant to happen and then disappear.

I think that's the reason why I was so drawn to writing and leaving the letters in the first place. I think it all comes back to presence. How nothing feels so wonderful as knowing someone, somewhere, is thinking of you. Even if it is just in a piece of stationery tucked on a train for a stranger to find. In a world that pulls you to look in thousands of directions, it's nice to know someone is out there saying, "Hey, I see you."

I will write you a love letter.

Those are the final words that came out in the last keystrokes of that blog post. *If you need a letter, if you need a reason to stand by the mailbox, I will meet you there.* I would break the anonymity of my letter-leaving excursions around New York City. I would finally be there on the other side of the page, signing my real name. I was ready to write back.

I left my e-mail address and I wrote that if someone wrote me an e-mail and supplied me with their snail mail address, I would write them that love letter.

I called it a love letter but I never meant it in the mushy, gushy way. When I wrote the phrase *love letter*, I simply meant the kind of note that says with each lettered limb of cursive, "Hey, you, thanks. Thanks for getting out of bed this morning. Thanks for rolling over, putting two feet on the ground, and getting out there to face the world today. I know how tough that can be. So thank you."

I pressed the "publish" button and then I walked away. I forgot about the entire thing.

In a matter of hours, everything shifted. When I published the piece, I thought it would be several friends and maybe a stranger or two who would request a love letter from me. I was not expecting this moment of tangled joy as I kept refreshing the inbox to see piles and piles of people who had read of my promise.

"The e-mails keep coming," I said into the phone. My mother was the first person I thought to call when I came back to the computer to find dozens of unopened e-mails from people who'd read the post. I tried to explain to her what had happened as best as I could recall it. "I wrote a blog post . . . and now there are all these people who want me to write to them . . . I don't know them . . . they keep coming." I kept clicking the "refresh" button and I watched another pile of requests stack on top of the others. I scanned through the subject lines:

Love letters.
Help.
Lonely and in need of love letter.

I tried to coach my mother through every curve of what had happened, but she kept stopping me, unable to understand how people who didn't know me could find me on the Internet. In case it isn't evident already, my mother isn't the kind of person who understands social media. She thinks tweeting is something only birds do. She didn't know back then that anyone could pick up content and pass it along. She didn't get virality. She thought my blog was between her and my aunts.

"So what are you going to do?" she asked.

"I'm . . . I'm not sure."

"Well, you could always write a love letter and then photocopy it," she suggested. "Then you could just mail out the photocopied letter to everyone and it would be a lot easier."

I thought of what I would write in a generic photocopied letter, what words I could actually mail to people I didn't know:

Dear You,

I'm sorry. I've let you down. Really.

Any effort to unload love on this page will just be unreliable and stringy and it won't hold. I'm sorry it won't hold. You have to know that I am just a girl. My knees shake. My hair curls. I still wince when I hear someone saying good-bye and I know that they mean it. I'm a romantic in the worst way possible and I have reached the point where I have stopped apologizing for it. But I apologize for nearly everything else. For standing in line for things that are mine. For wanting things I think I shouldn't have. I say sorry at least fifteen times a day and I wish I knew the root of it. I wish I knew the thread inside of me to pull and finally, finally be a mess of unsorry.

In the meantime, you should know that I give up on myself before breakfast. And I lose socks. Lots of socks. Gone. Poof. So please, don't think I can give you something that you cannot already give yourself. I don't have much of anything figured out for myself. You go off and live your life. I'll stay here and cheer from the background.

Love,
Me

It was only after I published the post that I wanted to take it back with full force. It was then, after it was already sitting out there in the world, that I wished maybe I'd said something else. Like maybe I probably should have warned people I wasn't a professional. I had no real reason to write them a love letter beyond the fact we both probably knew the smell of ashes and the blood of skinned knees. Nothing else really qualified me for the job.

But I remembered a story a friend had once told me about the day her grandmother was buried. She was twenty years old at the time. Single. Pregnant. Alone. Sitting beside her grandfather in the middle of this big Catholic church. Everyone around her was repeating the same verses but she couldn't make her lips move. She could only feel shame for being unmarried and pregnant in the middle of this church. She just sat there beside her stoic grandfather, who had just lost the love of his life.

"And when I couldn't do anything else in that moment, I just grabbed his hand," she told me. "I just held his hand. It's all I could do."

That's it, I thought. That was exactly it. These people in my inbox weren't looking for a guru. They didn't expect me to be a doctor. They were not putting faith in my writing to tell them things would work out if they just did A, B, and C. They probably just needed a hand to squeeze. In the middle of something really hard they couldn't wrap their minds around, they probably just wanted someone to halt them before they shut out the light for good and say, "Wait, I think there might be something brilliant inside of you. I don't always see it in myself but maybe we can both try to accept it and see where that takes us."

I didn't feel confident in much as I sat by the computer and my mother hung on the other line. I knew I wanted to be the kind of person who followed through with a promise. That was certain. If I was going to put an offer out there to write to anyone who needed a love letter, then I wouldn't just photocopy a generic piece of paper and send it floating into the mailboxes of hundreds of strangers. I had to follow through. It had to be good and genuine and true. Letter by letter. Bit by bit. Until my fingers swelled. Until my heart hurt.

"I guess I will write to them," I told my mother. "No . . . yes," I said again. "I am going to write to them."

I would write. I was tired of being the girl who never made a sudden movement because I already felt so sorry for my own existence. It was pathetic, and I could not possibly do that for the rest of my life, or else I would die alone. With lots of cats. And a crush on John Stamos. It would be a long life of litter boxes and Stamos marathons if I could not learn how to stop being sorry for myself and just step into the shoes of someone else for a little while.

I remember thinking to myself, *How hard could it possibly be?*

I guess I always believed the moments that would one day end up defining me would be loud. They'd be noticeable. I pictured fireworks. I thought I would definitely be able to point the moment out from all the rest if you put them side by side in a lineup. I'd be able to stand there, on the other side of the glass, and say, "That one. That one was loud and big and mammoth and I knew it would change my life."

As the number of e-mails continued to rise, nothing inside of me soared. My head didn't grow bigger. I wasn't watching myself from the rafters or feeling like I could barely get myself out of the fog. I heard no fireworks. It was actually the opposite feeling, in the most humbling and tangible way possible.

It felt like I was getting lower to the ground. Like when my knees kissed the tile floor there would be a bucket and rag waiting for me.

And something in my gut pushed me to take the rag and scrub the tiles of the past away, saying, "That's who you used to be. That's who you used to be."

I was scrubbing away the past and a purpose inside of me was beginning to rise. Someone, somewhere, was waiting for me to arrive. Dressed in twine and cursive, signed and sealed, someone, somewhere, was waiting for me.

Please Write Back

*Y*ou're no longer alone. That's the first realization you have when you promise love letters to any person in the world who asks one of you. You've never been alone. All this time there have been others, crouching off to the sides, who were lonely too. It seemed like everybody had stories of loneliness inside of them. There were so many of them. We could build entire cities out of the stories of loneliness. There would be bridges and fountains and libraries and cafés, all made out of the thick stacks of loneliness.

The day when the letter requests started coming was a turning point. I could never again claim I couldn't see people or their struggles. I had to see them. They were standing right in front of me holding up cardboard signs that spoke of loneliness and divorce and heartbreak and fear.

I was catapulted into the lives of people I'd probably never meet, and yet, at the same time, I felt as though we were sitting down to have a cup of tea as they gave me a tour of their life.

That's the only way I know how to describe all the letter requests. It felt like I was getting invited into the houses of strangers. Like all the houses were lined up down a single street. Some had the lights on. Some had candles flickering in the windows. Others were dark and murky from the outside and you could only wonder what kinds of things lived beyond the front door. Some would spend their entire lives working in that house of theirs, never once stepping outside to see what the world could offer them.

Every e-mail was another invitation to tour someone's heart, as if it were a home. Room by room, some would show you everything. "Here is the room where I keep all my shattered heart pieces stacked up. Here is the room where all the rejection gets stored."

People let me in. Square foot by square foot, I went touring through half-finished lives in need of new paint on the walls.

I started writing letters every single day. I would wake up early to write those letters. I would stay up late to finish them. I can't say I wrote good love letters. I don't think I even know what would need to be included for a love letter to be good. But I know with each request I pulled out from my inbox, I did my best to put my guts into it. I tried my hardest to just be there on the page and to not shy away from or ignore the details they were telling me. I don't know if I wrote the best love letters but I was definitely committed to those things in a way that made me come alive.

Some people kept the request for a letter short, with a blanket statement like "depression" or "loneliness" or "homesickness." Other people set out to break my heart and I know it, I absolutely know it, because sometimes they told me so. I got an e-mail from one girl who wrote she hoped when I read her e-mail my heart would break into pieces. She purposely wanted it to happen that way so she wouldn't have to stand alone in what she was going through, so she wouldn't have to feel like she was the only brokenhearted one. She'd fallen away from God and had been shunned by the church. She was so broken I didn't know what to write to her.

I'd get people's plans to hold on. I'd get people's plans to let go. I wish I could say a girl named Laney was the only one to ever drop into my inbox who said she hated herself. The cutting came from hating herself. The vomiting came from hating herself. The abuse she accepted and claimed as something she deserved came from hating herself. I wish Laney were the only one but that isn't true. There were dozens of Laneys living in my inbox.

And with every Laney I would stumble into—boy or girl, old or young—I just kept thinking of one quote from Stephen Chbosky's *The Perks of Being a Wallflower*: "We accept the love we think we deserve."

It helped me explain away every broken relationship I read about. Every reason why someone could not walk away. Why someone would choose to settle for less and learn to be thankful it was anything at all. I used it to explain away the people who showed up in my e-mail wanting to cling to other people, and all their imperfections, as if they could actually fix them. It had to be why maybe a lot of us have thought we are deserving of less. That we, ourselves, could never handle someone who thought us to be lovely and original and delicate all in one breath.

I wanted to believe there could be a bigger love, one that was so much bigger than we ever allowed it to be that could walk right up to us and say, "You know what? Screw your stupid limitations. I am bigger than you. I am stronger than you. And I have known you and what you deserve since long before you ever started passing your heart out to anyone who would pay attention to you; never mind if they would break you. You are more precious than you will ever give yourself credit for."

I could make all the jokes in the world about how I was writing love letters to strangers and people could give me every strange face in existence, but it didn't stop me from going home and being terrified by what was living inside of my inbox. I was terrified because it felt like I was holding a secret we never talked about and never got real about when we passed one another: "We are lonely." So many of us. We are lonely and we are just looking for whatever will be the opposite of that feeling. We are lonely. And sometimes it's bottomless. We are lonely. And yet life can still be the most miraculous thing from time to time.

Miraculous. That word just makes me think of one of the first letters in the batch of one hundred I mailed out that first October. It was a request from a girl in Toledo. She was in college and her best friend struggled with suicide attempts. Multiple suicide attempts that kept them swinging back and forth into two spheres: are you staying here or are you leaving me? I cannot imagine the ways it gave the both of them whiplash. Keeping life. Losing life. Keeping life. Losing life.

She wrote that if she wrote him a love letter, he would recognize her handwriting. He'd probably groan instantly. He was, after all, a twenty-year-old boy. But if someone else would write him a letter—a stranger, perhaps—he might think it was really cool. He just might think it was worthy enough to keep it on his desk or in his pocket or something.

When I wrote his name in big letters across the page, I already knew it would be one of my favorite letters of all time. I would remember this one. Don't get me wrong, I think it is all sorts of courageous people who can ask a stranger for a love letter they need to read for themselves, but I have never been more in love with the feeling of someone stepping outside of themselves to ask the question "Who in my life needs a love letter today? Who in my life needs me?"

This one letter request seemed to whisper from the screen, "Show up for him. Please, show up for my friend because I love him. And I need him to stay. I need him to stay here."

Tucked in the mystery of the letters gaining their own kind of life, there was Libby. Libby was the best friend of one of my roommates. She met up with us in Central Park the week we arrived in New York and though she'd just moved to the city a few months before us, Libby was already a walking and talking vault of knowledge when it came to New York. She wears bright yellow sunglasses and, to her, every stranger is just a few short breaths away from being a best friend, a soul mate, or a travel companion for a cross-country road trip. She's the only person I've ever met who treated online dating like an adventure. While I will be the one dry-heaving in the restroom of some Mexican restaurant, nothing daunts her about it because she sees every encounter for what it really is: A chance to learn more. A chance to see life from a different seat in the theater. Everything is a gift to that girl. She thinks it's all really precious and it's all really temporary.

In those first few weeks in New York City, Libby and I started meeting up in coffee shops strewn across Manhattan. She knows all the coffee shops throughout New York City destined to haunt you after you suck their mugs dry. And in one of those shops, she told me she was leaving New York. She had a plane ticket. She was moving to Italy three days after Halloween. She spent one of her semesters in college studying abroad in that boot-shaped patch of yellow and came back a different person. When she talked about it, she made me believe you could actually leave your heart in airports and on old Italian cobblestones and in coffee shops. That we have very little control over where our hearts choose to root themselves. Sometimes some places get superglued to your being no matter how you try to pry or tear them off you. Seemingly innocent dots on brightly colored maps do something to you. They turn you inside out. They make you question everything. Geography is severely underrated in that sense. When I asked her why she was going back now, she said it was for either life, love, or escape. Maybe all three.

As we sat and I listened to her tell me the anatomy of a cappuccino, I wondered why I always have a tendency to meet people right when they are about to leave and go somewhere else. It seems to be a thing. Honestly, I've stopped questioning it. Why the timing is off. Why right when you think you need a person to do something really crazy, like nearly complete you, they tell you they have a plane ticket. They're going away. But it's people like Libby who make me think that even if a person tells you there are only twenty-four hours left before a plane or a train takes them away for good you should still take the risk to just get to know them. They'll teach you much. And when that thing inside of them starts yelling, *Go, go, go*—there's no real choice but to let them go. I have yet to see someone go out there in the world—wholeheartedly searching—and not come back more capable than they knew themselves to be. That's what I think about people in our lives with plane tickets—you've gotta let them go. Let them see what's out there.

A few days after the explosion of love letter requests, Libby and I met up for coffee at a place called Neil's Coffee Shop. It's a cozy spot that has sat on the corner of Lexington and Seventieth for half a century. The vintage neon sign hanging above the brick building is all the proof you need that not much changes inside the place. It's a place for "regulars" and coffee and bacon.

We sat at bar stools and I ate eggs and she drank coffee and she asked me about the letters. She wanted to know what inside of me made me start leaving the letters and what was driving me to write to people I was probably never going to meet. Strange as it seems, that detail never bothered me. I didn't ever think about getting to meet someone on the other side of the letter. I just wanted to be something to someone, no matter how big or small it was.

"What do you think it is?" she asked. "What you do think it's going to be?" That's Libby for you. The girl is big-picture. Always. Big, big pictures with only bright colors. The girl cannot be bothered with blues or grays or browns.

Scraping my scrambled eggs around the plate, I looked at her and told her the truth: "It's a mystery. That's really what it is. I mean, I love writing the letters but every time I go to write another one, I have to stop and wonder, *What is wrong with this world?* Libby, they are the saddest requests I've ever read and I don't know why they are sitting in my inbox."

And this was just the beginning of the heartbreaking requests I would see come shuffling through my inbox in the next few years. For reasons I might never be able to explain, after that blog post was written, my inbox became this harbor of heartbreak and a holding spot for other people's hard days. The e-mails were sad enough to leave me sitting before the screen, staring down at the computer keys to confirm whether or not the "backspace" button still existed. It did. They could have deleted those words if they really wanted to.

I guess I expected people to think the prospect of a love letter in the mail would be cool. I never thought it would spark something inside of people where suddenly they were typing out their life story to me. Most of the e-mails had a pretty common ending: *I didn't mean to write that much. I honestly don't even know where that came from.* And yet, they'd let the words stay there.

There is something striking about the people who learn to let

things be. Just be, instead of taking a hammer and nails to every little thing in their life that does not look exactly as they planned it to
look. There's something about people who accept where they are for
the moment.

I was not one of those people, though. I could not even face my
own sadness, and here were people darting at me from every direction,
practically saying, "Maybe things are not going so right for me now, and
maybe I will cry myself to sleep tonight, but maybe I am taking one big
step in telling you all of this. Maybe I don't have to be completely fixed
and wholly whole tonight. Maybe I just don't want to be alone and I am
finally letting someone know that."

If I'm honest, I wanted that too.

"I mean," I continued, "who in your life never wrote you this love
letter that you needed to ask a twenty-two-year-old girl who barely even
knows what flavor of coffee she wants to write to you?"

"I think there's more to it than that." Libby smiled and sipped her
coffee. "Maybe you've tapped into something that's even bigger than
you know."

Even with Libby's steering me into all the right sugges-
tions for coffee shops, there was still something unbeatable about
the familiarity of a Starbucks cup in my hands. I have no shame in
admitting it made me feel like an Olsen twin. But in one of the Starbucks by my office in Manhattan, I overheard a girl beside me talking
on her cell phone. The tables were practically on top of one another.
My notebook lay open.

"You know," she said into the phone, "I am doing okay."

She paused. Someone spoke on the other side.

"It's just tough; I am going to have to prove myself. I just need to be
relevant in some way. The way I was in LA." Another pause. "It's just
hard being nothing at the end of the day."

Her words washed over me but I didn't flinch. I was holding a pile
of letter requests in my bag. They were mostly from young people who
would have described themselves in the same way. I guess that was the

most surprising part of the love letters, knowing the majority of the requests hadn't come for the reasons I thought they would. I thought I would be writing to people who missed snail mail, to the population of people who once wrote letters back and forth to one another as a main form of communication. But it was mostly a bunch of people my age sitting in my inbox. The ones who grew up in a world where our best memories played out on a screen. The generation of us who have never really known ourselves loved on paper. We were the millennials.

I'm mostly certain that 2010 was the peak of millennial bashing, but don't quote me on that. I think we all just naturally wonder if the media is this merciless with every generation that steps up into adulthood. We were the entitled ones. Self-absorbed. Impatient. Flighty. At the same time, seeing my inbox clogged with the e-mail handles of Ivy League schools, I couldn't help but think we weren't all that bad. From the looks of the stories, we were trying. We were young and doing the best we could with what we'd been given. We'd been told to get an education. We were told to take the loans. We'd graduated into a crashing economy. We were raised on the rhetoric that we could go out there and get everything we wanted. Except a lot of us didn't know what we wanted at all. Standing in a slush pile of stories written to me by girls and guys my age, I wasn't ashamed to be a millennial. I was actually quite proud.

As I listened to the girl at the table next to me go on speaking, I turned to a new page in my notebook and I started writing the girl a letter. I wrote that I wished she would not stay so small. My mother would say: be small or be beautiful. Beautiful is loud footsteps and knowing the weight of those footsteps. And though I couldn't give that girl the kinds of words I knew to be true for myself, I still wished she wouldn't walk through life trying to be an apology letter at every turn. That role would never fit her.

The girl rose up from her seat, still on the phone, and edged her way to the back of the coffee shop. I was forced to cut the letter short, knowing I wanted to actually leave this one in a place where she could have it for herself. I tore the sheet from the notebook and scrawled two words, *For you*, on the front of it. And then I gathered up my stuff—my bag, my earbuds, my iPhone, a tattered copy of *Beloved*, and my note-book—and headed for the door.

It wasn't until I was halfway down the avenue, walking fast, that my mind reeled back to the day in the Fordham library with Jessica. It was that day she told me she thought I was going to end up falling in love in a coffee shop after all.

"I think there is going to be an idea, some sort of idea you will have," she'd said as we sat together, surrounded by books. "You're going to fall in love with it in that coffee shop. And your life will change right there."

She was right. My life had changed.

Everyone

One afternoon, I got a call from my roommate about a package that had shown up at the immigration center for me. It was so heavy they had to get a man to carry it up the stairs. Cheryl and I were watching the kids weave in and out of the playground when the call came. We'd just taken the kids to visit one of the fire departments in the Bronx and we stopped off at a playground on the way back to let the kids run and unload some of their energy. October had brought the leaves down from the trees with a vengeance and Cheryl and I stood next to each other in a dampened pile of crisp reds and bright yellows plastered to the concrete. With our hands sunk deep in our pockets, I told her all about the letters, knowing the package was probably tied to them somehow. She couldn't believe it. She was speechless at the thought of that many letter requests showing up in my inbox. "We don't really do things like that anymore," she said to me. "Now it's all this." She pulled out her BlackBerry and held it flat in her palm. "It's all just this and we aren't paying attention anymore."

Later that evening, when I was on my way to the apartment, I called Libby and kept her on the line until I got up the three flights of stairs to the box waiting for me on the floor.

"Oh my goodness," I said.

"What is it?" she asked. "Do you know what it is yet?"

"This thing is massive," I said, surveying the box I could barely get my arms under to pick up and carry.

Kneeling before the box, I cut through the tape with my house key and flipped open the thick flaps of cardboard. Toys. Brand-new toys. Packaged and perfect and begging for the hands of little ones who would hold them and rock them and carry them and love them. Baby dolls with fat cheeks. Building blocks and cars and classic jack-in-the-boxes.

"It's . . . toys," I said over the phone.

"Toys?"

"Brand-new toys. All wrapped up and everything." I scrounged around the sides of the box looking for a note but found none. They had to be for the kids, I thought. I'd written about my adventures as a preschool teacher on the blog, and it was the only reason I could think of as to why a box of toys would be showing up at my front door. I'd never experienced an act of generosity like this before.

"Who do you think it could be from, Libby? It's like a couple hundred dollars' worth of toys." I pulled a doll with bright blond curls from the box and her eyes shot open, and then they rolled back in her head, long lashes brushing against her cheeks, when I placed her back down.

The line went quiet.

"Libby?" I waited to hear her say something.

"Hannah," she finally said. "I'm crying. I can't help it."

We both didn't say anything for a minute or two, the two of us holding postures of silence. Me on my knees before the toys. She standing off somewhere in the middle of Brooklyn.

"People are just good," she whispered.

"Yeah." I repeated her words back to her. "They are just good." I had nothing else to add.

The mystery of the box of toys at my doorstep unfurled that afternoon when a message shot into my inbox on Facebook. It was from a guy I'd gone to college with. He graduated the year before me. We barely ever spoke, but I pinpointed his face when I saw the message notification waiting. He told me he had sent along a package. It should be arriving any day. He wasn't really much of a love letter writer but he figured this would do.

I laughed when I read that message because even though he hadn't picked up a pen or a paper, he'd very much written me a love letter. This box of bright, new toys for the hands of tiny humans he'd never have the pleasure of meeting was definitely, definitely a love letter.

I showed up in Sister Margaret's office the next day and told her that I had this box of toys. It was for the kids. She immediately dove into the process of plotting to wrap them all up and give them to some of the children who wouldn't get any presents for Christmas. She sent two guys from the life center to pick up the box, and the toys were out of my possession.

As I watched Sister Margaret go through and touch the toys and realize how deep the box was, I could feel God. It was like He was setting fine fingerprints all over the moment. I could feel Him in it, as if He were saying to me, "Girl, I'm gonna blow the hinges off anything you think a love letter is, was, or could be. If you would just release the grip, I could turn your whole life into a love letter."

A few days later, another package arrived. This one was from a girl named Kaleigh. She'd read the post online from her dorm room in Virginia about leaving love letters and I think she had a dream of leaving letters across the big city as well. She was a few years younger than me, and I didn't have to read anything beyond her letter to know she too got love songs stuck in her head and couldn't get herself unglued from the constant quest to help other people find their place in this world. She tucked a note inside a small package of love letters that read something like, *I know you are leaving love letters. Could you leave mine somewhere too?*

The only thing I knew about her was she probably had the same fast heartbeat as mine, but I scanned the city for Kaleigh. I picked bookshops I thought she would like and left her notes there. I found coffee shops with lattes marked on the chalkboard menus she might adore. I found library books—ones filled with the kind of poetry that makes you have a hard time believing humans could stitch words together so well—and placed her letters there. I tucked her love letters throughout the city for her and it made me feel grateful to be able to do that for her. It was one of those surreal moments where I felt so alive and like I was living in the city of my dreams, in the city I once placed into every childhood prayer. It didn't always feel like a dream come true to be standing inside of that city, but it was reason enough to be thankful for all I'd been given that year.

A pool of black nail polish formed at my feet as I rode the 1 train down to Fifty-Ninth Street at Columbus Circle to the gala at the Time Warner Center—the one that brought on all the fitting rooms after the necessity for a black dress.

Dave and I were set to meet at the top of the escalator by the Bebe store at eight thirty p.m. I paced back and forth as his arrival grew later, checking my reflection a dozen times while hoping he might not show up. I stared at my phone, praying for a buzz to accompany some message like, "Sorry. Must work late. Need to cancel."

I didn't anticipate how uncomfortable the night would be. And the discomfort that snaked in around my ankles had nothing to do with Dave.

So I lied at the gala. And I barely spoke. And I wedged little shrimp appetizers into my mouth. And I looked down a lot. And maybe I was searching the floor for the courage it would have taken to tell Dave how I felt at the event: like I was the secondhand green flannel in a closet full of silk. Like I was less than these people. Less than their luxuries. Less than their conversations.

I stood off in the corner of the room when I could, holding my ground beside a slide show that flickered black-and-white images of the women benefiting from the silent auction. Their skin was leathered and anguished. The children in their tired arms had cheeks stained with tears that looked like they never stopped coming on strong and salty. I didn't want people to look close. I was afraid that if they did, they'd see that I didn't belong there.

I pushed away from the crowd at one point and walked over to a giant glass window overlooking a Manhattan that was postcard beautiful that night. Dave joined me a few minutes later to sit by the window.

My heels were kicked off and to the side, already taunting me with threats of the blisters I'd get on the walk back to my apartment that night. We said nothing for a little while, the both of us staring at the quiet view of the city left untouched by the sirens and the car horns that roared beyond the glass.

"So," he finally said. "I heard you're writing love letters to strangers . . . Well, I didn't hear it . . . I mean, I read it."

He kept looking down. I could feel myself blushing, inside and out. My cheeks turned scarlet. No matter how many times I heard words like those, *I'm reading you*, I always felt undressed before someone. Vulnerable. Naked.

"Yeah, there's been dozens of requests. My inbox is full of them. It's kind of beyond what I thought it would be."

He went to stand and reached into his back pocket to pull something out of his wallet before sitting back down again. In his hand he held a folded book of stamps. Liberty bells adorned the front of them. They looked like they'd been wedged in his wallet for a tiny eternity— begging to be pressed on an envelope that would take them sailing to states they'd never visited before.

"I've had these things for a really long time," he said. "I just keep thinking there will be a reason for them. Like the perfect occasion." He turned the weathered stamps over in his hands. "But I think you might need them more than I do now."

He dropped the stamps in my lap. We sat really still before I ever touched them. I could not help but wonder if maybe I was holding the secret to a lot of things right there in my lap: Tiny things like this keep a person moving. Tiny things, like his believing in me, would keep me going. Tiny things keep hope flickering and they light the journey just when you think you've reached a patch of darkness.

At the start of the night, I'd thought about ditching him. I could complain I had a terrible headache and I just couldn't make it out to the gala. I didn't think there would ever be a real reason for my going there that night. But as I walked away from the evening with blisters kissing the backs of my heels and the tags still hanging on the inside of a dress I'd return in the morning, I felt like I was holding some sort of new truth in my fist: when people believe in you, that's the real fire. I would have licked a thousand envelopes just to have him drop a book of stamps into my lap and hear him say, "I believe in you. Go on, you crazy girl. I believe in exactly what you are doing. Don't stop here."

I was settled beside a demon-like thing and a skeleton wearing Converse sneakers when the text appeared on my screen. It was midday on Halloween. The subways were full of people dressed in costumes. A little witch scampered around the train in tiny circles but her mother kept drawing her back and in closer. The green face paint was barely still on the girl's face.

"Hey, stranger!"

It was Nate. Seeing his name show up on the caller ID flooded me with relief. A tiny dose of home. It was strange that I'd become so distant from my friends back home. I felt like I was worlds away from them, even though they were just a phone call or a text away. That's the thing about the service year I didn't get warned about—you're still you. But you're changing. And you're trying to process everything around you. And it's overly confusing for anyone who is outside of the experience of the year and never fully understood why you chose to take a year of your life and make no money voluntarily or live attached to an immigration center just to pass the time. I knew, already, there would be stories I would never share with my friends back home. It wasn't like they wouldn't care, they just wouldn't understand in the way I hoped they would.

Nate was an exception though. He was always the exception because even if he didn't understand something, he wanted to. And he would plant himself down into any chair you placed in front of him and just listen to you for hours, if you needed that sort of thing. That's Nate for you. Even though he wasn't with me on the subway, and there was a demon in the place of where he would have been, I still felt safe just seeing his name come on the screen.

Nate and I grew up together. I mean "grew up" to say we became friends during that awkward Grand Canyon–size chasm between being a kid and wanting to do kid things and being a teenager and wanting to fit into that role too. We met when the hallways buzzed with first kisses and second bases, when metal filled our mouths and most of us could draw constellations out of the pimples cascading across our noses and foreheads. Awkward times, yes, but it was also in those early teenage years when you started to pick out the ones in the groups of classmates who would naturally grow up to be good people.

Like every teenage girl, I felt unnoticed and was trying to figure out how I was going to fill out this lanky body God had entrusted to me. But Nate noticed me. And picked me out from within a crowd. And joked with me. And checked up on me. I like to think I reciprocated in some way. Perhaps with obsession. Because I was obsessed with him. And you would say *obsession* was an understatement if you were there to witness my tiny heart attacks every time I'd hear the sound of a door swinging open through the computer speakers and see Nate's screen name appear at the top of my buddy list, where I kept all my secret crushes. How I would wait approximately three to five minutes, let him get settled online and check his mail, before remaining cool, calm, and collected enough to type, "Hey," and send it wafting through cyberspace over to him. Or how I would print out every one of our conversations and keep them in a bright yellow folder beneath my bed. I would want the memories when we got married; that was my thinking.

I wouldn't be surprised to find there are a hundred yellow folders out there dedicated to Nate. He noticed everyone. He talked to everyone. His actions just sort of blurred the lines of popularity. While we all seemed to care so much about that word, he just wanted everyone to feel wanted. Needed. Like they had a reason to be there. That's a big thing when you're fourteen years old.

"HEY!!!" I wrote back to his text. The train had just risen aboveground by 161st Street. That's the memorable part of the train ride when you're finally in communication with the outside world again. All the texts and tweets you'd missed while you were underground would come flooding back when all the AT&T bars of service reappeared in the corner of the screen.

I typed out "How are you?" but debated deleting it. My thumb hovered over the "send" button. I hated asking him that question. That was the question all of our friends were asking on a continual basis, and I hated that too: *How is Nate doing?*

Just two years earlier, a phone conversation changed every "How are you?" that would follow. It was one of those conversations where the ink of its memory stays on your fingertips long after it's gone. I've learned to be wary of the kinds of conversations where you remember everything—where you were standing, what you were wearing. Those conversations become a part of you. Like a second skin.

It was a phone call to Ronny, Nate's best friend. I was standing in the middle of my college dorm laundry room. I was folding shirts. I told Ronny I'd heard a rumor about Nate's being sick. I was asking him to confirm it wasn't true. I just needed him to confirm that. He couldn't. Nate was sick. Really sick. It wasn't a rumor. Cancer.

We're supposed to be invincible, I remember thinking when Ronny hung up that night. We were twenty-one. This had to be nothing. This would be just another bump in the road and we'd all be sitting around a table in a few years, talking about things we were just so happy to leave in the past. Like flare jeans and the time we thought it was cute to wear hooker-style prom dresses. Cancer would be just one of those things. Because cancer wasn't the sort of thing that could touch us. We were too young. We had too much to do. I guess you never think cancer can touch the people you love. Until it does.

I saw Nate for the first time a few weeks later. He made a joke about being only 136 pounds. I could see it in his face. We sat at the town diner. I tore at the edges of my chicken fingers. He slurped soup. I wished I could fast-forward to a moment when we'd both get to see the adult versions of ourselves and how we'd turn out on the other side of this. I think I just wanted to know we'd both get there safely.

He told me everything in that old, familiar diner booth. How his semester had been fine. He'd secured his major. Everything was normal. And then came pain, excruciating pain in his side. He stopped being able to hold down foods. He had a high fever. He coughed so hard he broke ribs. It happened fast. All the tests and blood work led up to a Monday morning where the words dropped off an oncologist's lips:

"Just by looking at the scans, I can tell you have colon cancer that has spread to your liver." Colon cancer. Stage IV. Advanced.

I guess that's the root—the root of what made me hate asking the question "How are you?" I didn't want to be asking it now that he was sick. Maybe it was my fear or maybe it was his wanting to forget about it, but we didn't really talk about the sickness. And when I wanted to know the real truth, I would read the blog he wrote to keep his family and friends updated on his treatment.

For a long time, I carried a printed copy of one of his blog posts in my purse. It was about this random day when he caught a glimpse of his face in the mirror. He stared for long enough to recognize the fire in his eyes had gone missing. *Gone, gone, gone.* "I did not like this person that I saw in the mirror . . . in fact I hated him. It was the sight of a person so close to giving up that I was ashamed of myself. What would my family say, what would my friends say if I simply told them that I give up, that I can't do this."

And, out of that desperation, he stacked the wood and he found the fuel to make something burn. He didn't focus on his doubts or his fears. He wasn't waiting on others to rebuild his faith and hope and trust. He just started stacking the wood and this one word started to appear: *relentless.*

It began showing up in conversations. In writing. It showed up again. And then again. *Relentless.* It kept coming out of him. Eventually it morphed into a mission statement. And then Nate built it into a non-profit, one that would soon grow too big for his own two hands. It was like our town's little miracle. A way for us to keep coming back to one another. That was the best part about Nate. He let us rally with him for this cause. He let us stand behind him and make a lot of noise. Yes, we all loved Nate and wanted to support him. But people love, more than most things, to find themselves in bigger missions. We like to find ourselves fitting into a bigger story.

Another text from Nate appeared on the screen.

"I'm doing good. Hanging in there. How about you? How is the big city treating you?"

I felt wrong even typing that I was struggling, that I was having a hard time. I felt like I didn't even have a right to say those sorts of things to Nate. But I sent the text message anyway. He wrote back immediately. "Well we are all so proud of you over here. You're doing what you said you would do. Remember, *bigger than this.*"

I bit down hard on my bottom lip and tried not to cry. My mind was flooded with the memory of when he first said those words to me. We were seventeen. Just on the fringe of senior year. It was summertime. One of those nights where we'd all ended up in someone's garage, cracked open a few cases of beer, and let the sounds of O.A.R. stream through the speakers of a stereo hooked into an iPod.

"I'm going to get out of here," I said to him. "I'm going to get out of here and I don't think I'll look back."

We were off to the side of the party sitting in plastic lawn chairs. You could hear the sounds of laughter mixing with the rhythms of Ping-Pong balls hitting plastic cups and people shrieking, *"Rack 'em up!"*

"Yeah," he said, looking down into his cup. "I don't know if I will come back here either. We've both got good things ahead. Bigger than this."

If I believed anyone when they said that they were going to get out of our small town and find bigger and brighter and better for themselves, it was Nate.

We sat side by side that night, a slow kind of buzz between us as we held red Solo cups and I felt my shoulder against his. I kept tracing his words into my memory, hoping I wouldn't forget them by the morning. *Bigger than this, bigger than this.* It was a lullaby to the summer night, a promise made between the two of us.

You need that sometimes. You need one person who comes up beside you and validates you, tells you you're not crazy and that they too want to fly away sometimes. Otherwise you forget gravity is something you're supposed to go up against.

Libby showed up at our apartment that night fully clad in a Batman costume. She'd come from a Halloween party. In the morning she would leave for Pennsylvania, the home that existed to her before New York City. At five a.m., she'd be gone. The city would mourn the loss of another dreamer.

"There's like fifteen locks on our front door so I'll just wake up to let you out," I told her the night before. "Otherwise, you'll be struggling until the people show up for ESL classes in the morning."

I couldn't sleep that night. Something made me restless. Sitting up in my bed, I pulled my laptop from the armchair beside me and opened it up. I plugged my Christmas lights into the wall to shed light on the bedroom with the red curtains. It might have been two months too early but I keep white lights strung around my bedroom all year round. The wireless was patchy, at best, in my bedroom, but I logged on and typed in the address for Nate's blog. He'd published a post just a few hours earlier. I'd say it was a strange coincidence the post was there just hours after we talked, but I've since stopped believing in coincidences. The post was about angels.

He wrote about how he was never sure angels existed but he wanted to believe in signs from God, or whatever it was that was out there. He didn't want to boil things down to strange coincidences. He wrote about how on the day he walked into the hospital for his first treatment, people who were certainly angels met him. Angels. They talked to his family. They shared their stories with him as if to say, "Here, here is a rope . . . grab on tight and let it pull you to the other side." He honestly didn't know where he would be without those angels during that time when he was sick and terrified of the road ahead of him. He wrote that someday, maybe, he could be an angel too.

"You already are one," I whispered into the room. My hands were pressed against the computer. My eyes were closed, as if the whole thing were a prayer. The room felt holy and cloaked in the kind of light only Christmas lights in October can give you. "You've always been one to me."

He was an angel. Not the kind of angel you meet in Sunday school or at the Christmas pageant with the cardboard wings and the white robes and the glitter in their hair. I just mean angel, as in a person who shows up right when you think the ground might fall out from underneath you.

Libby was still wearing the Batman cape and matching boxers when I met her in the hallway the next morning. It was five a.m. and still dark outside. We didn't say much as we walked down the three flights of stairs to the front door. I hugged her good-bye. I told her to be safe and to look for her heart, or whatever she needed to look for when she got to Italy.

"Here," she said, handing me a long skinny envelope. "This is for you. Read it when I leave. I know how you like your letters."

I hugged her again. I peeked my head through the window to look outside and check for anyone out on the street as I unbolted the door. A thick coat of freezing air lay like a cloak on the sleeping borough.

"No," Libby said, pushing in front of me before I could open the door fully. She stepped out on the stoop. "No."

Strands of things lay all around her trunk and the door to her backseat. Someone had broken into her car. Pieces of Libby's existence were strewn all over the sidewalk. Bits of broken glass trailed back from the shattered window in the rear of her car.

"No." She ran toward the car. Her voice was tight. "Please, no."

In those moments, you can't do much. You stay quiet. You think about the things you should have done differently. We were dumb to leave her car parked outside full of stuff. We should have parked her car inside the gate. She should have thought to take her valuables inside with her. We were too trusting of the neighborhood. Of course this was going to happen.

You stand there and you try to let your mind trail off to a quiet space where you can count all the other blessings you've got. It doesn't work for long. The whole experience feels violating. You feel really small and helpless standing inside of it.

Back inside the life center, Libby rummaged through the bag she'd found on the ground minutes before.

"I need a piece of paper," she said. She started scribbling things down furiously. I sat behind the desk that would be occupied in just a few short hours and wrung my hands in my lap.

"There's this . . . and this . . . and this . . . ." She was totaling things. "Okay," she said. "It's stuff. It's just stuff. It can all be replaced."

She was calm and collected. I know it sounds impossible but she looked blessed, even with nearly a thousand dollars' worth of things gone from her possession. I would have probably been throwing things and barreling down the street to wait outside of pawnshops, thinking the thief would show up soon. Libby was quiet. It was just stuff to her. Just stuff. And all the stuff she cared about, all the things she really wanted, weren't tangible. It was sights and it was sounds and it was familiar voices and it was all the things she was traveling back to Italy to find. It was never going to be about the stuff.

She eventually left to file a police report. I stayed in the empty hallway of the immigration center after she was gone. I sat down in the middle of the floor and I opened up the letter carefully. It was several pages long, front and back. I read the words out loud to no one, feeling like each one was echoing off the walls of that place.

> *I know things have been extremely hard lately and I can't really say anything that will change it but you need to remember the only thing we can strive for perfection in is seeing the potential we have to really make a difference. We're always looking for perfection but we need to look for potential instead, one little bit at a time.*
>
> *You'll find happiness. I know you will. Just try to leave any worries, any fears, any doubts, in a closet full of all the other crap you're getting rid of.*
>
> *Even if you need another day to go back to those fitting rooms to just sit there and think and cry to realize it, you do have a place and you fit perfectly in this world.*

Find happiness and keep doing what you're doing. Everything you are doing . . . you have to believe it matters.

I'll be following from across the Atlantic,
Libby

Out of the letter dropped a bright blue check. Libby had scribbled the amount of $100 in ink. An investment, as she put it, in what she knew the love letters would become one day. Maybe she'd believed in that "bigger thing" all along.

I stayed still for a few minutes, soaking in the quiet of the immigration center before it opened. Holding the bright blue check, I thought about Nate and the angels he wrote about. He was so right to think they were everywhere, helping us stand when we feel ready to crash. Libby was most certainly one of those angels.

The Tale of the Yellow Towel

Club di Giulietta (the Juliet Club) is a real spot in the town of Verona, Italy—the home of Shakespeare's Romeo and Juliet—where thousands of letters arrive each year, all addressed to Juliet, a gal who seems to know her way around heartache.

As the story goes, people began tucking and leaving these notes for Juliet at a local landmark said to be her tomb. So many letters started arriving in the mail they eventually made an office, packed it to the brim with fifteen secretaries who I imagine have great handwriting, just so they could answer back every single letter. Those secretaries do the work for free. The town pays for postage. And yes, every one of the six thousand letters that come into the Juliet Club every year gets a response.

And while I was holed up in the Bronx, checking my mailbox regularly to find stamps from strangers who were cheering me on, what I really needed during that time was a trip to Italy to meet my doppelgänger homegirls. I needed someone to show up at my door with a plane ticket and say to me, "Here, go hang out with the secretaries at the Juliet Club and see the way they operate. Hear their stories. Figure out how to write better things."

I liked to imagine I was a part of their club, or at least an estranged sister who was thousands of miles away. And if I'd gotten the chance to meet any one of those women, I would have asked them the questions that were constantly on my mind: How do you keep going?

How do you keep this letter-writing thing fresh? Don't you ever just want to stop?

That's where I was at the middle of November. The first hundred or so love letters had been good. I was new to the thing. But as the numbers rose up to nearly two hundred, I was losing steam. I was sounding unoriginal. I was wondering how someone else might handle this sort of situation. Every bit of heartache that came into my inbox was original but I was having a really hard time valuing the letters and responding with the same sort of originality. People deserved the best of me but I didn't always have the best of myself to give.

Looking back, it was the best thing that ever happened to me. The desire to just give up and walk away needed to sweep in for me to ever truly understand the real makeup of commitment. I guess I'm now starting to understand why that word—*commitment*—seems a little jacked up and flimsy in the world today. Because real commitment— hands all-in with no hope of turning outward—is not always what you'd thought it would be. A lot of times it's tears. And it's telling yourself you have to keep going. And it's reminding yourself you are not the center of the universe. And quitting shouldn't always be your option.

So I kept going. And I kept writing. And I just looked at every letter as a chance to be more honest than I was in the last.

On the topic of honesty, I should say this: the misconception would be I started writing love letters and the depression skipped off to haunt some other body. That isn't true. I'm not an expert on depression, I just know it's not a one-size-fits-all sort of deal. And I am only saying this because I don't ever want to belittle the beast that is depression and how it manifests in so many people.

If I could, I would draw a map of depression—I'd draw out the high highs and low lows. The valleys of it and the deserts. But you see, there's the catch. Maps get drawn to lead you somewhere. Maps get drawn because there is an X to mark the spot or a tiny house planted in the corner that symbolizes, "This is where you will end up."

That is the trickiness of depression though. He doesn't easily let you draw maps of him. He won't tell you where you're headed. You might have forests and I might have bogs. The most important thing is you just keep going. With no map. And no compass. And sometimes not even real truth to guide you. You just have to keep going. And along the way, you find things to hold tight to. Hope. And good conversations. And people who stick with you until morning. You find things to clutch. For me, that was a yellow towel from my mother.

It arrived in my lap just a few hours before our Thanksgiving Eve festivities began for the night. As part of the requirement of the service program, we were asked not to go home for Thanksgiving that year. The holiday would be spent with the community we lived in to encourage solidarity and to respect those who couldn't travel the long distance to make it home. The tradition at my program was that the Bronx service site and the Lawrence, Massachusetts, service site would have Thanksgiving together. So on the night before Thanksgiving, four of the service volunteers from Massachusetts were due to arrive on our doorstep.

Earlier that afternoon, my preschool classroom had spilled over with volunteer room parents and heavy serving platters of fried chicken, plantains, and corn bread. If I had never read the textbook story of the first Thanksgiving feast, I would have believed the first Pilgrims and Indians shared *arroz con pollo* and Capri Sun while singing to Justin Bieber. All twenty-six kids sat around the collection of tables mashed together into the center of the room, wearing hats Cheryl and I had spent the entire week making for them out of construction paper, and we held hands. I watched a tiny Pilgrim slip her hand under the table to find the grip of a little Indian whose headdress was held up by plastic flower hair clips.

We went around in a circle saying out loud what we were most thankful for. A parade of *Mommy*s, *Daddy*s, and *Titi*s spilled from their mouths and each child listened intently to the others. No one even squirmed. There is something so mysterious about gratitude that makes even a circle of twenty-six four-year-olds hush. When the circle of hands reached me, and Josue squeezed my hand and told me to go, I said I was thankful for home. Whatever that looked like. Whatever that was.

After several Thanksgiving feasts that day—another one with some of the students from the ESL classes at the immigration center directly after this one—one of my roommates came upstairs from her classroom holding a package. She handed it off to me. I took one look at the familiar scribbles on the front of it and knew instantly it was from my mother.

I tore the side of the package open and found all the typical essentials of an "I wish you were home for the holidays" care package. What stood out from the insides of the package were a copper plaque and a bright yellow towel. I turned the plaque over in my hands. It had a Native American Indian etched on the front of it. Like most times when my mother sent me something, I couldn't get inside of her head to know why. She likes to be random like that. My only thought was of my grandmother and the ongoing joke in our family that she always believed she was a Native American. On and on she would go about her tribes and her heritage, her apartment draped with Indian décor, but there wasn't any real evidence she was being truthful, especially in light of her Irish heritage. We were pretty sure she wasn't Native American, but we all went with it anyway. For a couple of years in middle school I told everyone that I was a Native American too. I thought boys would think I was exotic and might want to date me. The pale skin and freckles weren't to my advantage, but I still tried with gusto to be some sort of Irish Tiger Lily and score mad boyfriends. The act was dropped shortly after, when there was no proof of my heritage. You can't get college scholarships unless you can prove what tribe you're from.

I picked up the bright yellow towel in the package and tucked it against my cheek as I read the note she'd put inside:

When I was in New Mexico, for my first holiday away from home, I remember a package my mother sent with a beautiful yellow towel in it, so I will continue the comfort and color of this tradition.

I hugged the towel closer to my chest. It's amazing how an item that holds the smallest amount of significance—an item that normally just hangs on a hook and pulls the sopping water off your body—had so quickly and so suddenly become the most important thing in my orbit.

My mother didn't have to write a thing more in that note. I was thankful for her few words. She didn't use the moment to remind me of how hard the year had been. Come to think of it, she never did that at any point. She never told me to get stronger. She never asked me to get stronger. She'd been young once too. She'd been a girl just trying to find her way once too. Everything about the towel in my arms seemed to say, "It's fine to miss home. This life thing, it's tough. I get that. It doesn't always lend you much control. It's okay though. You've always been okay to me."

The night unfolded pretty seamlessly after our guests arrived. We plotted where to go to celebrate Thanksgiving Eve and our mini reunion, since we hadn't seen one another since August. And somehow, a stroke of sheer genius in the planning process led us across the street to the bodega to buy several cans of Four Loko.

I'll be honest—it does not even feel classy to write the name *Four Loko*, never mind consume it. I don't have much pride when it comes to this decision. It tasted like a combination of malt liquor and an energy drink. Apparently the drink was so dangerous it was eventually banned by the Food and Drug Administration for its combination of caffeine and other stimulants. I knew nothing about the drink at that point beyond the fact it was mentioned in a lot of rap songs, and that made me feel really legitimate when I took the first slow slug from the neon-yellow can.

We decided on Woodlawn for the evening, an Irish-American neighborhood that sits at the end of the line of stops on the 4 train. I was nauseous before we even got to the pub. Ten minutes into our big night out, the dimly lit bar was spinning and I clutched the table, hoping the twisting contortions of the atmosphere would subside. It wasn't long before one of my roommates brought me outside for air and hailed a gypsy cab to take me home. Gypsy cabs were the best option if you needed to get around in the Bronx since yellow cabs never made their way out to the borough. The only difference is that the cabs were actually illegal, and you had to pray you were getting into a gypsy cab and not just some strange black vehicle that would drive you away from your friends and family forever. You'd propose a fee to the driver and they'd either accept it or look at you like you were crazy and then speed off.

Inside the gypsy cab, I sat in the front seat alongside the driver. My insides somersaulted. The cab driver made sharp turns. I kept my head against the cracked-open car window as I pleaded with the driver to never consume Four Loko. "It will make you feel absolutely awfulllllll," I moaned.

I barely even reached the top of the stairs before throwing up. I got safely into the bathroom off the side of my bedroom. There was vomit. Lots of it. Plus tears and some snot. Mascara dribbled down my cheeks. My hair slopped up in a messy bun. My insides on tumble dry. The works.

My phone buzzed. I looked at the screen. It was the barber Juan from across the street. I'd forgotten I even sent him a message earlier asking him if he had ever tried Four Loko. He responded by telling me I was stupid if I ever thought to try it. Too late.

"Where r u ima go get u." His message showed up on the screen.

This cannot be happening, I thought to myself. *This isn't happening.* The bathroom was spinning all around me. I could barely type the words out.

"With my head in a toilet. It's wonderful," I wrote back.

"Omg can I take care of u?"

I pictured everyone coming home to find Juan holding my hair in a jumbled ponytail as I dry-heaved into the toilet. I wondered if it would be just like the moment I prayed it would be when I plastered the quote *I want a guy who will hold my hair back when I puke* in bright pink Comic Sans lettering across my language arts binder in the ninth grade. More than anything, I pictured the horror on Juan's face when he would see the shriveled mess of me in party clothes with makeup smeared all over my face. That image of horror on his face caused me to respond: "Really. It's fine."

* * *

The vomiting continued. Over and over again. To the point where there was definitely nothing left inside of me and I might have been coughing up parts of my organs. I was too afraid to move even just a foot away from the toilet in case the violent heaving should strike again.

This is what you deserve, I kept thinking to myself. *You deserve this for thinking Four Loko was a brilliant idea.* It was that criticism on repeat, back with a vengeance. Head in a toilet or not, a Hunger Games battle of small voices raged in my head, like kids from all the districts flinging themselves around the arena: *You're so dumb. You're hopeless. Good job. No, great job. You're all alone. You're always alone.*

I passed out sometime in the middle of the night, my body curled around the toilet, my face down against the tile floor. I woke up instantly to the sound of screaming.

"I'MMA KILL YOU. GET OUT HERE NOW."

The yelling pushed through the open bathroom window and grew louder and louder. I could hear banging. Clattering. The sound of glass breaking. I couldn't move. I just lay there on the ground wondering if this was the end of my life. Would it end this way? Was the world ending on this day before Thanksgiving in 2010? Would someone invade the home and just take us all? I had no idea what time it was. The yelling continued.

"JUAN, GET OUT HERE!!"

The man's screaming got louder. He was screaming for Juan.

No. No. No, I thought, trying to push up on my hands and sit up. The white walls danced all around me. I crawled out of my bathroom slowly and into the room closest to the street to get a better view of what was happening outside.

The man was screaming up to the window of the apartment where Juan lived. He kept pulling the door by the side of the barbershop open, the one that led upstairs, and going inside but coming out again. He was yelling for Juan. He was threatening to kill the man who had just basically proven to me chivalry wasn't dead as he volunteered to come take care of me.

No. No. This cannot be happening. It has to be a dream. This must be a Four Loko dream. I crawled back to the toilet. I had to vomit again. The banging continued. I went back to the window. The man had someone in his grip. He was shoving the man up against the wall and punching him. It wasn't Juan though. He kept yelling for another fifteen minutes or so. I went back to the toilet. The incessant cussing blared through the window.

Is this happening? Maybe this isn't happening. Maybe I am hallucinating. I felt awake. I knew I was awake.

This is it, I thought. *This is how it will all end. The barber will be dead in the morning. I'll somehow survive. It will be Thanksgiving. We'll be sitting down to have some epic turkey feast and there will be this banging on the front door. And it will be the police. With handcuffs. Coming to cart me off to prison as I was the last one to ever talk to Juan and I never called the cops. This is it. It's over. I've tried to be good for so long. I didn't think it would end this way.*

And it's always in those moments when the cute barber across the street is being murdered and your insides have been wiped clean by guarana that you begin mumbling things up to the ceiling that look like prayers in the dark.

It's always in those moments when you've shunned God, or you've gone ahead as if you don't need Him, that you find yourself crawling back with pathetic little attempts to get His attention because suddenly you're weak and you need to convince yourself you're not alone on the bathroom floor.

God . . . sir . . . God . . . Mr. God . . .

The room was quiet and still spinning. I covered my eyes to shield them from the bright lights of the bathroom.

Father . . . Daddy? Daddio? God . . . Just God . . . You up there? I hope You're up there. I know people say You're always up there but I don't always feel You . . . And I understand if You ignore me . . . Could You like, um, send a sign? Make the lights flicker or do something funky to prove to me You are there?

Nothing.

Okay . . . So You're there. Let's just go with that. Plan B. You and me.

Sorry? I guess I should say sorry? And I don't want to be sorry because I feel awful right now and I think everything inside of me is sitting in the toilet. I want to be sorry because You're probably embarrassed. Because I've probably disgraced You. 'Cause I'm like . . . Your child.

I've thought about it and honestly, I feel embarrassed for the woman whose child throws a temper tantrum in aisle nine by the cans of soup. I cringe for her and on behalf of her. So I legitimately cannot even fathom what God must feel with His billions and billions of children. Everywhere. Making a mess of themselves. I think if I were Him, I probably would have paused the whole creation story and tied Eve's tubes right then and there, saying to my foolish little leaves-for-clothing jungle children, "Y'all can't even handle not eating fruits off one tree in Eden? I don't even want to see what a whole population of you fleshy messes in Michigan and China and Canada will do combined."

My barter with God continued.

I feel really, really, really awful. And I know Four Loko is probably the devil's soda pop. I get it. It was dumb. But just let me survive. Don't make me throw up again. Please. I will be indebted to You. Forever. It won't happen again.

I thought about all the promises I could make to Him. I'd open a soup kitchen. I'd get *Amazing Grace* tattooed across my forehead. I'd sell all my belongings . . . No, wait, I'd give them all away. I'd become a nun. Whatever He wanted of me. To just make this feeling go away.

Part of me expected I would wake up in the morning and walk out into the living room to find my stationery gone. I would check my inbox and all the letter requests would be deleted. It would be confirmation I had gotten a chance to do something really wonderful and I had botched it. I had ruined it. The emptiness of the moment was punishment enough. But I felt guilty for everything. It was like a dangerous concoction that looked like one cup of disobeying God, a half a cup of failing Him, a pinch of wondering if He was even there. Stirred and stirred until it was frothy. And then iced with real thick and sugared fear: *What if You give up on me, God? What if You're looking at me right now and saying, "You think I will use you? Why would I even love a little thing like you?"*

The only other time I think I've lain helplessly down on the floor like that was in the summer between my freshman and sophomore years of college. I had not been looking for God. I'd spent the whole year trying to play God to my own circumstances and keep a four-year relationship going off the strength of two kids. My boyfriend and I finally reached that point where *good-bye* has to mean everything. You suddenly have to put your whole body into that word because it kills you both to think of trying to string the pieces back together. And so *good-bye* has to mean something more than a quick wave and a kiss on the lips to last you until tomorrow. *Good-bye* has to mean you're forgetting the taste of his ChapStick.

My best friend and I had had that same kind of breakup in the same week. Suddenly, we were both one person. We weren't kissing someone else good night. We weren't waiting for the call at the end of the night to talk about how the day had gone. We were adjusting to the fact that it takes a split second for you to go from two people down to one.

I remember being right beside her after it happened. We got together to talk and ended up just lying in the middle of the dance studio in her basement. We didn't have much to say. We just kind of lay there. And hot tears rolled down our cheeks. It felt like a weight was sitting on my chest. Like there was no real way to wash away the pain of missing someone you loved. *I could change this, or I could do this better,* I thought in my head. *He'd take me back. He'd take me back.*

"How long is it going to hurt like this?" she whispered in the darkness.

"I don't know. I really don't know."

We wanted an expiration date. A day to mark on the calendar when all the tears would shrivel up and we'd be whole again. I think it was one of those realizations for the both of us that love isn't a seamless kind of thing. It was the first realization that sometimes we give ourselves to each other and then we learn to live with the fact we aren't getting everything back.

"Do you think God sees this kind of stuff?" I squirmed in even asking the question; she and I had grown up with different kinds of Gods.

"This?"

"I know that's kind of crazy. But I always wonder if He maybe is up there crying too."

"I don't really know," she said. I felt stupid for even bringing it up.

I lay there and wondered why I had thought of God in that moment. I hadn't opened the door for Him to arrive at our pity party with a red-carpet entry; I had not even scribbled out an invite and dropped it in the mailbox for Him. And yet He, and the thought of Him, hung in the air like lanterns that night, wiping out the darkness, the pain, and the fear of being alone. Something inside of the moment with my best friend made me whisper when I was getting into my car that night, "I hope You're here. I hope You're really here."

The same feeling of hope huddled inside of me as I lifted my head from the floor and crawled out of the bathroom. I moved toward the package sitting by my bed. I pulled out the yellow towel from my mother. My teeth chattered together as I wrapped it around my shoulders and curled up in a ball in the middle of the floor. Trailing off to sleep, I woke up a few hours later to find it was quiet outside. The fighting had stopped. I checked my phone. No messages from Juan. I pulled myself up off the floor and got into bed, wrapping the blankets around me, still clinging to the yellow towel. The morning would come.

"I hope You're here," I whispered into the newly silent night. "I hope You're really here."

The police never showed up. And the morning did come. I, however, did not get up for the majority of Thanksgiving Day. While my room-mates and our guests got up at around four a.m. to head into the city for the Macy's Thanksgiving Day Parade, I lay at the mercy of a stomach bug and a 101 degree fever. I'll never know if it was the Four Loko that caused the sickness or if I'd just been getting sick all along. But the only time I got up that day was to walk across the street to the bodega. I kept my eyes closed tight as I reached into the refrigerator to get a red Gato-rade, praying a Four Loko drink wouldn't be staring back at me.

As I snapped open the cap of the drink and stood outside to get some air, I noticed Juan. He waved and smiled as if nothing had hap-pened the night before. He was very much alive. I looked deathly. I asked him a few days later what had happened that night. He laughed and told me it was just his friends being "mad stupid." I only agreed with him. Yes, death threats at one a.m. are mad stupid. We never talked about that night again and I like to imagine we both washed it from our memory as the holiday season walked on in.

There is a definite romance that buzzes and ticks and takes you by the elbow when Christmastime arrives in the city. It's something about the lights. The way the wreaths dress up the streetlamps. How everyone seems to commute home at night with much more purpose, and I often found myself wondering what they were barreling back for. If it was a tree that needed to be decorated, or cookies needing to be frosted, or just someone worth holding all winter long.

While everyone else around seemed to grumble about tourists taking over the city so much, I loved watching all the red cups cradled between people's hands and the little girls in their peacoats holding American Girl dolls close to their sides. I loved the tune of "Silent Night" streaking through the halls of Grand Central. I loved the Santas you found throughout the day—plump and skinny, full beards and fake ones adorning the street corners.

I got into the habit of stopping at a specific Starbucks on Lexington Avenue a few days after work that season, ordering a misto (regular coffee with steamed milk totally fits the $25 budget) and just sitting on one of the bar stools by the window watching businessmen go home. I'd bring a stack of letter requests with me in my bag and I'd just sit and write to people, imagining the letters showing up at the doorstep of a house strung with lights in Idaho or waiting in the college PO box for a student stressed with finals, ready to travel on home for turkey feasts and nights by the fireside.

While the letters filled me with a sense of purpose, it was the women at the life center—Sandra, Shelley, and Sister Margaret—who filled me with perspective that season. A perspective I didn't even know I needed when I walked into the service year, just so eager to do something that mattered.

I was learning how to stick with things. When finances were frail or when efforts were being exhausted. And while I'd grown up with the "do what you love" mantra in my head, that season the message slowly morphed into something different for me: Don't always get so caught up in doing what you love. Instead, do what is necessary. Do what others need. Whether that's holding a child as they whimper throughout nap time because no amount of *A Charlie Brown Christmas* will make them fall asleep or it's helping to file invoices that have needed a home in a three-ring binder for the last six years. The point isn't to be above any work or grumble over any task; the point is to do the stuff others need of you and trust it will somehow matter. Do what needs to be done to keep something bigger than you moving and shaking. Show up for your role even if it seems small—small like the part of a shepherd in the Christmas pageant. Still show up. I think that is the real heart of doing something that matters.

As I showed up for whatever Sister Margaret gave me to do, I stopped trying so adamantly to find all the answers. I wasn't getting all the answers but I was getting a lot of choices. Some mammoth and massive. Others tiny and seemingly minute. I was beginning to see each one mattered, though. Every single choice, every task that does or does not meet the to-do list, would ultimately stack up and answer one big question: has what you've been doing meant something?

I wanted it to mean something. So I did whatever I could.

One morning that season, I sat in Sister Margaret's office brainstorming ideas to fund-raise for the life center. The topic of money was always coming up and Sister Margaret would worry about it so much it made me feel like I needed to put an idea forth every once in a while. It was better than avoiding the subject entirely, which is what I really wanted to do.

"We could write a letter."

Suggesting we write a holiday letter to fund-raise was my weak addition to the conversation.

"I don't know when you last wrote a letter to the people who have supported you in all this, but people love mail."

Sister Margaret's eyes got big when I said it. Moments later, I was back in my tiny office space, beside Sandra, scribbling notes furiously into a yellow notebook as Sister Margaret dictated what should go in the letter.

Hundreds of labels and envelopes later, we sent letters with dancing candy canes around the edges sailing into the mailboxes of nuns and priests around the country. Sitting beside Sandra, licking envelopes, I remember talking so fast. About everything. I felt fuller than I'd been in a while. Letter writing all on my own was a good feeling, but I was addicted to this feeling—I was a part of something bigger than my own efforts. I didn't feel alone.

Waiting for the mail to arrive every afternoon quickly became the best part of the day for Sister Margaret and I. The days I was at the center, I'd wait to hear the creaking of the wooden floorboards as her footsteps took her down the narrow hallway and into the doorway of my office.

"We got another one!" she'd say. "Another check!" She looked so excited, so surprised by people's generosity. It sounds corny to say, but every dollar was its own version of Christmas morning to us. We were giddy and glowing and fist-pumping, silently and not so silently, as I added the numbers into an Excel sheet and watched as the contributions reached over seven thousand dollars. The total wasn't earth shattering. It was probably a small pocket of cash compared to what we actually needed for the center. But it was money that hadn't been there yesterday. Funds seemed to just appear the second we reached out to people with a simple letter. I went back to Staples for another few stacks of candy cane paper.

As I waited to cross Grand Concourse to get to the department store, I thought about Ryan. I can't say what brought the thought of him back with a vengeance as I watched for the glowing walking man to appear on the other side of the intersection. It happens like that though. You're walking along, on some busy street, and you see something as small and irrelevant as a food truck. Or a window cracked open and a familiar song coming out. And just one of those things triggers a memory and you remember a person's face or a conversation. Memories can be cruel little tyrants like that.

There'd been so many moments throughout the last few months where I'd just wanted to pull my phone out and call him. Or shoot him a simple text. This was one of those moments where I wanted to tell him exactly what I was doing and hear him tell me, one more time, he was proud of me. I probably didn't even need it to be him on the other side of the phone, I just wanted someone to reach out to and say: This is what I have done this year. I am trying. I am trying for you.

When I got back to the office, I pulled out my phone and scrolled through my contacts to find his name. I opened my notebook and wrote his number down on a piece of paper, then quietly deleted the contact. The texts. All of it. I ripped out the piece of notebook paper and folded the scrap into fours. I could have thrown the paper out but instead I shoved it deep into the pocket of my sweater. When the sweater with the swirls of yellow went into the wash, it would be good-bye. The suds, the water, and the tumble dry—the gods of detergent would rip him away and it would be done.

Those seven numbers, swooped thick in Sharpie, would only draw me back into someone I was meant to let go.

Shortly after, Celia arrived in the Bronx for a visit.

It was the start of her holiday winter break. I stood in the middle of one of the classrooms of the immigration center, anxiously awaiting her arrival. We hadn't seen each other in five months. I remember being afraid we'd be different, afraid something might have changed between us in the span of a semester. I wanted to still be the same person for her.

When the car pulled up, I bolted down the steps of the stoop, barely waiting for her to pull her weekender bag from the backseat of the car and say good-bye to her dad before I squealed and pressed into her. Juan and the other barbers looked on.

We're back, we're back, we're back.

I had the weekend all mapped out. We would spend the majority of Saturday and Sunday in Manhattan. We would soak in all of it. We would tour through the Upper East Side. We'd hear violins howling to the tune of "O Holy Night" in Central Park. We'd head over to Serendipity 3, fingers crossed that the line wouldn't be too long, to sit inside the scene of one of our favorite holiday movies—*Serendipity*—together. We'd watch skaters dance on the ice. It would be a classic tourists-in-New York City weekend. And while we did do a lot of those things, I think the need to stay busy fell away right when she got there. There'd been so much life wedged into the last few months that we needed to sit, and talk, and sip coffee, and just pretend like nothing had changed. So I took her to the Blend instead.

The Blend was a little coffee shop Libby and I had discovered as we made our way toward Arthur Avenue one morning—a stretch of delis, bakeries, and cafés at the foot of our neighborhood that prided itself on being the real Little Italy of New York. From the front window, the Blend is deceptively small. At first, we thought there was only a front room, but when I went back to the coffee shop the next time, I watched a slew of students in Fordham sweatshirts disappear through a black curtain by the cream and sugar into a wide-open room full of tables and black leather couches. It was a refuge for dozens of students with noses sunk deep in their textbooks.

With cups of pumpkin coffee between our hands, slush on the bottom of our boots as we propped them up on a low coffee table and we sat shoulder to shoulder on one of the black couches, Celia and I eventually reached the point where all the small conversation fizzled out and we started talking about the good and crazy things we hoped to do in the world one day. It was a conversation we both already knew by heart, but it never seemed to get old—our hopes of finding love, of one day having families. Her hope for a wraparound porch and wide-open fields for her kids to run through. My hope to write books and travel to countries where even asking where the bathroom is sounds romantic. I could trust Celia for that reliable kind of conversation. It's those kinds of conversations that always manage to keep you hopeful for what's to come, even after you both say good-bye at the end of a weekend.

"Do you still talk to Ryan?"

She looked down at her cup when she asked the question. I knew eventually we would arrive at this point. I could tell by the way her voice stood inside of that question what she already hoped my answer would be. She'd been in Prague the semester I met him and was hurt to find I went to him first with a lot of things. Even when we Skyped, her stance toward Ryan never changed: "You really don't want to do this, Hannah." I didn't really listen.

"No," I said. I could see her shoulders relax when the word slipped out. "I don't. I haven't. I just cannot go back to that. I get so on the verge of saying something to him when I see something stupid that reminds me of him around the city, but I don't even know if he would respond."

"I think he would. But I don't know if it would be a good thing."

"It wouldn't be. I am learning that now. I should have never even started the thing. It should have been over before it even began."

"Yeah, but it wasn't an easy situation for anyone," she said. "You could not have known it would happen that way."

"I know. It just makes me wonder why things happen though. You know? Like why do we even have to go through meeting people when we know they aren't going to stay in our lives?"

"Or I sometimes wish you could at least know the purpose someone served," she added. "I think about that all the time, why some people come into our lives and we can't manage to shake them and why other people leave."

We sat still for a while and didn't say a thing. I could have kept talking, but I just stayed silent. She is the only person in the world who gets to know me better when I say nothing at all.

"I think a lot about letting go lately. What that really looks like," I told her.

"What do you think about it?"

"I don't know. I am trying to figure out if I believe there is such a thing as closing a door for good."

"Closure," she said.

Every time I heard the word *closure* my mind wandered back into my eighth-grade body, sitting beside my best friends as we hosted these things we called "Closure Ceremonies." If you can picture a bunch of teenage girls with metal in their mouths swinging a hammer wildly through the air to crash down on lockets and bracelets and the voice boxes of teddy bears that died with the muffled and mangled words *I love you* on their breath, that was us. We thought that if we tried really hard, we could make the closure tangible. It could be just like slamming a door and walking away for good. We burned love notes. We screamed and cussed a bit, feeling empowered as forbidden words dropped like bombs off our tongues. And then when we were exhausted from all the crying and rage, we just lay and cried beneath stars as ballads from Selena and the nightly radio show "Love Songs at Night with Delilah" trickled through the stereo. We didn't attempt to give answers we didn't have. We didn't act like a broken heart was the oldest thing in our books. It wasn't. We just acknowledged it felt like all the oxygen had been sucked from the world and then we embraced one another.

"I deleted his number," I told Celia. "I thought that would do something but it doesn't really. I still think about him. I wish I didn't want to call him whenever something good happened."

"I guess deleting a number doesn't do much if you keep holding out for someone to call," she said.

"Liz Gilbert says in her memoir that when you think about that person, the one you're trying to get over, you should send them lots of light and love and then let them go."

"Have you tried that?"

"Yeah, but I feel like I've given him way too much of my own light and love." I laughed. I thought of Ryan—all filled with too much light and love for his little lungs to handle—and I pictured him smiling. Because he had a great smile. And I tried, for the moment, to be content with the real truth: just because something breaks, or comes to you broken already, doesn't always mean you should script yourself an invitation to go on and fix it.

"It's kind of helped the hurt go away," I continued. "Yeah, I'm sad. Yeah, I thought I would get some sort of different ending. But it reminds me that I always wanted the best for him. Even when I wrote him a letter on the day we said good-bye, the whole letter was just about him finding happiness. Having the courage to do that for himself."

"You deserve that kind of happiness too," Celia said.

An awkward pause stood over us when she said that.

"I know," I said.

As I sat beside my best friend, our shoulders touching but saying nothing, I remembered the night Ryan had stood by the window overlooking our campus at night.

"I want to know how your story turns out," he'd said. He made me feel like I was a *Dawson's Creek* character, surprised to find I was standing on the wrong side of the creek. At the time I thought I would have done anything just to live a good story for him. A story where he chose me in the end.

But this was the story. All the details were unfolding all around me. And it had nothing to do with being chosen or not being chosen. He hadn't written the letters for me. He hadn't braved loneliness for me. And that's the truth I needed to swallow: people don't step out and live for you; that's on you. You have to be the one to get down deep enough and whisper the words people can't always say for you—whether you believe in them fully or not—"I choose you. I choose you."

"Here's to the year and to New York," Celia said, breaking the silence between us and lifting her white cardboard cup into the air like she was making a toast.

"To New York!" I followed her, shooting my cup into the air. "And here's to calluses and two hundred seven love letters in the mail!"

"Really?" She turned to me. "That many?"

"That many," I said. "I put the last couple dozen in the mail right before you got here. I am going to take a break for the holidays but I think I will keep it going. I just wanted to say I got them all done. I wanted there to be something for us to celebrate.

"I can't believe I made it to this point," I added.

"What do you think you've learned from all of it?"

The question caught me off guard, though I am not sure why. It was just like Celia to ask that sort of thing. Celia is one of those constant reminders that we never stop learning, no matter where we go.

Nothing inside of me had ever paused to process what all the scribbles might actually mean for this time in my life. I'd been so focused on just finishing the letters that I hadn't really thought much of what I was learning.

I could say so much though. I could say it was surprising to find myself capable of writing so many letters. I could tell her I really had no idea how much heartbreak existed in the world. Like, so much heartbreak. Like, so much so that it was tempting to start a club, at least a welcoming committee, for newbies to the feeling of broken pieces. You'd think within a world that gives us genius little smartphones and turn-by-turn navigation we'd have created some sort of community for the ones who just need to hear these words after their heart is gouged out: "Hey, you're here. You've arrived. Don't be ashamed. You're in for quite the journey back to wholeness. It gets better. I promise. You're not alone, toots. You're not alone."

But I didn't say any of those things to Celia. My answer was simpler than that.

"I think maybe I've learned my way around loneliness," I said. "Just that loneliness doesn't always have to be the worst thing in the world. I guess none of this would have ever happened if I hadn't been lonely. I want to be thankful for that."

It was true. It took loneliness to make the first couple of love letters come out of me, to realize something so much bigger than what I thought was just my own loneliness: we've never really been alone. Maybe lonely, but never alone.

Strega Nona Grace

I went home for Christmas a few days after Celia left and stayed through the New Year. On Christmas morning, my mother handed each of my family members a gift to unwrap. All you could hear for a few moments was the crinkling of wrapping paper. My brothers each held up a pair of yellow boxer shorts. My mother held up her own pair of yellow underwear. I opened mine and kept them tucked in the wrapping paper, embarrassed to take them out.

"I found the idea in a magazine," my mother announced to the room. "It's a tradition in Venezuela. People wear yellow underwear into the New Year to bring them good luck." She was beaming over the idea, over all of her most treasured people together in a room holding pairs of yellow underwear.

I looked down at the yellow underwear, small white polka dots speckled all over them, and thought it was a strange tradition. The whole thing was strange. But I guess it is no weirder than all the ways I convinced myself that come midnight on January 1, I would magically be a different person with resolutions. More rules and better eating habits.

I looked around the room at my entire family, all of us tethered together by some Venezuelan tradition and the commonality of yellow underwear in our hands. I was suddenly okay with the weirdness of it all. I let the wrapping paper fall to the ground. I just said thank-you.

And then I said thank-you again, loud enough so my mother could hear me.

At the start of 2011, I didn't make any resolutions. I didn't go to a bar wearing a sparkly miniskirt and pumps like the year before. Instead, I sat surrounded by some of my closest friends from the town I grew up in. We ate off cheese platters on the living room floor. We watched the ball drop and drank from champagne flutes. I brought crowns for us to wear.

I decided instead of making a resolution I knew I would not keep, I'd just pick a word. One word to carry with me into 2011. That word wasn't *comfort* or *success* or *excellence*. It wasn't *confidence* or *resilience*. The word was *serendipity*. Serendipity. The act of finding something valuable and delightful when you are not looking for it.

There was no ruckus or kisses at midnight. No confetti caught in my hair. The New Year came in quietly, almost like if the crowns hadn't been there you wouldn't have noticed the shift at all. I wore the yellow underwear.

A week later, I was back in New York City. Back at the desk in the small office of the life center. January is merciless in the Northeast. It's a heartless month. January is basically the love child of Satan and Sallie Mae. I marveled at the way New Yorkers were so quick to heave their Christmas trees to the sidewalks. That's all I saw on the way to work that whole first month of 2011, evergreens crying out to be resituated back in warm homes and decorated with bulbs. They seemed to whimper as I passed by, "You wanted me once. And you were so quick to let me and my little branches go the day after Christmas."

You see, this is the point where I want to lie to you. I want to present you with a magical turning point where I skipped through the streets of New York with zest and feistiness and all the other peppy adjectives I can place in this spot. I think it's the world's fault I want to paint such a pretty picture for you. At least I am choosing to blame a world that always manages to convince me I should always be soaring. If I am not at rock bottom, I should be soaring. Thriving. Succeeding. In actuality, I was okay. I was just okay. And I was trying every single day to not let little things unravel me. And I was in a state where I knew if someone told me to "get stronger," I would punch them. Because sometimes we don't get stronger right when we want to. And sometimes an attitude change isn't as simple as we think it can be. I think it's more than okay to wake up some days and just be "okay." Not amazing. Not having the best day of your life. Life is just hard sometimes. And people deserve more credit for even getting out of bed sometimes.

On the plus side, I was making pretty awesome friendship bracelets at the preschool—being quite the gangster when it came to beads and black pipe cleaners. And I was getting involved in committees at the United Nations, specifically ones that dealt with the injustice of girls being left out of the classroom and not afforded an education. I was making the most of trying to create work for myself and ended up joining a committee to help plan a daylong conference for two hundred fifty girl delegates who would visit the UN from all over the world for the fifty-fifth Commission on the Status of Women—a solid two weeks dedicated to gender equality and the advancement of women. Basically, those two weeks at the UN were to me what Shark Week is to other people.

And, as for the love letters, I started writing them again. I took a short break for the holidays but felt forced, more than anything, to re-open my inbox for more letter requests. No matter how I tried to write about other things or try out other projects (I actually don't recommend asking your blog readers to mail you peanut butter and jelly so that you can feed all the homeless of New York City)—the love letters were what stuck. It was the thing people wanted to read about the most. I didn't get why at the time but I let that compartment of my life be just what it was: a mystery.

Even in all the goodness, I still struggled to get up most mornings and I still cried. Too much. I won't deny that. The tears were just sort of there. For reasons and for no reasons at all. I worried the tears might never stop that January. They came so frequently, rushing through my eyelids like shoppers into stores on Black Friday, I wondered if I would be the first girl to cry for all of eternity. I'd eventually be forced to take to the streets as a public spectacle, more prominent in Times Squares than the Naked Cowboy. People would board trains and planes just to meet me, to touch my cheeks and see for themselves if the droplets were real. I would cry so much that books would get written about me. And nursery rhymes.

Even Aesop would have struggled to make a moral out of me.

I was sitting at my desk one morning and I honestly didn't even know I was crying until I felt this warm hand on my wrist. I looked over to see Sandra, one of the women from the office at the life center, staring at me through her glasses. She gripped my wrist tighter. Her other hand stayed resting on her keyboard. She just held my wrist for a while, not saying anything at first. It was like the world paused, and we were both standing still in the clutter of a busy morning. No phones to be answered. No e-mails to be sent or texts to be read. It was just us and the slow hissing of the radiator you could always hear when the office was quiet in the morning.

She finally spoke. "Darling, you go home tonight and you pray and pray and pray until you fall asleep. And then you are going to get up and do it all over again. Okay?"

"Okay," I said.

It was gentle and forceful, all at the same time. She wasn't throwing anything in my face. She wasn't telling me to stop crying reckless, purposeless tears. She was just holding my wrist and telling me to do something. Even if praying feels like nothing, do it and see if you can prove yourself wrong.

It made me think of that old scripture from Ecclesiastes, the one in chapter three about seasons that everyone loves cross-stitching onto pillows and making the background of their computer because it feels so peaceful to think everything happens in its right time. It's like a gateway verse. Something we can agree upon whether we have a beef with God or not.

But I think the words of that Bible chapter are so much more powerful than just saying there are seasons for everything under the sun. If you read the first eight verses, you'll see a bunch of verbs. *Plant. Harvest. Search. Quit searching. Grieve. Dance.* It's a massive batch of action verbs. It's like God's strategy. It's like He's saying not only, "Hey, I made you," but, "I am at the helm of this whole thing and every season I bring you through is only to polish you up and refine you even more. There is no time to ask why right now. Don't ask why. There is only time to do. You don't want to miss what is going on here."

Sometimes asking why is like being a wallflower at a dance party because no one invited you out to dance. Sometimes you just need to say, "Screw it," and plow onto the dance floor anyway.

I feel like I am networking with the God of the universe.

That was the basis of my thoughts the moment I got down on the floor and tried to make prayers flood out of my mouth the way Sandra suggested.

All the words just seemed to slam into one another in my head like how the kids at the preschool would thrash into one another the moment we'd do a practice fire drill. (Thank God we never had an actual fire. Those were messy times.) I was shifting from side to side. I got down on my knees by the foot of my bed because that's how all the Precious Moments dolls pray. I stood up and raised my arms to the ceiling. I took out a Bible, dropped it down onto the floor, and silently hoped it would open to a page where God would speak to me. But nothing availed when I tried to let it all out. This all seemed so much easier in points of crisis. Otherwise, it felt like I was walking up to God in the same way I approached professionals in stuffy dress suits with my résumés and business cards in hand. I didn't even have a laundry list of requests for Him, I just wanted Him to like me and think I was doing an okay job on this little planet He'd created.

But every time I tried to utter something out loud, my mind kept retreating backward to one of the conversations I had with the girl from the religious group in college. It was probably two weeks before my planned baptism. We sat outside together in the pathway between my dorm and hers. It was ten at night. We'd ordered a pizza. The stars were out. It was the kind of night you find wedged into the chorus of a Taylor Swift song.

"It's strange. I just don't feel God in any of this," I told her honestly. "I thought maybe I would feel Him more."

I remember her saying God was distant for a reason. I wasn't in communication with Him yet. I wasn't in the light yet. I wish I could remember the exact words but they hurt me more than I could express in that moment. Like God hadn't chosen me. I think that's probably the hardest human feeling to swallow—the feeling of not being chosen.

She eventually took the box of pizza and the few stray slices inside. I stayed out there on the ground, looking up at the stars. I didn't have the answers but I had so many questions: How is God not reliable? How is God picky and choosy about with whom He wants to speak? I felt disappointed in God that night, more than anything. Disappointed He was so exclusive.

I just remember thinking the stars were so reliable. I felt it as I drew my legs in close to my body and wrapped my arms around them; the stars are reliable, unlike any other thing in this crazy world. Leaves fall off the trees. Snow melts. Rain washes away all the things we wrote on the pavement. But the stars are relentless in shining.

When it came to talking with God, I wanted to believe He was like those stars. If I looked, He'd be there. I'd lost a lot of things in the years that led up to this point—shoes and keys and books and boyfriends—but I never lost that hope.

I got up from my knees and went on the computer after a few minutes. Libby was online, somewhere over in Italy. I pictured her hanging out in an Internet café with cute Italians who spoke the kind of broken English that could make your mouth water.

Hannah: Can I be honest with you?
Libby: Always.

Hannah: I'm afraid I will never be happy again.

Libby: You will be.

Hannah: I'm petrified that I am never going to get back to normal. I never wanted to lose myself so fully.

Libby: Well, I don't think anyone wants to lose themselves fully. I don't think you've lost yourself, Hannah. I think you are just on a detour to finding yourself. And sometimes we have to go through that. You learned a lot. You learned you like living in a city but you want to be living on more than $25 a week. You found out something about yourself. That isn't the same as losing yourself.

Hannah: I keep putting my arms up asking God, "Like seriously? Seriously? Do I really need to keep falling apart for the last months of this thing?"

Libby: Have you written him?

Libby: I'm serious. Have you written him a letter?

Libby: I mean, you and him seem to be good friends. I think he will respond, though it might not be clear, but he will somehow write back if you believe him enough. See, if I wrote God a letter, I'd never get a response because I don't have enough belief . . . but you do.

Hannah: Ok.

Libby: Write the letter. I have to head out.

Libby: Va bene. I will talk to you later.

I X'ed out of the conversation with Libby and took out a piece of printer paper. I prepared to write God a letter. I wanted to reach Him. Like, really, really reach Him.

You might call it crazy but I just call it hopeful. Hopeful that in a world where we can e-mail anyone, find anyone, tag anyone, poke anyone, tweet at anyone, reach anyone, we could reach God too. Like those stars. And He would read me. Digest me. Click me open on His iPhone. And, even before I thought to click "send," He'd respond with a love so mammoth it'd blow Arial and Georgia and Times New Roman straight out of the font family tree.

It became evident pretty quickly that God didn't need me to write Him a letter. It was 2011. It was the age of technology. God was a pretty savvy dude. He already knew lightning speed. So God, of all people (beings? things?), should have an e-mail address, I decided. I would create an e-mail address for Him.

I went back to the computer. As I signed out of my own Gmail account to create one for God, I pictured Him slugging a pumpkin spice latte in the square of January, checking His e-mail and watching it flood over with petitions from His little ones. I pictured Him fist-pumping when the Super Bowl was finally over with a sigh of relief: the end of one-liner prayers for victory. I could see Him creating folders like "Broken hearts" and "Cannot seem to find Me lately," while taking minimal breaks to watch viral videos and laugh over the fact He'd known what the fox says all along.

Just five minutes later, HolderofYourHand@gmail.com was born. God's e-mail address. A way to finally slingshot my prayers into the atmosphere and have them all caught in a password-protected vault that no one else had to know about.

Strangely enough, I didn't hesitate when it came to sending Him an e-mail. I thought it was going to be awkward, like the way it would probably feel to respond to one of the messages I got on dating sites where the man on the other side of the screen seemed to be sitting on the "emoticon" button as he filled my message box with wink faces.

There was that initial "How do I address Him/can God and I make nicknames for each other?" awkwardness, but a few seconds later I was getting personal.

I started unloading junk and worry and desire and fear. It was unexpected, but it was pouring out from me. It was skittering away from my own hands. It was like God and I were standing in the kitchen together and it started with a comment about His not doing the dishes and exploded into all these other things I hadn't brought up with Him.

Send. Send. Send. Send. Send.

I didn't feel the need to filter anything or fear anything. There was no "Am I doing this wrong, God? Am I not getting this whole prayer thing right?" I could be clear-cut and eloquent with my prayers if I wanted or I could send Him blubbering petitions and heavy one-liners if I wanted that too. The white space was mine. The communication platform was there. It was like gathering up the courage to finally send a message over Facebook to a guy you've looked at for too long from a distance at a coffee shop. It was the anxiety of wondering how he might think to read you. If he would read the whole thing. The anxiety of wondering: *How could he respond?*

The next night I was sitting on the subway, waiting to reach the Fordham Road stop. A little boy was sitting next to me, slowly nodding off to the pull of the train. He must have been about seven years old. His feet dangled off the floor. With the jerk of the train, he heaved into my side but didn't stir when he fell into me. He stayed wedged into me sleeping, his face half-buried in the collar of his puffer jacket as the train kept pulling uptown. I looked around in the packed subway car for someone to approach me and scoop the sleeping child up into their arms. No one flinched.

On any other day, I would have worried my life was about to morph into one of those Lifetime movies where a woman finds an orphan child and must take him into her home. On any other day, I would have wondered how to feed the little boy, and clothe him, and be a broke Daddy Warbucks to him and his bald little head that I am sure the barbers across from us could have shaven stars and planets into. Normally, I might have nudged him away or gotten up to stand. But on that night, he was warm. And he fit right there. And just his sleeping beside me—a little child who barely knew the frown lines of worry—took some of the hiss out of January's voice.

He and I, we didn't move for a long time. We just stayed that way. And I closed my eyes. He didn't stir. The subway crawled uptown as my breathing reached a synchronized rhythm with the little boy's. For the smallest pocket of time, the two of us were cradled and rocked in the arms of the transit line.

I thought back to the e-mail address I'd created, how I wondered what kind of response I might get, if any, from God. Would it show up in a conversation? Would it be staring me in the face when I opened a book of hymns? Or was it right here, in the heavy breathing of this little boy?

This was grace. And I say that with hesitancy because grace has always been a tricky word for me. Growing up in church, it always seemed like people had such messed-up portion control when it came to grace. Who got more? Who got less of it? To some, grace was everywhere. To others, it came in spurts, like quick drips from an eyedropper. I even had a friend once tell me that an elder of the church announced to her, "There is less grace for you because of your sins." She repeated the idea out loud, "There is less grace for me," like she actually believed it. Like slowly, in time, it would become a melody to her and it would trickle into all the things she did, and the relationships she kept, and the things she thought she was capable of.

God is a lot of things to a lot of people but I don't think He is a cheap party host with limited grace to give out. I think He'd laugh uncontrollably—with a very robust godly laughter—at that one. Like, "Oh no, sorry, I managed to stitch legs upon the spider but I have to give you a smaller portion of grace. You've messed up too many times, and though I am like a schoolboy infatuated with your heart, I've capped off My grace quota! Be sure to apply next year!" I didn't think it worked that way.

This was grace. All of it—it was grace. The boy. The subway. The sleeping. The breathing. Being tired. Worn. Tumbled dry by a long day. And not needing to do anything but close your eyes and listen for the slow click, click, clicking of the subway tracks. Just closing your eyes. Not heaving. Not pushing. Not striving to be anything else in that moment.

Grace is letting something else—something so much bigger than you—carry you home. It's having and wanting nowhere else to be but in a moment that wants you and takes you just as you are.

As I kept sending e-mails to HolderofYourHand@gmail .com, grace kept rushing in. Grace rushed in and made herself known— as if she were an old Italian grandmother who knows all the names of her grandchildren, all the Alessandras and Antonios and Vitos skittering into alphabetical order. I pictured Grace in that way. With these wrinkled hands that once held knotted-up laundry with a furious grip. She kissed everyone several times before leaving a party. She had secrets tucked inside of her—secret recipes and secret sauces scribbled on scraps of paper coated with flour and remnants of old spices. Grace would be the kind to sit with you after the sun went down and hum slowly to all the things you told her and the words that stampeded out of you until you reached the point in the conversation where you realized it was safe and you could say just about anything, and she would not get up and leave you there alone.

That sort of grace rushed in. Grace with the mean table setting. Grace who always pulled out a chair for you and was delighted to see your tired face among the dinner guests. I don't know why but I pictured Grace as looking just like the storybook character of Strega Nona with the magic pasta pots, whispering and taking your hand to say, "Baby, you can't make me want you less. I know only more. I know only how to want you more."

Grace was everywhere. I was seeing her in everything. But I say that only after I admit I had to take the first step for myself. I had to do something I hadn't done in a long while as I sat and stewed in my own sadness and tears and pathetic wallowing—I had to look up. That's the one thing that changed inside of me. It was like a bridge I crossed over. First, I decided: look up. Second: pay attention. Maybe it is easier to plug into other things or stay staring down at your phone, but you really need to pay attention to what is happening all around you. Otherwise, you'll miss her.

You'll miss Grace, and all the wonder she brings. You won't look closely enough at the businessman shuffling through the *New York Post* to notice his bright blue and yellow pin-striped socks poking out from underneath his pant legs. You won't see the precisely painted watermelons on the fingernails of the girl who types frantically throughout the entire train ride. Nails so intricate you can see the little seeds of the ripe melon dancing by her cuticles.

You'll miss the man across from you, wringing his hands in his lap like he's anxious. You won't even look. And when you miss him, you won't pray for him. And though you might think your prayers are no answer at all, every form of prayer is a chance to slip outside of your own chaos to ask that someone else be overwhelmed with a little goodness and favor that day.

And, if you aren't paying attention, you'll miss the swift second when the subway flies out from beneath the ground, right before Yankee Stadium, when you can see the most remarkable sunsets just beginning. The way the sunlight lies like blankets on the building tops. Blankets of yellow and gold. At the same moment, your phone will flood with those precious bars of service and all the text messages that piled up while you were in the dead zones will light up the screen. But just watch the sunset instead. The messages will be there, they won't change, and you'll see one of those things the older people always say they wish they'd noticed more of when they turn ninety-six and younger people start asking them, "What would you have done differently?"

She

I used to think about heaven a lot. What it looked like. What it smelled like. For a long time, I imagined it would be just like the movie *Titanic*. I watched that movie so many times I was convinced we'd all get that grand-staircase moment. The very last scene. Where Rose walks in and she's standing at the foot of the stairs and Jack turns around—looking just like the Jack she fell in love with so many years ago—and his face is all scribbled with a thousand different sentiments: "You're here. You're finally here. I knew you would come. I've been waiting for you."

That was heaven to me for the longest time. Mind you, I was eleven years old and only wanted to go to heaven because I thought Jack Dawson would be in attendance but it was before the time of all the books written about visits to heaven. Back then I wondered if maybe after that moment, God would show up on the staircase and whisk me away to this big, private movie theater and we'd sit and He'd recline His chair and say something like, "How was the ride? Did you enjoy it?"

And I could only hope I'd have good things to report back to Him about the people I met and the things I did. That's a weird feeling I still feel sometimes, like I want to make God proud. I pictured God holding this big, heavenly remote control and pointing it at the screen before us.

"Just watch this," He'd say. "It's time for you to know all the impact—big and small—you made just by showing up and being human."

With a slug of His raspberry blue slushie and a massive handful of buttered popcorn, maybe He'd say, "Your life served purposes beyond what you could have ever known."

I don't know what actually goes down in heaven, if heaven has a grand staircase or a theater where you get to see your impact in a *Crash* kind of cinematic adventure, but I do know our stories work that way—the imprints of ourselves we press into the palms of others have the power to be passed and passed through the hands of many. That the smallest things we do, never thinking twice about them, might be the very things that keep a person alive, and breathing, and standing on that day. I've stopped doubting that kind of impact because believing in it— believing in miracles in the mud of the mundane—gives you so much more purpose than not believing in it at all.

And if there is a movie theater, and a God who is like a tour guide for halls of other people's memories, then I know He has probably reached a woman named Hélène Berr already. And He has told her my name and all about the day I met her.

It was a Tuesday. The UN was hosting a Holocaust remembrance week specifically to honor women who'd lost their lives or who fought with dirt beneath their fingernails to just keep life in their grip between 1933 and 1945. For the entire month of February, the main lobby was transformed into a memorial for the victims and the survivors.

I cleared my calendar for that day. I was ready and excited to see the transformation of the lobby. When I first arrived, the room was quiet. You could hear only footsteps walking around the exhibit after you got past security. I stood at the front entrance and sucked in the silence as I walked beneath an imitation of the gate at Auschwitz that read, *"Arbeit Macht Frei,"* or "Work Makes You Free." I remember thinking all these crazy things as I stood beneath that gate. I wondered about the people who made the gate. The people who chiseled the twisted letters. If they knew how many people would be transported through that gate and how many would not walk out again.

Drawings sketched by an unknown prisoner of Auschwitz stood in the center of the lobby. I stayed to the side of the room, noticing some sort of script paneling the exterior. I could see cursive. Shreds of what I thought from a distance had to be a diary.

My first thought, naively, was of the diary of Anne Frank. That was always my first association between a diary and the Holocaust. I've asked people in the years that followed just to make sure I wasn't the only one. And, through my research, I have learned there is a legitimate not-so-secret secret society of people who love and adore the Anne Frank diary. They're everywhere. The story of Anne Frank can run a dinner party. It's more than just the story of a girl. She was with so many of us when we were growing up—a copy of her tattered diary in paperback form handed to us at the stroke of middle school when we were just being introduced to puberty and French kisses and back acne. And suddenly, there was Anne and her diary, Kitty. And we got this secret lens into her life and we sat with her on the page. And then Anne was with us again when we got older and we read her diary for a second time and things popped out to us that we'd never seen before.

But Anne was just one of the people who struggled, and tried to pin hope down to the floor, and maybe thought in darker corners, "Will anyone ever know my name? And what they did to me?" I've always made heroes out of those people, though I'll probably never know all their names. They were heroes just by being there. Just by standing in the face of other humans stripping them of their dignity.

As I got up closer to the diary paneling the white walls of the lobby, I discovered the diary actually belonged to a woman who, in 2008, was called "the French Anne Frank" when her words were finally published and put on the shelves of bookstores. She'd been at the same concentration camp as Anne Frank. They died just weeks apart from each other. No one might ever know if the two exchanged glances—or sat so close their elbows touched—when they were contained inside the fences of Bergen-Belsen.

Her name was Hélène. Hélène Berr. She was twenty-one at the

time. She was studying English literature at the Sorbonne in Paris, France. She was a Parisian. Living a good life of abundance. She wrote things that made my head spin because I didn't know the footprints of the Holocaust could sound so eloquent when they stomped on through.

Only a year younger than me. The same initials. The same deep appreciation for words and the power they could hold when you strung them together just right. I was drawn to her story instantly. She was like a friend you've always expected to meet. Like someone who gets you at your core and suddenly you feel known.

As I walked panel to panel, she held my hand with her storytelling. She tore back the curtains of her life. She showed me the orchards she used to skip through. I shook hands with her fiancé, Jean Morawiecki. I stood two feet from the oppression and I screamed her name when she left me there, standing alone and wondering how things like this happened. How life ended in this way. I swallowed the mouthfuls of her fear.

I know why I am keeping this journal, she wrote on Wednesday, October 27, 1943. *I know that I want it to be given to Jean if I am not here when he comes back. I don't want to disappear without him knowing everything I have been thinking about while he has been away.* She spent the next few paragraphs going back and forth, back and forth, on whether she should just start writing as if Jean were reading. But writing *darling Jean* would make her feel like a heroine in a romance novel. Jean would have laughed over that. She wrote she would have laughed at that too, if she thought she'd remember how to laugh again.

She knew. I said it beneath my breath. Tears filled my eyes, even though I already knew what had happened to Hélène. It was even more heartbreaking to know she knew that evil was coming for her. That she might never get to see her fiancé again.

She knew what aisles would never be walked down and what babies would never be held. And still, amid the dark reality, she came back to the pages of her diary, day after day. Not to relive memories. Not to hash out details. It was only so he could have something of her to hold when he could hold her no longer.

I don't want to disappear without him knowing everything I have been thinking about while he has been away.

Chills streamed down my arms and legs. The diary wasn't about her. None of it was ever about her. She recognized the heartbreak of her fiancé long before she even acknowledged her own—the fractures of his heart he would carry with him always. She'd found a way to place herself on the back burner and her life became a quest to create something that mattered to someone she loved too deeply for words.

And then it was over. Suddenly. The last panel felt like it came too quickly. I was standing face-to-face with Hélène's ending. I touched three fingers against the wall where the last three words of her diary lived.

Horror! Horror! Horror!

Famous words of William Shakespeare. The cursive of a girl who deserved all the oxygen the Paris air could give her. The last entry. February 15, 1944. My mother's birthday. *Good-bye, sweet girl.*

Stepping back from the wall, I stood in the middle of a crowd of other people—quiet and pensive as they read the pages of her diary—questions swirling in my head: *Why am I here? What am I doing? How is anyone ever going to know that I was here? That I lived? That I loved? That I danced? That I cried? That it was hard? But it was worth it.*

Hélène hadn't been whining. She hadn't been complaining. She'd been so intentional with every step. She never even wrote with a full diary in front of her; she just kept on delivering the batches of pages to her cook—someone who was not Jewish—so that the cook could keep the diary safe until Hélène's fiancé came back. If Hélène had never done that, never submitted those pages bit by bit, no one would have ever known her story in this way. I could not let go of the fact Hélène never actually learned of the nobility in her own story. I guess when the story isn't for you, it probably doesn't matter how many lives you will touch. She would never know a twenty-two-year-old girl who wanted to uncover the strands of bravery in her own life was reading her diary, that parts inside of that girl were getting stronger because of her words.

Finally, finally, this is what bravery looks like. This is what courage looks like. It has nothing to do with dominating the day, every single day. It has to do with showing up and speaking truth. One true sentence after one true sentence.

You changed my life, I wanted to tell her. *You changed my life, Hélène. And I realize something I didn't see before. It's not about me. It's really not about me.*

It was like that was the light switch flipping on. And either I changed or things changed around me, but I started to see people differently. And I started to meet different kinds of people. My friend Clifton calls these people the "rare exotic goldfish." The ones who never were fine with just fitting in the tank. They are the living, fleshly personifications of a Steve Jobs quote because they push you and challenge you and force you outside of the boxes you built for yourself out of other people's expectations.

More of those sorts of people kept strolling into my life. Tammy was one of them. I met her through the United Nations, while I was doing work on the committee for the girl delegates. Back then, Tammy was just at the beginning of a dream that would take her into a whole new life. She dreamed in a way that made me jealous. She never did wait for someone to invite her into a life she wanted. She went after it every day. And I learned from her that it is one thing to be the girl on fire, but it is entirely another thing to be the girl who manages to set the world on fire with all the quiet and beautiful things she does.

At the time, she was still the social media editor for one of the top fashion and lifestyle magazines in the industry. When the first rumblings of the words *social media* started popping up, Tammy saw the real power and potential behind it. She knew, with the kind of nagging in your heart that doesn't learn how to stay quiet, that this thing would be so much more than a tweet or a status update or just another way to make the world jealous with your wedding plans. If we used it well, we could change the world. She loved that job, but I could see a different kind of love in her eyes every time she talked about the nonprofit she started, She's the First. It was a nonprofit that helped to provide scholarships for girls' education all over the world.

I became a researcher for her nonprofit, keeping up the communication between our organization and the schools we helped to sponsor girls in Tanzania and Indonesia. At a leadership summit for all the team members, I found myself standing beside Tammy next to an array of burritos and tacos during lunchtime. I remember having all these questions to ask her: How she created something that mattered. If she ever surrounded herself with people who made her feel like she couldn't accomplish things. If she ever just wanted to give up. But before I ever got to ask a single question, she wanted to know about the love letters.

Too nervous to really tell the story, I tried to rush from start to finish, but I ultimately told her the whole thing. The woman with the red hat. The blog post. The hundreds of letters. The number was getting to the mid–two hundreds. I probably tried to wrap the whole thing up with "Yeah, I really have no idea what I am doing with it."

At the end of my rambling, she didn't say much. She just had this genuine smile on her face as she held her plate. And she told me it was the sort of story people needed to hear. For reasons I may never know, Tammy continued to invite me to different places and our friendship grew.

One morning she invited me to have brunch at her apartment. She lived up near Columbia University, just a few blocks away from an entryway into Central Park. It was myself and three other women. We sat around a table fully stocked with orange juice and strawberries and bagels and cream cheese, taking turns with sharing who we were and what we did.

I told the women about the love letters. And nearly instantly, the conversation morphed into the kind where everyone just gets real focused. I never could figure that out, why the story of the love letters would open such a wide door every time it tumbled out of me. But I understand it better now. Now I know the truth: it wasn't me or my story that came in to steer the brunch conversation—or any other conversation where the love letters came up—in a different direction. It had nothing to do with me. It had everything to do with the real hot-shot in the room: love. It wasn't about my struggle. And it wasn't about depression. It was about love. And what happens when you let love loose.

We scraped our plates clean. I think all of us sat there for a lot longer than we expected. But what I remember more than the tiny details of that day was how the pressure to be someone other than myself wasn't in attendance that morning. It was like insecurity forgot to show up on that day. I was surprised to find the feeling of "enough" spreading all over me because I was surrounded by the types of successful women who normally would make me want to start pulling out the measuring cups and rulers, as if I were going to pass them out to everyone at the table and say out loud: "Measure me. Make me feel like I am enough for you." That's just who I was used to being—someone who could change who she was in five minutes. If you told me to be someone different, I would have listened to you. I would have swallowed hard and listened to you. Even if you and I never held hands or kissed cheeks or knocked knees beneath glass tables, I still would have wanted to be enough for you.

But in that semicircle of women, our plates in our laps as we talked about old love letters, there was no need to measure myself. There was no need to compare. I was surprised to find out these women and I had so much more in common than we had things that would split us apart. We might have had different paychecks. Different motivations. Different job titles. But it seemed like every one of us at that brunch wanted things that were simple and the same. We wanted a life that was full. We wanted to be able to balance it all. We all had trouble letting go. We wanted love. We wanted to be necessary somewhere. That was the common thread. Necessity. It sounds like such a simple thing and yet it sends a lot of people to crying themselves to sleep, asking God or the ceiling that holds their prayers, "Am I there yet? Do I matter yet? Am I wanted yet? Am I enough yet?"

It was an honest and strange conversation within a group of women I'd never met before. None of us had all the answers. That didn't seem to be the point for them. I needed to witness that—I needed to witness what it looked like when you eventually stopped asking questions and just started living the answers out loud.

Throughout the entire month the Holocaust remembrance exhibit was at the United Nations, I kept going back. I kept going back to the main lobby to read the pages of Hélène's diary once and twice more.

I called my mother one evening as I got off the train and headed for my apartment after I attended a panel on some of the heroic stories of women who played pivotal roles during the Holocaust.

"I don't even know why it is hitting me so hard but I just sat in this panel surrounded by people who were so much older than me. Like seventy and eighty years old, and I couldn't help but think about them being dead soon."

"Well, that sounds fun," my mother responded. Sarcasm dripped in her tone.

It was all I was able to focus on throughout that whole panel though—I was one of the youngest people in attendance. The survivors up on the stage had a slowness to their voices and I knew soon they would be gone. This generation of survivors—of the ones who felt the Holocaust with their own two hands—was trickling away. I was squirming in my seat. Looking around. Trying to listen. Wondering if anyone else was as worried as I was. These people were dying. Old age was sweeping in to take them away. I was legitimately panicking.

"Mom, this is terrifying." I talked to her in my "You need to understand your daughter right now because the world is crumbling all around us" tone. That's the thing about me—I'm always the one having an earth-shattering crisis while everyone around me is content to just go on with their day. I encounter something as simple as a story that might give you goose bumps and it leaves me feeling mangled as roadkill. I will not shake the story off me for days.

"Like, how is anyone going to ever know about them? How will people know their stories? An entire era of people who survived this horrific tragedy is dying."

"Well, that's what diaries are for. And photo albums. And letters." She wasn't concerned in the way I was. I couldn't let go of this sorrow inside of me at the idea that things would be forgotten, that Hélène's story had been just inches away from never being published.

"But then it made me think about me," I continued. "And my generation. And how we have all these crazy social media tools we could be using for such good purposes and we use them to whine and complain and make a lot of noise. And what if that is our legacy? I mean, for the ones of us that don't do anything off a screen, what if that is how we are going to be remembered?"

"Well, I'll just be thankful that isn't me then," my mother answered. I expected her to say more, but she didn't. My mother never bought into the pulls of social media. And so she didn't seem to notice the day when social media raised up its arms and announced to the world, "I ain't so social anymore. Me? You've morphed me into a flickering slideshow of other people's highest moments. You've started living through me. And I get to keep you from people. So what do you want to do now?"

I think that's what social media really does these days. More than it connects us. It claims to bring us together but I think we're too distracted to see it's ripping us away from the one thing that really matters: one another. And how much we desperately need to show up for one another.

One week later, everything my mother said to me on the phone call made sense as I stood off to the back of the room at my mother's surprise sixtieth birthday party. I got permission from the program to travel home for the occasion. My aunts threw the party for her in the basement hall of one of the town's Catholic churches. We hung stars from the ceiling. Old photos were scattered around the room in white IKEA frames. My mother's high school yearbook photo stood at the center of one of the tables: proof she was a babe. Major babe. There was a DJ. It was the culmination of all the things my mother considers life to be: a party, a dance floor, and a beach.

The walls of that church hall were packed tight with people and laughter. I kept being approached by people who just wanted to tell me how much they loved my mother. I wanted to answer everyone with the same response: "I know. She is everything. She has always been everything. I understand why you love her so much." The rest of that night, I watched my mother sashay around the room. It might have been her sixtieth birthday but she took the room like she was still twenty-two.

Toward the middle of the night, she approached the front of the room to make an announcement.

"I was on my way to the doctor the other day because of chest pain," she told the crowd of nearly one hundred guests, as if it were an intimate secret. "Thankfully, it turned out to be only reflux. But I was driving and then panicking, thinking to myself, *Did I tell everyone that I love them? Do they know how I feel about them?*"

Her eyes scanned the room, falling on coworkers and sisters and best friends and nephews. "But you're here now. You're all here now. And I get my chance."

I watched my mother turn her own surprise party into a celebration of other people. She'd already become who she wanted to become in this world; I guess all that is necessary to do after that is say the most important things—"Thank you" and "I love you" and "I believe in you and I hope I always find the time to tell you that."

My mother might never know it, but I stood at the back of the room, shifting back and forth in my black heels, wanting to become someone different that night—the kind of someone who realizes what she has when she has it. The kind of someone who actually sees the people surrounding her. She's actually there for the big moments. She wouldn't miss them for the world. I wanted to become her. At the very least, I was ready to become the person my mother had always known I was.

Now You Are Ready

The week before I traveled home for my mother's surprise party, I roamed through the aisles of Target trying to find her a gift. I'm an awkward gift giver. For as long as I've existed and birthdays have been rolling up to the front of the calendar, she's been at the mercy of my awful gifts. One time I drew her a sixteen-page comic book about a hypothetical situation where all of my family members would become the next contestants on *Survivor* and what would or would not happen when we needed to vote one another off the island. In it, our seventeenth dog (we had a lot of dogs that mysteriously died . . . a lot . . .) ended up winning the whole game. You might be thinking it's sort of cute, and it probably would have been if I hadn't been sixteen years old at the time.

Needless to say, I was roaming around the store for a long time, but no coffeemaker or sun hat or normal gift was jumping out into the aisle and screaming, "Take me now!" I didn't know how to gift a woman who would have told you, very honestly, that she already had everything she needed.

Standing in the middle of the stationery aisle, I noticed a plastic container full of cards. It was a pack of one hundred, all in bright shades of yellow and gold and purple and green. The idea showed up instantly.

After all the years she'd written me letters and mailed packages and tucked notes into my suitcases, I would write back. I would write for all the times I should have thanked her or paid more attention when she wanted to read me a passage of scripture that spoke out loud to her. I would write back for all the times she stopped me in the middle of the kitchen and asked if I would pray with her. There hadn't been many of those times. But it pains me to say I always told her no. "That's just weird," I said. "Prayer is a one-person kind of thing." For all the times I hadn't said the words that were sitting in the room like those elephants they always talk about—*I'm going to miss you; I already do miss you*—I'd write back.

I sat on the floor of the prayer room of the life center that night with the stationery, a gold marker, a spool of ribbon, and a box to put all the letters inside of. I wrote her letters, one by one. I sealed each letter and labeled the outside of the envelope with a special reason why that letter, more than the others, was ready to be opened. *Open me when you've lost your way a bit. Open me on a day when the tears won't stop coming. Open me when you need a reminder to follow your dreams*—that was maybe my favorite card. It was bright orange.

I wrote to her about how I hadn't forgotten the nights when I was home from college for summer break and we would go walking around the neighborhood. It would be late. And the heat would be so bad that you'd have to take a dip in the pool after you reached home again. I hadn't forgotten those nights where only the streetlights and the cicadas heard us when she said she still dreamed about going off to an orphanage in South America. That had always been her dream, the one she kept on the shelf for when we all got older. I wrote to her and told her we were older now. She could go if she needed. I know she didn't need my permission but sometimes it means the world to people when you free them with the word *go*.

On the last card, I scribbled on the outside of the envelope: *Open me when I come home for good.* I don't know that my mother or I anticipated how quickly that letter would become relevant. Both of us had no idea that just a month and a half later, she'd be opening that letter.

"So what do you want to do? When all of this is over, what do you want to do?"

That was Libby talking. She'd come from Italy and now was sitting across from me in the downstairs of the immigration center late one night. She only stayed in Italy for a few short months, but while she was there, she packed in a lot of life and cappuccino. Like, a *lot* of cappuccino. She devoted a whole entire Blogspot space to cappuccino, and on Christmas Eve she live-streamed a cappuccino crawl from Italy. If you've never heard of such a thing, it's because Libby made it up. The tradition in Italy on Christmas Eve is to have seven courses of fish and since Libby didn't have fish for seven courses, she decided to have seven cappuccinos instead—all across the city.

"Are you on cappuccino number three or four?" my mother had asked to the live-streamed version of Libby, who was parading around the streets of Italy in a Santa hat.

"She can't hear you, Mom," I told her. "But I think it is number four . . . her face looks kind of red. I think she might keel over."

"*Drink some water!*" my mother screamed at the screen. Miraculously, Libby made it through all seven cappuccinos. And she came back to the States a month and a half later.

"Well," I told her, "I still have a few months until this year is over. So I think it's too early to even start looking."

"But really though, that aside, what is it that you want to do?"

"I'd want to work in a place like this." I turned toward the computer and typed the website address of a nonprofit that was based in Connecticut. "I love what they do. I love the human rights work they are associated with. And I think it would be a lot different than the job I am doing now. They might even have windows in this place."

I clicked into the section of the website titled "Careers," as I'd done several times before in that last month, and scrolled through the job descriptions.

"Even if I can't apply, I just keep looking, thinking maybe something will show up. But all of it just requires experience that I don't have. Wait . . ." I paused. "This one wasn't here yesterday."

I turned the computer to face Libby and together we read the job description for a communications associate. It had just been posted in the last twenty-four hours. The job was an entry-level to a junior position for someone with several years of experience. The person would join the public relations team at one of the largest nonprofits for children in need around the world. They'd be in charge of helping write informational publications, pitching to the press, and helping to come up with creative media campaigns.

"That's . . ." Libby looked for the words. "That's you, Hannah. They wrote that description for you."

"But I can't apply. I wouldn't be able to start for several months."

"You have to apply. Regardless. They wrote that job description for you."

So I applied. And I received an initial informational interview from the recruiter who found my résumé in the pile of applications. And then I waited for something else to move.

Weeks went by and I heard nothing about the job. The recruiter kept contacting me, letting me know they kept running into different hurdles but I was still a candidate. I had started going to this church on occasion with a girl I met through Tammy. The church was tucked into the nightlife of Chelsea. I liked going to the church because it was like nothing I'd ever experienced before. The music was actually good. The lights were low. The messages were relevant. I found myself going back from time to time.

It was raining one night when we went. I had debated canceling. It'd been coming down all day and it was the kind of rain that tempted you to drag your finger across the part of the Bible where God makes a promise to Noah that He'll never cause such a storm again. "Really, God? Really?" It was the kind of night where you just might have seen a maniacal man herding elephants and tigers into a boat, two by two, down by Chelsea Piers.

On this night, the girl and I realized we were late as we made our way into the empty foyer. We poked our heads into the sanctuary and stood in the back of the room for a moment before heading to the balcony. The worship had already begun. It was my favorite part about the whole thing. There was something electric about everyone lifting their hands up to the ceiling as if they were trying to pull things down from heaven. They reached and they reached and I couldn't help but wish I would find a reason to reach my hands up too.

I think the reason I kept going back to that church is because it made me feel less crazy, less alone. Not in life, but in God. In finding a way to sit comfortably inside of those three letters. Probably just like too many of those twentysomethings in the pews, I'd grown up with choices. Too many of them. And the more choices I'm given, the harder it becomes to actually commit solidly to something because I never want to make the wrong choice and I don't want to miss out. I'd rather have free trials and compare products and models before investing. So on some things I choose and other things I never choose. But to scan through the packed room, so packed people were forced to the balconies, and to know people were there to choose God—that was mind-blowing to me. That kind of commitment was unfathomable to me.

We slid into seats in the balcony and began pulling the wet layers from our bodies. The scarves. The drenched jackets. Before I could fully peel my jacket off, a girl appeared on the stage below. A single light poured down on her. She was wearing a dress. Her hair was in curls. And, without notice, she started speaking into the microphone she cupped with two hands.

I'd never seen anything like it before. Like every word had been strung together so intentionally and she'd memorized the whole thing and given it a rhythm. I'd learn much later—from a cluster of viral videos—that what the girl was performing was called spoken word. That first, a writer sits down and creates the poem and then they perform it out loud. And with the tone of their voice and the intentional movements and pregnant pauses, the poem grows arms and legs and it sprints into you full force, wearing all the armor of good diction and solid alliteration, until you're paralyzed by the performance of it all.

I could not take my eyes off the girl. I was bartering with God up in the balcony. *Please, God. You are using her so mightily. You are shining so brightly through her. I wish You would use me in that way.* Her hands swept through the air like they were cutting chains. The pleas continued: *I don't want another rule book. Please, not another relationship filled with rule books. I just want that, whatever that is. You are using her and it is breaking my heart.*

I wanted to be a light like that.

The girl told a story through her poetry. She led the crowd of hipsters in the pews as she described what she called "the car crash in [her] soul." She illustrated the space inside of her and I saw wreckage when I closed my eyes. Caution tape roping it off. A foggy night. The kind of cold that sits in your bones. Cops standing all around the scene as the rain steamed off the pavement. She said it was this hidden space inside of her she never wanted to talk about. It was where she kept all the wounds, as if you could keep all the ugliness locked up in a box that sits square in the center of your chest. She tried to act like it wasn't there but she said it was the place inside of her God wanted most to go. He wanted to shine His godly flashlight on all the damage and she wouldn't let Him. She was too ashamed of that place, that place inside of her where she felt as though she'd failed God.

I know that place, I thought. *That place inside of me that makes me cross my arms and whisper weakly in my prayers, "God . . . if You only knew this, You would leave me. I know that You would leave me. It's dark. It's cold. You'd see I am no good. So please, please don't come all this way here if You're just going to leave me."*

In a matter of seconds, a pastor replaced her on the stage. He stood at a pulpit with an open Bible in his hands. The message that night was on surrender. I remember thinking *surrender* was such a Christian-ese word. The word seemed so weak. But I couldn't focus much on why I was offended by the word before I was scribbling furiously into my notebook, trying to catch every word he said. He told a story of Jesus that happens in Mark chapter 10. When he asked us all to go there, you could hear the sounds of Bibles flipping open and pages turning. Down below, a blanket of glowing screens appeared as people thumbed into their Bible apps.

Jesus is on a roadside and this man comes at him rambling. Nowhere in the Bible does it say that the man looked like Joe Pesci—the short burglar from *Home Alone*—but that's just who I've always envisioned when I've read this story on my own. So the Joe Pesci lookalike is breathless before Jesus, asking him how he could manage to get eternal life. And Jesus just acts like he's really annoyed with the guy and starts shooting back commandments. But right before he tells the man he needs to go and sell all his belongings to follow him, there's this really strange sentence. It's like it doesn't belong there. It's easy to miss. "Jesus saw him and loved him." The line was staring back at me through my screen. He saw him. And he loved him. Instantly. Like it was that easy. Like the man didn't need to do A, B, C, and D to just be loved. He was loved. He was seen. He was known. Already. He just had to show up and annoy Jesus. Showing up was all it took. And then being willing to let it all go.

When the music cut in, the pastor invited us to say our own prayers and have our own time with God. We stood. The worship flowed. The room got dark and quiet. I closed my eyes and just let this peace wash over me. There's no better way to describe it than just peace.

It wasn't judgment. It wasn't fear. It was just this peace, that if this was God, then He was the kind of God who would have driven forty-four hours (or however long)—all through the day and all through the night—just to show up at my door. He would have made a nearly constant road trip out of finding me there. Pounding His fist against the oak, this kind of God would have vowed He would not walk away come morning. He would not walk away. He would wait until I unlocked the door and let Him in.

I lifted my hands to the rafters and imagined the laughter of the city nightlife creeping up all the walls of that church, but I wasn't afraid. I was giving up. I was giving up control because I didn't know what else to do. Surprisingly, I didn't feel weak or fragile in the way I thought I would feel if I ever put a white flag up to surrender. *Surrender* actually felt like a strong word in that moment. Like I was finally saying out loud, "I just don't feel like holding all the pieces together anymore with weak forms of glue."

I don't know how to describe it as anything more than that. Anything more than a girl up in the balcony of a church in Chelsea, New York City, making statements she never thought she'd actually say out loud: "I'm not going anywhere. I am going to stay right here. Use me, God. Use me. Love me. Show me if You love me. I'm not going anywhere."

It wasn't a magic potion. It wasn't like God barreled in unexpectedly and smashed my little life into pieces and made me holy. I still made mistakes. I still misjudged the amount of tequila I could actually handle. I still hurt people for no good reason. God hadn't magically reduced all my problem areas. He was more like the Ray LaMontagne song, the one you never know the name of, that plays in the middle of the coffee shop but you're too distracted to hear it. You're too busy tapping and typing and watching the people around you. And then, just toward the end of the song, you look up for long enough to think, *I really like this song. I have always liked this song because it's simple and beautiful and true.* And then the song ends. And you sort of miss it. And you spend an extra minute or so wondering why you don't listen to that song more often. That's what God felt like to me in that church.

Like if He were the type to say really pretty things in a moment that makes you want to fall to your knees with the peace of it all, then maybe He'd have cupped His godly hands and said into my ear: "You're okay. You've always been okay to Me. Not a piece of you is missing. Not a thing you lost was wasted. You lost nothing down the road that couldn't be renewed, restored, remade. You are whole. Stop looking for a reason not to be."

After that church service in Chelsea, everything started moving faster than I expected. Several interviews later, and after a visit to the office, I was accepting a job offer with the nonprofit. I moved home a few weeks later.

I left New York City on the Tuesday right before Easter. I wish I

could make it seem more whimsical than that. But that's just life sometimes—transitions are not always slow and swooping. Sometimes you
only get the breath to pack your bag and clear out the hair elastics you
find scattered beneath the dresser and in the corners of the closet before a new thing is waiting for you up ahead.

So there wasn't an interlude or an orchestra or a chapel choir lining the streets as I rolled my suitcase down to the Fordham Road
subway station and waited for the 4 train to take me to Grand Central. No birds chirped. It wasn't long or drawn out or cathartic for
the soul. It looked nothing like the television good-byes. No one
waited at the train with a sign that read, STAY. I watched too much
Dawson's Creek and imagined I'd get to have all the long, grueling
departures one day, just like Joey Potter. I thought that would be the
real golden egg of adulthood—when people found it terribly hard to
release me.

It isn't. And Joey Potter should have just been honest and told us
all the truth: Good-byes hurt. And they happen too much. And there
is nothing in the moment that makes walking away seem reasonable.
And people find a way to live without you. That's a hard truth to swallow but it's not a reason to stay in one place—just so you can never
give someone a reason to forget you. Sometimes you have to go . . .
ready or not.

The only thing I know for certain about this whole good-bye thing?
You have to say it sometimes. You have to get real brave, and bite your
bottom lip, and let people go sometimes. Fully, fully. Whether you feel
ready or not, you're still going to grow up and use that word a lot more
than you ever expected to.

I wanted Grand Central station to be the last place I said
good-bye to. So I had one last dinner with my roommates and then I
headed for the train that would take me to the station, so I could go into
the Main Concourse and say good-bye to the big clock and the staircase
and the little shops that jutted off and huddled close to the entrances

for Lexington Avenue and the 4-5-6 trains. It seems silly, to want to say good-bye last to a place made out of concrete and bricks, but I will always get to claim that so much of what would happen next was because of Grand Central and how the love letters really started there. I think I will always love that they started in a place where everyone is just waiting for something. The waiting that happens there is no different from what happens in an airport terminal or another train station, but everything feels heightened and buzzing because that's just New York. She doesn't play small, even in the places where people are waiting for someone to go and someone else to arrive.

I walked toward platform twenty-one to board a train that would depart for New Haven in the next twelve minutes. I said thank-you for the clock one last time, because I'd once waited for something to happen in that place too. And, as silly as it is to still admit this, I wished I could write one last letter and somehow find a way to get it into the weekender bags of all the people who found themselves coming here, walking through this same foyer, in hopes that New York City would learn or remember, or maybe even forget, their name:

> *To whoever finds this letter,*
>
> *I have high hopes of one day being a car wreck of a romantic. It's crazy to admit that to a stranger but I want it all. I want the passion that is fast and the commitment that is slow. I want the grit of it. And the beauty of it. And I believe that one day I will lend this heart of mine out—like a well-read library book—to someone who'll decide to rip the return date straight out of the inner binding and never let me go. But before I could ever find a love like that, I had to go out there and see what was really sitting behind that first love of mine—New York City.*
>
> *When I moved to this city, I carried with me three letters, tucked in a notebook to be easily accessed: a letter from my best friend, a letter from my mother, and a letter from my aunt. My best friend told me to fall in love with this city, however I needed to do that. My mother told me to find God in this city, however*

I needed to do that. And my aunt's words were too perfect to do anything but plant them here: "The real answer to all of this is to find your gift and give it, whether to a million or a few." That's the core of it right there: give of yourself in this place, however you need to do that.

I can't predict what might happen for you here. This city might break your heart. You might find yourself, really find yourself here. You might become someone new. You might spend too much time clinging to the old. All of this could happen. So much more than this could unfold. But, in the mix of it all, take a step back sometime. From the noise. And the lights. And the hustle to be someone here. Take a step back and you will see that this city is really just one big dance. And you'll be the blessed one if you get to just be in the middle of that dance for a little while.

So dance. And one night, when a soft layer of snow coats the city, take the subway to Fifth Avenue and just walk for a while in the streets. New York City will never be so quiet as that one sacred chunk of time when the snow is falling and the world just seems to still a bit. There's a Hungarian pastry shop right by Columbia; go there too. Visit the cathedral on Amsterdam Avenue. Find the Poets' Corner, where you can read some of my very favorite words. Head to the Strand. Get lost in the books for hours. The Grey Dog is one of those coffee shops that will haunt you long after you leave. And Alice's Tea Cup is a legitimate wonderland—you deserve to feel like a kid again for at least five minutes, or however long it takes you to devour the scones and have a spot of tea. The MoMA is free on Friday nights but you never have to pay a cent to sit in Central Park and watch pieces of art go by for hours. All the holding, the kissing, the passing, and the greeting—it's enough art to be locked up in a museum and never let out.

Just get swept up in it all for a little while. No matter what. You may never understand the things you see. The things you feel. The places you go. The hands you hold. But you should still see, feel, go, and hold anyway. This is life. You're right inside of it. And life is exactly what people will say New York City is after a first glance: Crazy. Intense. Magical. Wild. Unreal. Big. Loud. Worth it.

Welcome to it. Now you are ready. Now you are.

Love,
A girl just trying to find her way

Section 3

To Practice Dancing on the Ground

Coming Home

At the foot of the door of the house with turquoise shutters—the home I'd grown up in—I remembered a promise I'd made to my mother before I left for New York. It'd been a heated promise I made last summer, resentful for having to move back for the four months wedged between college graduation and moving.

"I will never move home again."

That promise came rapping its fist on the door of my memory as my mother helped me lug my two suitcases up the same stairs my brother and I used to ride down on couch cushions. I was home again. There was no real other option besides moving home once I left New York City, so I was thankful to have one. And after making no money for the year of service, I couldn't really go off on my own and start paying rent on top of $400 in student loan payments every month. The cost of living wasn't feasible. I did come across a tempting offer to live in an apartment and pay no rent as long as I promised to be the other person's "boo thang." I think I'd make a great boo thang, but that's beside the point I'm trying to get at.

When all of my stuff was back in my childhood bedroom my mother asked if I wanted a cup of tea. I did. I wanted to tell her I was thankful to be back in a place where the porch light was always left on for me, a place where the kettle was always waiting to be heated up. I didn't though.

Surprisingly, there was a humility that surged inside of me when my mother left me in my room to go downstairs. I stood silently in the middle of a room I'd outgrown, watching thick, black hand-painted Chinese symbols dance on the walls around me. I needed to repaint. Wash over the days when I actually thought Chinese symbols and pagodas were cool to paint on the walls of my bedroom.

"It will only be for a little while," I told her as I stirred two packets of Sweet'N Low into my tea a few minutes later. "Once I get enough money, I am planning to move closer to work."

"It's for as long as you need it to be," she said, not even looking toward me. I know she wasn't fazed in the way I was. "I'm proud of you."

We sat on the couch that night and watched *General Hospital*, and my mother caught me up on the life happenings of the main mobster, Sonny, and Elizabeth and Luke and all these other characters she'd followed for the last twenty years of her life, waiting until the end of each day to make a bowl of yogurt and fruit and spend time with her friends from Port Charles—the imaginary town where all the characters lived. I decided to make a conscious effort to be fake friends with all the characters too while I was home. In the morning, she and I would talk about the characters as if they were our real friends. It was a common and reliable bond between the two of us and I've learned to try my hardest to keep those sorts of things alive.

In the first few days of being home, one of my friends' mothers passed away. I hadn't even unpacked my suitcases yet when I was forced to pull the shreds of black clothing I owned and call up friends I hadn't talked to in years to ask them if they were attending. I saw so many people I knew that night. I told all of them that I was moving back to New York City; it was just a matter of time. I didn't actually want to go back; I just didn't want to stay there.

I remember going to TGI Fridays after the funeral and a few of us talked about how sometimes when you see someone you used to love after a long while—someone you used to know so well—you convince yourself you can still be the same person for them. You could try so hard and just change back.

"Yeah, but people change," one of the girls at the booth said. We looked so depressing in that moment—a booth full of black and eyes puffy from all the crying, twirling drinks around the table.

"I think that is the pain of leaving a place," I said. "You always come back different and are forced to see things through new eyes."

It was in that moment I realized I had to be there. New eyes or not, I had no real choice but to make the most of being home.

I flung myself back pretty easily into life with my old friends. I started a new job. Life became a shuffle of happy hours and coffee dates. I was making new friends. I was rekindling old relationships. The letters continued. Upward and upward the number spiraled until I made the decision to stop at four hundred. The plan was always to stop at four hundred love letters, or at least that became the plan I wanted to stick with at letter three hundred fifty. I'd get a dozen or so requests a week but I didn't know how long I was supposed to keep the letter writing going.

I learned something about myself in the five months of being home that led up to the four hundredth letter: I like being in control. I like controlling the elements around me. And even if I give it up for a little while, I am really good at taking back control. It's like I am the girl who sells everything to you at a tag sale—refrigerators and old desks and books—and I'm all like, "Take it! I don't want it! It's been good to me but now it's yours." And then I show up at your house in a terrifying ski mask in the middle of the night to take it all back. You catch me by the computer, unplugging the lamp I sold you from the wall. That's me. I release things out of my hands and then I take them back full force.

It's funny, because I am all-in with a lot of things. If it's a relationship and I love you, I will love you until your face hurts. But when it came to God—this omniscient being in the universe—I was noncommittal. I was flaky. It was conditional. That has always been my biggest struggle when it comes to God: letting Him stay in my life. And isn't that the biggest obstacle that hides behind most relationships? One person wants to be let in. The other person struggles to just unlock the door. But there is a sprawling beauty that exists inside the relationships where the one who is holding back finally finds the courage to mouth, "I'm all-in."

I've learned it's easy to be all-in with the things you can dictate and control. It's when you have very little control and no idea where life will take you that going all-in is so terrifying. But what if it's in those spaces of no control that a brave life actually begins?

I wondered that on the night I found a church at home. Just like the Chelsea one, the unconventionality of this church is what swept me into the chaos. There were no red hymnals sitting in the pews. There actually were no pews. There was no fear that the people in said pews would pass away from old age and bad music in the middle of the offering. There was a dude in skinny jeans preaching from a cardboard pulpit who used the words *jacked up* a lot and would sometimes cry onstage in a way that really disarmed me and made me think, *Wow, he really is all-in.*

And there was a rock band. That's actually the root of the church—a rock band that used to travel the world playing shows. They did that for years before the crowd of twenty- and thirtysomethings decided to settle in New Haven, Connecticut, and plant a church. They will tell you it was the last thing on their agenda, to actually plant a church. But I think a life on the road, in and out of different venues, made them crave the kind of growth you could actually see. That's the hard part about traveling—you sweep in and out of places and it's really hard to see if something shifts in the atmosphere once you leave.

They launched their first church service on Easter weekend of that year, right when I was moving home from New York. It was held in one of the dirtiest and yet most legendary venues in New Haven: Toad's Place. It's nasty to even think about the things that would happen on a Saturday night in the building that we'd have to try to scrub from the surface come Sunday morning, but I loved the heart of the idea:

Church isn't a building. It isn't where you meet. It's the people you stand next to, if enough of something stirs you to believe they're actually your neighbors.

I found the church near the end of August, about a month before they started weekly services. They'd host community groups on Tuesday nights where ten to fifteen people would sit around talking and occasionally someone would strum a guitar and people would worship. It took me a while to get into that because for me God had always sort of been a one-person kind of activity, if that makes any sense. I always just thought you pray alone, and you sing in rooms where people can't hear you're not actually talented, and you keep your journey with God pretty down low so as not to offend others. For a while in those jam sessions, I'd just tap my toes. Eventually I opened up my palms.

On the first night of the community group, after all the awkward introductions, the leader passed out neon-green sticky notes to the circle. His name was Chuck. He was one of the pastors of the new church.

"Tonight we're going to share a bit," he said to the group. "I want you to take a Post-it note and write down on it what you think God's plan for your life is."

I looked around the room at the people sitting on chairs and couches. No one seemed fazed by the question. I wondered if he was kidding. I think I laughed out loud and then looked down at the tiny green square like, *Really? You really want me to try and write that into a square?* I had no idea what God's plan for my life could be. I just knew I was a girl who only ever knew how to want big things. I remember lying barefoot on the hardwood floor of my childhood bedroom, palms up to the ceiling and whispering, *"God, I don't want to know about your line-up. I know there are a million other people out there who you could use before me. People who haven't screwed up as much as me. But if you pick me, if you use me, I won't let you down. I promise."* I didn't make promises much when I was sixteen but I felt like I could keep that one.

I listened to people open up as we went around the room and they shared parts of their story. They talked about struggles. They asked for prayers. And, fittingly for the new girl, I was the last one to share. I'd already torn the edges off my note out of nerves and started rambling about just having moved home from New York City and probably not staying for long because the plan was to go right back. I didn't want any sort of roots in this place. I didn't want anyone to get too close and ask me to stay or something.

"I don't really know what God's plan for my life is," I said. "I just wrote down this quote from Mother Teresa I've always really liked."

Written in swirling handwriting on the Post-it note was a paraphrased version of the quote I'd found: *I am a little pencil in the hand of a writing God, who is scripting a love letter to the world.*

Without warning, a massive amount of word vomit flew out of me as I started telling people about the love letters and how I had no idea what the point of them was. I was at letter 397. I would stop at 400.

"But I almost wish it would resolve." I found myself surprised to say it out loud. "I wish I knew why I wrote any of those letters in the first place. It feels weird to know it's just going to end. And it will be over."

That was the plan though. I imagined life pushing in to slowly cover up the story—the one of strangers and stamps and New York City. New relationships. Job promotions. Life shifts. And eventually I would forget about those love letters and the place they held in my heart.

But in that room full of strangers hearing the tale for the first time, I felt like that wasn't the full story. It was just the first few notes of a song. It was just the first paragraph to what should really have been a longer letter. That pathetic little half ending tore through me though as I opened my palm to the group to reveal the crumpled green note.

Chuck stopped me. He stood up from the table he was sitting at.

"I just need to tell you that you need to do something with this. You need to. So many people want this," he said. "I don't know if you see it, but so many people want what you just had for the last ten months."

It had never been phrased to me that way: You're lucky. You had something really lucky happen to you. And whether you see it or not, those letters were a blessing to you at the lowest time in your life. They were a life jacket in a lot of senses. You were never the life jacket. They were. And people need life jackets.

Chuck pulled me aside at the end of the group and we talked for a few minutes. Without even knowing me, he looked at me like I was equipped for whatever would happen next. He looked at me like I already knew the job description was getting placed into my hands. I just needed to act on it.

"Turn this into something bigger," he said. "Keep the focus on love. Nothing else but love."

That night, I tore valiantly into the house with my fists in the air declaring to my mother that I was going to turn my love letter writing into something bigger than me. She barely even looked up from her latest issue of *Parade* magazine.

"But you said you wanted it to be over." Her eyes focused on me through her red-framed glasses.

"Yeah, I know I said that," I said quietly. "But what if I miss out on this? What if creating something bigger is what I'm supposed to do?"

I wrestled with my thoughts that night as I tried to sleep. My mind found itself in the middle of a massive tug-of-war, both sides strong. It would shove far to the right side for a few minutes: *This idea is too big for you. It's too big. What if you can't make it work?* And then the opposing side of me would tug even harder: *What are you thinking? You're crazy to think this idea is bigger than you. Why are you even doing this? This is too small of a thing. It won't make a difference. The world doesn't need more love letters. The world needs education. It needs clean water. It needs less distraction.*

I didn't want to add to the noise. I didn't want to create something the world didn't actually need. I'd already tried that before. When I was living in New York I thought I was going to create some website full of interviews of women who were movers and shakers that would change the world. I had the whole thing mapped out. I tried desperately to force ideas like that one out into the world but they never did take flight. I'd make spurts of progress but the execution of the whole thing wore me down. It left me picking the thing up and putting it back down, picking it up and putting it back down again—like trying to haul a kayak up a hill.

I knew what was wrong with all those things I tried to force out into the world: they were fueled by the parts of me that just wanted gold stars. I wanted to be the important one. There was this aching thing inside of me that just wanted to be known and loved and adored and worshipped for something that came from my own two hands. A feeling like that can start off as small and innocent but it will grow into something that leaves ugly stains on your heart. The fuel will run out. The plans will grow sour. And you'll burn out quickly trying to build a temple for your own sense of status.

The following afternoon, coming back to my cubicle after lunch, I clicked into my e-mail. At the top of the pile was a message with the subject line *WSJ Reporter*. I looked up toward the ceiling of my office and mouthed the words, "You're kidding me, right?" It had to be a joke. Twenty minutes later, standing on the boardwalk behind my office building, I realized it wasn't a joke. The reporter was real. She was writing a piece on how we use social media to keep the handwritten practice alive. She'd heard of me from someone who had recently gotten a love letter from me. I somehow came to fit beside a slew of other letter writers who could still distinctly tell you about the ink of their letters and the scents of their paper. I was the millennial in the piece, trudging through the thick of something I wished my generation could rekindle and call its own.

The piece for the *Wall Street Journal* would be out in the next week. I saw only two options: decline the story, and participate in the piece and get dozens more letter requests. I would then begin naming the calluses on my fingers as they became like children to me—Jenna and Paulie and Middle-Finger Mitchell—eventually quitting my job and ending up on a street corner somewhere scribbling love letters to strangers on cardboard, and enduring the hisses of tourists who passed by saying, "Oh, I heard she used to be perfectly normal. Poor, poor love letter lady."

Either I was going to create something bigger than myself or I was going to pretend like no letters had ever been written. I stood at the fork in the road between these two choices. I didn't know back then the choices we make—the small ones we deem insignificant—become something. And, a lot of times, they determine if we become someone we always said we wanted to be.

"So what will you do next?" my friend at work asked, not even letting the question exit his mouth fully before taking a bite out of his burger.

He and I had taken our lunch break one afternoon and gone off to explore a new burger joint down the street from our office. As we stood in the line that snaked around the building, somehow the love letters story slipped out and the questions he started asking me made it impossible to retreat backward.

I tried to keep that part of my life boxed up and far away from my new job but somehow a thread in the conversation was always pulled and I found myself spilling my guts about stationery, stamps, and strangers all over again. It was like having a child I didn't tell anyone about. People would nod and ask questions and then other people would show up at my cubicle asking to hear the story they just heard from someone else down the hall. No matter the ways I tried not to tell that story, it always pushed its way out, as if to laugh in my face and say, "You don't own me, girl." Still, I kept trying to pretend it wouldn't really faze me if the love letters were no longer a part of my life.

"So what's next?"

I shimmied my pickles around the plate when he asked the question. I tried not to look up at him as he waited for an answer.

"I think it's over," I said. "I mean, what more can I do? It's kind of done."

"So wait," he said. "You're telling me that you think the story is over?"

"Well, yeah . . . I mean, I have a new job here. I want to do other things. It was great for a specific time in my life but I think it is time to do something new." I filled in the gaps of silence with more confirmation that it was done. "So, yeah. I think it might be over."

"Oh, no. No," he said. "You can't. I mean, if this were something you were trying to push around for the last ten years and never got it to lift off the ground, I'd maybe say stop. But you are young. This is that time to make the mistakes and go after crazy things."

"But I have no idea what to do."

"It doesn't matter that you haven't figured it out yet," he said. "Here's what you don't do: you don't kill the story. No one kills a story right when it's about to get to the good part."

As we were sitting there, half-eaten burgers before us, my mind reeled back to a memory of my sitting in a local coffee shop with a mentor of mine right before my college graduation. I write the words *coffee shop* hesitantly because it's not a coffee shop in the sense that there are cute booths or brown-eyed baristas or the kinds of cappuccinos that arrive at your table with all sorts of shapes in the foam. It's more like a Dunkin' Donuts knockoff. The menu is full of a lot of ungodly combinations of chocolate and peanut butter and chunks of shortcake mixed into the coffee. Last time I went back, they had a warning up on the door about massive chunks of cookies floating in the drinks just so that people wouldn't choke.

But somehow, my mentor and I always found ourselves at this coffee joint sitting between some sort of Asian mafia that frequently congregated there and a window with mysterious bullet holes in it. Even with the sticky tabletops and the unsettling bathroom off in the corner, the place strangely felt like home. And so much of life's resolutions and revelations met us at those dirty tables.

I remember watching her hand dip down to touch the table several times as she told me a story called the Parable of the Talents. The story is about a man who gives talents to three of his servants. It took me years to figure out talents were a form of money in biblical times. All the while, I thought this dude was passing out secret talents to his servants—like the gift of juggling and the talent of singing. Wrong talents.

Anyway, two of his servants are very wise and they go out into the world and multiply their talents. The man is pleased with both of them. The third servant becomes anxious, afraid he might lose his talent, so he buries it in the ground for safekeeping. The man who gave out the talents is pretty irate over the situation when he finds out. I can't help but picture that man rage-caging with the servant, like, *"Dude!* You buried it in the ground?! It's not even a seed! What is wrong with you! Get a safe or a diary or something better than the ground!"

I never asked my mentor why she was telling me that story of all stories that day—just a week before I put on a cap and gown and crossed over the stage into a life with fewer grades. But I think she was trying to warn me of how easy it is to be the third servant. Or maybe she was warning me of how hard it is to step out and take a risk when you're faced with someone getting up real close to your face and saying, *"Ha!* Forget about it. Get practical. You're not good enough. You're wasting your time, kid."

I didn't want to be the third servant. I don't ever want to be the third servant with the talents or the gifts planted in the ground just because I am fearful of what would happen if I tried to multiply them.

But that was the decision to be made: either focus on the possibility or focus on the fear of failure. Failure and fear, they go hand in hand. They're like dance partners with great rhythm. Fear has been hoisting failure up into that one *Dirty Dancing* swan-dive move for years. And people love to talk about the two of them. Fear and failure, they're more popular to gossip about than the vampire celebrities. But here's the thing, and maybe it's a secret: people will always talk about failure but no one might ever think to turn their head, look you straight in the eye, and ask you how broken your heart would be if you never even went out there and tried.

Bigger Than This

With five days left before the article would be published in the *Wall Street Journal*, I decided to build a website.

Besides my own blog, the only other time I'd built a website was back in the sixth grade. I actually think it was a decently successful "Dear Abby" website but there weren't any metrics back then to tell. I know I hailed myself as some sort of guru as I answered questions people e-mailed to me about French kissing (which I had no real experience with) and posted tips and tricks on how to style your hair so that all the popular girls would notice you. (Yes, I am aware I added so much to humanity at the young age of eleven.) I just remember never telling my friends I was going home after school every day to sit with the questions of other people. But nothing filled me more than those hours in front of the screen, figuring out how to tell people they weren't alone. I was only eleven years old. I think that would have made me even more of an oddball than I already was. So I kept my "Dear Abby" business pretty quiet.

Either way, I knew I had to create a website. And I had somewhat of a plan for how this website would work. I imagined there being two pockets of people: letter leavers and letter writers.

The letter leavers would get their own stationery, take out their own pens, and start leaving love letters all over whatever community they belonged to. I envisioned people finding letters in baseball fields and restrooms and bookstores, just in the way I left love letters strewn across New York City. The only difference would be that people could track the letters by writing, *If you find this letter, please contact MoreLoveLetters.com*. That way, we could post the impact and we could share the stories of where letters were left and then found again.

And then there would be the letter writers—the pocket of people who wanted to show up for strangers with stories so similar to the ones I found waiting for me in my inbox after that first blog post. I envisioned people being able to come onto the site and nominate a family member or a friend or a teacher or someone in their life who needed a reminder of how strong they really were. Whether they were facing cancer or sickness or depression or loss, I would then go through the stories and pick several to put up on the website and then invite the rest of the world to script a handwritten note and send it to a PO box. From there, I could take all the stacks of letters and mail them off with a letter on top that basically said, "Hey, someone in your life loved you so much—and wanted to prove it so extravagantly—that we rallied a bunch of people from Australia and Texas and Canada and Mexico to remind you that you have to keep pressing on. We really need you to keep pressing on. It matters that you are here." We could call the pile of letters a "love letter bundle."

There is something remarkable about just the thought of someone sitting down for you. Taking out a piece of paper for you. Focusing their mind on the words they write for you. And through sloppy cursive and a cramped hand, they manage to tell you all the things that have ever mattered, in between the lines: "I care. I'm here. I see you. You're more than just words on a screen to me."

The whole idea seemed crazy. But what felt crazier was that the whole thing might actually work.

I unpinned the bright blue check from the bulletin board above my desk, the one Libby had written for me right before she left for Italy, and cashed it. It was an investment. I used the money to buy all the things I thought I'd probably need to make this bigger than just me. A notebook. A domain name for $15. And a PO box at my town's post office.

And I won't act like it wasn't the proudest day of my life to get that PO box. It was. It felt like I was the owner of a new car or a new home or a pet dog. I was so proud to own that post office box. No matter how small it was (very, very small—like, you-can-only-fit-a-dozen-envelopes-or-so-inside small), Box 2061 was mine. I registered it under the name *More Love Letters*.

A day later, I sent out a tweet:

"I have a crazy idea about these love letters."

Within minutes, I got an e-mail from a woman named Becky. Becky was a blogger I'd been reading for the last few years. We caught each other in passing through tweets and blog comments and it was surprisingly enough for me to feel like I kind of knew her and her husband, Ben, and their cute, cozy apartment, and their dreams for the year ahead. Even if those weren't details she told me directly, I still held them like they were treasured things I needed to take care of—whether I read them on a blog or not.

I want in, she wrote. *Whatever you are going to do with these love letters, I want in.* She didn't even need convincing. She was ready to push forward.

And though we'd never really talked before, we let the cosmic-sounding ringtone of Skype lead us into a conversation about those love letters. I poured my heart out to her. I told her everything. I was a rambling mess of stories that somehow added up to wanting to create this thing—this website—where other people could write love letters and leave love letters and bless other people.

I noticed as I spilled my heart out to her that I was already so protective of this thing I hadn't even created yet. Already I was approaching it as if no one was going to understand it the way I did. I think, in all of this, I was just waiting for someone to mouth the words *You're crazy* to me.

But that wasn't Becky. From the other side of the screen, she just laughed. She laughed and she nodded her head a lot, as if she understood me better than anyone else.

"I mean, I know what my letter did for me when you mailed it. I'd love to see what that could do for others." Her words caught me off guard. It was a detail I'd overlooked. When I got off the Skype call, I scrolled through my e-mail to those first letter requests that trickled in when I published the blog post nearly a year earlier, and I noticed something: Becky was the first. She was the first of the hundreds to request a love letter. The first piece of stationery. The first person to ever get a love letter from me. She'd stood by the idea the whole time. And now, nearly a year later, she was about to become my biggest cheerleader for the road ahead.

The phone rang one afternoon on my day off. It was Ronny. I knew he was calling about a wedding we were going to in a month.

Ronny and I have been friends since high school. Our common thread was Nate. The two were best friends. Meeting Ronny helped me understand more about Nate. Nate held the moral compass and Ronny instigated the memories that will probably never be fit to leave the two of them. Ron will tell you Nate made him better. Nate would say the same about Ronny. I think that might be the golden core of real friendship: When you make each other better. When the two of you are whole—completely whole—but you each make brilliant add-ons to what the other brings into this lifetime. Ron will kill me for saying they were like peanut butter and Oreos, but they were like peanut butter and Oreos. They both stood on their own. One just naturally made the other one better.

And then our common thread became attending the same college, even though he transferred after one semester and we only ever saw each other approximately three times in that first semester. Still, one of those times was after my first my-heart-has-been-steamrolled-into-the-ground breakup, just one month into college. I showed up at his door. I didn't know where else to go. If ever a storm were to cut across my memory and make me forget crazy little details, there are things about the moment in his doorway I would give everything to save: The way he took me into his arms. The way he didn't ask any questions beyond, "You're okay? Right? You're okay?" And how that one steady question became a confirmation beneath his breath: you're okay. How he said that to me over and over again. How he said it until I believed it.

"We have a wedding to talk about. We have a dance floor to hit," Ronny said when I first picked up the phone. The sound of his voice on the other end of the line was one of those quick juts of peace. The kind that came randomly and reminded you to just be where your feet are for the ten or twenty minutes it takes to have a conversation with someone you've missed. Not five years in the future, not two years in the past, just right here—catching up with an old friend.

We talked about random things. The kind of gift you're supposed to get for a wedding. Whether we'd match or not match. What color my dress would be. At the tail end of the conversation, I asked about Nate. I always hated asking but I knew Ronny knew exactly how Nate was doing.

"He's hanging in there. You know him, he's a tough one. The last few weeks have been a little hard but he's coming back around."

"Yup, that's Nate," I said. "For sure."

"I meant to ask you how the job is going these days," Ronny asked, changing the subject. "Any new crazy things in your life?"

I have to be really honest: I told Ronny about the plan for the love letters on purpose. It was on my mind, all along, to tell him the plan I hoped to execute in just a few short days. And that's because Ronny, if anyone, would criticize it. Not in a mean way; he'd just be the one most likely to tell me if something wasn't a good idea.

"So wait, you're going to have to explain this to me." The tone of his voice sounded skeptical. "You're going to start a business? With love letters?"

"I mean, it's not really a business. I guess I don't really know what it is. Or what it will be."

It could end up being nothing. It might make no impact. No thud. No ripple effect. I didn't really know.

"We are going to create these things called love letter bundles." I told him that when people first started e-mailing me to ask for a love letter there was always something about the people who requested a love letter for someone in their life. It made the whole process feel different. Each word became much more intentional, knowing someone would be holding that letter soon and asking, "Who in my life loved me enough to ask for this letter?" If that kind of feeling could get stirred by just one love letter showing up in the mailbox, the impact of a couple hundred love letters might leave a person speechless. They might actually feel wanted, and sort of invincible, at the end of that day.

"Hannah . . ." He paused. "I think you're onto something . . . I mean, love letters are totally for women who are insecure and like to eat their feelings. And people like you . . . So yeah, that just goes to say that I myself am never going to need one of those things." He paused. His voice lowered. "But I can see why other people would want these love letters . . . I think this is really going to go somewhere. You can't back down from this, Brencher."

I thought Ronny would be the critic. I was waiting for him or someone else to tell me not to let this crazy idea go any further. I know that if someone had told me I could not make it happen, I would have used it as an excuse to shrivel right back into the body of a girl who believed her footsteps were not capable of making an impact. I would go right back to being the girl with the apologies all stuck in her throat.

When no one came forward this time to tell me "no" or "stop," I realized I was the only one waiting to stand in my own way. I didn't really care how many pep talks throughout a given day I would have to give to myself; I wasn't going to let the fear of failure win.

With Ronny's confirmation that I should move forward, I set out to finish building the website. I won't even try to make the inner workings of that statement—"building the website"—seem like a romantic one. I had no real knowledge of what I was doing. I took out books from the library on HTML and soaked in tutorials. Day and night. Before work. During lunch breaks. Nights that would crawl into the two a.m. and three a.m. hours. I learned all sorts of new cuss words getting so frustrated with layouts and themes that didn't work. I gave up on myself at least fifty times before breakfast every morning. I think the creation process of anything is brutal. There are false starts. There's getting so far in the process of creation and pulling back. I've learned you have to invest in armor to plow through those battlefields of doubt and fear. The battlefields don't go away. Not ever. They might only get bigger when they see what kind of drive you've got building inside of you.

Ronny's words, his belief in me, stayed in my head as I reached the later hours of my quest to figure out website hosting. And whenever my thoughts ran over to Ronny, they ultimately got all tangled up in Nate. And so I thought about Nate as I tried to keep my eyes open past four a.m.

Bigger than this, bigger than this. The words trailed back to me as I put my head against the desk and slowly waited for the patience to flood back into my bones so I could keep coding. *Bigger than this, bigger than this.* I could feel the whispers coming in: *It's not about you. It's not about what you want. Look for that selfless place inside of you and just start stacking wood for the fire there. Search until you find that place, though it won't be easy to find. Still, be relentless in finding it.*

Build from the selfless place inside of you that is not big or loud or selfish or proud. Build from that little spot inside of you that burns quietly and unceasingly for others. Remember: whatever is burrowed deep in one hungry soul is bound to be tethered to the hearts of many, many more.

The website building was finished with a letter. It was the final step and the hardest step. It was the tension-filled moment I think most of us encounter somewhere in this lifetime—a moment when you're ready to tell the people you love about an idea you have and you're just bracing yourself and hoping they'll go with it. I think that's one of our most vulnerable moments in life—the moments when we hope we'll be understood.

I think there is a place to reach inside of yourself, a place where when people tell you that you can't make a difference, you politely tell them no. And you top it off by not wasting too much time trying to convert people into your cheerleaders. Not everyone will understand you. Wild hearts are necessary though. The world needs wild hearts.

The letter I wrote was simple. It read along the lines of, *I've created something. And now I'm crossing my i's and dotting my t's and passing the work along to you.* I had no big, inflated hopes. I just didn't want to be the girl who never shared the life jacket that once saved her.

The world didn't need another website. It didn't need another app or another tool to make the day-to-day run more efficiently. The love letters were never about efficiency. So why did I think a website should be built?

Love. That was the "why." It was the "what" I found hiding behind all of the letters. Love. Simple. Bare-bones. Often forgotten in the race to be liked, and followed, and friended by the world. Love. Pure, old-fashioned, never-goes-out-of-style love. A ridiculous, oozing, cannot-pack-this-thing-into-140-characters kind of love. Fearless, bold, unstoppable love.

Love. It's crazy to think it took me that long to figure out the one thing to make this all spin and go. It might have been the only thing that mattered the whole time. Not me. Not the stationery. Not the stamps or the strangers. Just the love we learn to give one another when no other motives stand on the table.

No matter how much I pretend the world might be about something else—something bigger and brighter and shinier and more perfect than that—I think love still wins in the race to steal our hearts.

I pressed "publish." The site launched on the day the article for the *Wall Street Journal* came out. I sat on the train that morning, slurped my coffee, read the piece, and tied the rest of my feelings up with a final prayer: *If someone needs this, please find them.*

They Call Her Love

I didn't know that fourteen days later, there would be a day where my life split in two. At 2:07 p.m., two weeks after the website launched, life would sneak up from behind me and tap me on the shoulder.

"Psst . . . ," life would say, nudging me hard. "Take this."

I'd turn around to find life holding a black Sharpie marker in its right hand.

"What do you want me to do with that?"

"Take it and draw a big thick line down the middle of me," life would answer. "From this point forward, you won't ever look at me the same. Part of me will be 'before' and the other part of me will be 'after,' but I'll never be just one thing again."

Pensacola has love letters, the subject line of the e-mail read. It stood out among the clutter of other e-mails in my inbox. The day was otherwise ordinary and uneventful.

And even though my body was curled up into an office chair in Westport, Connecticut, every part of me that had ever wanted something—anything—when I wrote the first love letter on the 4 train in Manhattan was suddenly standing in the middle of a bathroom stall in Pensacola, Florida, with a girl named Brittany.

She told me everything. She wrote in the e-mail that she was having one of those days. It was one of those days where the bullies that rattle inside of your head are merciless in making you think you are not good enough. Not skinny enough. Not pretty enough. Not doing enough. It was one of those days where the gods of Not Enough seem to rally all around you and nothing you do or say or try will ever be sufficient. I imagined her walking through her campus in Pensacola that day and turning into one of the bathrooms. As she went to leave the bathroom, she noticed something small propped up on the sink. Folded up like the notes you used to scoot across the desk to a person you liked in science class. It was a love letter, left by a stranger. The letter told her she was enough. She was worthwhile. She was doing just fine.

Your love letters are in Pensacola, Florida, she wrote as she signed off. Someone in Pensacola must have found the website. They must have decided to start leaving letters on their own. Whoever wrote that letter, it made the difference. All of the mayhem started right there.

E-mails began rolling in from people who were finding letters in the crooks and curves of their own cities and communities. Letter writers were popping out of the folds of Tennessee and Pennsylvania and Canada and London. I started reading and sharing stories every single day about individuals who went out and wrote love letters and left them all around the world for other people to find. People across the world were finding love letters and keeping the notes of strangers on their dressers and their bedroom mirrors. I don't know that I'll ever get over the fact that someone can write *I love you for all the things you think no one notices* and leave that message on a park bench, and how someone else can find the letter and get all choked up over the words. I'll never say the world can't use more of that.

I read about this one girl, Erin, who always had a fierce desire in her heart to do something really wonderful. Like most of us, it was embedded inside of her and it kept her up at night. She was living in Dubuque, Iowa, wondering how she would make an impact and change a life. She stumbled on the love letters and she decided she would leave them tucked throughout her campus for others to find. Well, she didn't get very far. She only left a few notes before one morning she walked out onto the quad and found love letters hanging from the trees, tucked in the bushes, and on benches. One of those letters she wrote must have sparked a bigger movement.

And then there was a girl named Sara—a young twentysomething brimming with an unquenchable passion for classic novels and Taylor Swift—who started to take Manhattan by storm, dropping the same kinds of letters as I once did around the lonely city. She plowed onto the streets in boots and a brightly colored hat and she wrote words into her letters that could sting a city slicker good. *Sometimes we lose sight of really taking hold of life. We get lost in the 9 to 5 jobs and the daily commutes. We get lost in our smartphones and avoiding eye contact. We get lost. We forget to say "hello" and "good-bye." And "please" and "thank you." How are you today? Sometimes you have to reach out and ask that question. And you could change someone's day, just like this letter changed yours.*

And just a day later, a tweet came through. One of Sara's notes was found in Rockefeller Center station. She hadn't left it there to begin with, so one can only guess it floated and passed through at least one other pair of hands before it met the one who would take it home.

It was that same Sara who knew her best friend's heart had been broken. She heard it crack and burst when it hit the ground. There were tears and tissues and vats of Chunky Monkey ice cream. And then Sara got an idea: a breakup survival kit—crafted with carefully constructed playlists and best friend coupons (the kind with no expiration date)—rounded out by a stack of letters from people around the country. We posted a quick note on social media with her address attached. We said there was a girl, off in Pennsylvania, and we were determined to keep her from feeling all the red-hot pains of a broken heart alone. Sara watched her mailbox flood with all the best breakup tips and notes to soothe a broken heart, all written by people who would never touch the girl's hand or know the girl's heart or kiss the girl's head. None of that mattered.

My favorite part is knowing Sara brought the kit to her best friend and, in the car of a mall parking lot, they read letter after letter. And they cried. And they laughed. I like to think they probably had no reason to touch their phones or stray far from each other in that moment, and they marveled at the way love reaches and stretches far beyond what we ever come to expect of it. Just a few weeks earlier, love had been the thing that swept in like a torrent and broke that girl's heart, but now it was putting her right back together again.

My heart sank a week later as I walked into the town post office and unlocked PO Box 2061. It was nearly empty. There was just a single yellow slip.

It was my first attempt at creating a love letter bundle. I'd picked a girl named Briana to be one of the first recipients after one of her friends nominated her through the website. Her friend wrote that when she met Briana, she noticed her infectious laugh first. She swore everyone in a ten-foot radius of Briana would stop what they were doing just to get a glimpse of the girl. Recently, their relationship had been mostly confined to Facebook because of distance, but she'd started to see a downward spiral in Briana's Facebook posts. She wrote that regardless of the trials Briana was facing, she was strong. Even though she was about to be a single mother with not enough money to pay her rent, she was strong.

I held my breath when I typed out Briana's story and published it on the website. The plan was that at the end of the month, I'd take all the letters and mail them to Briana.

I brought the yellow slip to the man at the front of the post office.

"This was left in my box," I told him.

"Oh, box twenty sixty-one," he said. "We've been seeing a lot of mail for you." He walked away from the desk and came back holding a key. He slid it over to me.

"You got too much mail, dear," he said. "We moved you to a bigger box."

Let's just say I walked away from the post office that day with a lot of mail and a lot of conclusions about humans in general: mainly that they're really cool and if you give people something to do, a mission, they will show up. They will do more than show up. They'll find a way to blow the ballet flats right off your feet.

Those feelings only expanded as I read through the letters. Scanning the pile of mail, I realized the letters were coming from everywhere: Missouri. Delaware. Canada. London. All of these strangers were showing up for Briana, not because they would ever meet or laugh over cups of coffee but because they had found one another. Finally, they'd found one another by way of letter writing.

At the end of that month, I marched the love letter bundle for Briana proudly up to the front of the post office and mailed it off to her.

I got an e-mail from her best friend a week later. Briana and she had cried in their own corners of the map over the arrival of the mail. Briana's friend wrote to me, *It's not that the letters heal you. They show you're not alone and that you're not struggling for nothing. And this is something so big I can't help but want to be a part of it.*

Nate

"I need you to take my credit card information and book the hotel room. Book whatever. And just let me know."

That was Ronny talking. He was frantic as he spoke. It was the end of September. The wedding we were going to was a week away and we needed to book a hotel room.

"Is everything okay?" I asked him.

I could hear him pacing and moving in the background. "I'll be in touch soon. I am taking a leave of absence from law school. I am going down to be with Nate."

"Ronny?"

"I need to get down there. So I'm gonna call you later and keep you posted. Just take down my credit card number for now."

At the time I didn't even know if I'd copied down the numbers right. I called my friend who was also in her first year of law school. I asked her if people typically do that, take a leave of absence. She told me no. It had to be something really serious if he was going to leave. So I waited. I knew what I would probably hear when Ronny called but I didn't let my mind go there. To me, Nate was getting better. He would get better. Cancer would lose. He would win. Because that was how I'd ended the story a dozen times in my head. *He will win*, I thought. *I know he will win.*

I kept that stance even when Ronny called me that night. I kept that stance even when the news of Nate's going into hospice became real. I kept that stance even when Ronny texted me and I stood there, my phone in my hand, wondering how some messages don't break the screen with their delivery:

"Hannah, I need you to write the best love letter you've ever written. For Nate. I'll get the address to you."

"Maybe you should write," my mother said when I showed her the message. She said that to me three times. I remember it was three times because the pressure to write just kept getting heavier and heavier each passing day. And I'd let it go on for three days, making all sorts of excuses for why I couldn't write.

"I can't write yet. I don't know what to say," I told her. "So when I figure out the right words, I'll put them down."

The truth is I tried to sit down multiple times and write the words, but they didn't come. Instead, I waited. Studied my phone. Texted people who didn't even matter—the kinds of people you only text because you're bored and you want distraction. Wrote other letters. Made phone calls. Checked e-mails. Googled random things like *What is a cornucopia?* and *Were Ben Franklin and George Washington friends?* Scribbled notes on a page. Checked the weather. Avoided praying. Avoided conversations with too much eye contact. Avoided people who tend to see my soul within the first three breaths of asking, "How are you?" I would have cracked like a sidewalk. I made plans. I scheduled meetings. I tried to make the reality go away.

And I kept making excuses. I didn't have the right stationery. And if I just had the right stationery, then I could write. That became it, the major excuse: I need the perfect stationery. The boy was too perfect for any element to be imperfect. So I had to find the perfect stationery. And yet, nothing about this situation was perfect. Not the way it had happened. Not the diagnosis. Not the thirty months of hurting. Not the fact he should have just been healthy.

"You really shouldn't go anywhere unless you write first, Hannah." My mother said it as she watched me pack a bag after work. I was headed to see friends from college. It was alumni weekend.

"I'm going to write it. Stop trying to control the situation." I turned for the door, mad she'd brought it up again.

"I'm not trying to control the situation," she answered me. "I just think you should write the letter already."

I don't remember what I said to her. It was probably something snarky like, "I'm twenty-three and I know how to live my own life." I didn't see it in that moment, but I look back on the image of my mother, standing by the kitchen door stirring black beans on the stove, and I think maybe she was trying to teach me a lesson about regret. Maybe she was trying to save her daughter from recognizing, and realizing with her own two hands, that regret is a very human thing. Regret takes so little to put on, but it might take forever to get it off. You'll spend years trying to rub those sorts of things off your skin.

I still wonder if her mind was swept with memories of loss and things she wished she'd done differently. I wonder if she was looking at her daughter, with the same curly hair and the same long legs she had, and wishing we were still at the crossroads where I wanted to take every one of her life lessons with me.

It rained the majority of the alumni weekend. A pile of us lay on the floor of our friend's apartment the following morning, watching the water drip against the window and trying to muster up the energy to go out and get some breakfast.

"Hey," my friend said to me, coming out from her bedroom. "I have a box of stationery. I have no real use for it, if I am being honest. Do you want some?" She placed a crate down in front of me.

"Yeah," I said, sitting up and combing my fingers through my hair to get the pillow knots out. "I'll have a look at it."

"Take whatever you want . . . seriously."

I tucked a strand of hair behind my ear and began flipping through the piles of stationery clumped together. Flowers adorning the top. Strange kinds of fruit baskets in gold on the front of them. I was just about to give up on the pile when I came across a manila letterhead, a quote cascading the front of it in black ink: *Someone is sitting in the shade today because someone planted a tree a long time ago.*

I immediately thought of Nate when I read the line. It was as if the stationery were created for him. Crafted for him. Everything suddenly clicked. That's the only way to describe it. Sitting there on the floor of my friend's apartment, hands sunk deep in a bin full of reject stationery, with a rainstorm pushing against the pavement outside, it all clicked.

Bigger than this, bigger than this. I remembered Nate's words again—how those were the words he repeated to me every time I would start to doubt.

"He knew," I whispered. It's like he knew what was coming all along. It's like he knew we all eventually reach this crossroads at some point, forced to fumble with the strangeness of a word like *good-bye.* It's like he expected the hard stuff to come and yet he never gave himself an option to stay angry at the world. I still don't know how he did that. I think it's easy to stay angry at a world that never promises you invincibility but still manages to break your heart with the way some moments can make you feel so infinite.

He didn't get angry though. And he didn't stay in one spot. And he could have chosen to never move forward and I know I would have never loved him any less. But no. Nate created something really tangible for the people he loved. He gave the whole rest of his life to that. He found no time to get scared or look back or decide he couldn't do it. He just got down on the ground, hands and feet sunk into the dirt, and went about planting trees—creating something that would outlast him—for the benefit of other people. It all clicked—this world, this life, has nothing to do with me.

"I have to write a letter," I announced to the room.

"Who's the letter for?"

"A friend," I said. "A really good friend."

I picked myself up off the floor and I left the other stationery in the box as I went into a corner of the room to write the letter. The words were coming. The words were finally coming.

* * *

I've learned as the years have gone on that writing love letters to strangers is easy. Maybe not the easiest thing in the world, but you eventually get over the initial challenge of it. You stop asking, "But how am I supposed to know what a person I've never met needs?" It'll seem challenging until the day you have to write to someone you do know and the pen burns in your hand because you realize your words mean everything and nothing at the very same time. A letter to someone you love so much you memorized the way their hands flail in the air when they get all flustered in conversations, that sort of letter could just as easily go unwritten. It would be easier to not find the words for people we love. You have to force those kinds of words into existence, as if your whole little life were depending on their reaching another person.

Here's what I've learned so far: If you sit down, the words will come. Not always at first. But eventually they'll come. You'll sit there for a while and tear at the page. You'll start to write. You won't like the pen you're using. You'll change pens. You'll make a mistake. You'll realize there is no "backspace" button and you'll go to grab another piece of paper. You'll make a comment about how awful your handwriting really is. You'll groan. You might howl. It might be an overly dramatic process. But if you sit there long enough, the words will come. I think the hardest part of the whole process is sitting and paying attention to your own heartbeat for that long.

It's easier to let fear win. Even though love covers all things, fear is what keeps us silent and keeps words unsaid. Fear keeps us standing in one place. Eventually, when it wins, it means we never got the courage to say what we needed to say. But the words are needed. They won't always fix things or mend things or make things better. They won't bring someone back. They won't stop a good-bye. They won't be perfect. But they'll be true. And maybe that is all we have ever needed from one another: true words written with a love that feels too big to pin down to a page with measly little syllables.

I wrote the letter to Nate tucked in the corner of that room and I took it home with me. I found a stamp for it that night and dropped it into the mailbox the next morning on the way to work. I kept the reminder from Nate close to me, like it was the sort of thing you could slip into the pocket of your jean jacket: this life has nothing to do with me and love still wins.

He never got the letter.

It waited in the mailbox the next morning with the red flag up. It's strange to admit but I drove into the office that morning and somehow knew he was already gone. I could feel it in the way the sunlight poured through the window of my car and how this strange sort of feeling seemed to cover me and almost made me feel like Nate was in the car that morning, sitting right beside me in the passenger seat as Jack Johnson played. Even waiting in the traffic that always piled up three exits from where I would get off the highway, something about the morning just seemed to fill me with this sense he was gone.

I was at my desk only long enough to turn on my computer and see the shuffle of Facebook statuses left by Nate's siblings before my phone lit up and I saw Ronny's name on the caller ID. I knew we didn't even need to have a conversation. He didn't have to tell me what was happening. I was already sobbing. I already knew.

That morning was a blur. I left e-mails unanswered and calls unreturned as I got into the car and just started to drive. I stopped at the nearest store, right off the highway. I went inside and started pulling dresses from the racks. These were the rhythms of a familiar habit. It was an extra layer to add on to the tears and prayers. Those fitting rooms always held me, and they never asked questions. But they did sometimes give answers when a person in the room next to mine would find something that fit them just right. In the multiple forms of joy and hallelujahs exchanged between friends, I sometimes got all the answers I would ever need: Things will fit eventually. Maybe not right away. Maybe not today. But as long as you keep trying things on, and shedding things, you'll eventually find the right fit.

I don't know how much time passed inside the room. I tried on one green corduroy dress. One green corduroy dress with the most beautiful blue tulle beneath it. It was the kind of dress where when you spun in a circle, the dress would flare outward and the tulle would dance all on its own. I listened for people outside the room. They were laughing and carrying on a conversation. In the moment I couldn't understand why the world was still moving. That's something I may never understand, how the world still moves when someone you love isn't there anymore. I don't understand how people still find ways to get out of bed in the morning or go through the checkout line. Put books on hold at the library. Grab takeout on the way home from the office. When a tragedy happens, it feels like everything should stop. At least pause for a little while.

The two kept laughing. I stood in the mirror, forgetting the blue tulle beneath the green corduroy dress. Suddenly, the feeling closed in all around me: *He's gone. He's not here anymore.*

The night before the funeral, I took a notebook and walked to the baseball fields about a half mile away from my childhood home. Those fields pulse with memories for nearly everyone who lives in our tiny town in Connecticut. There were so many first kisses and secrets shared and hopes invented in that place where four fields sat adjacent to one another and you could just loop the perimeter of them for hours after the sun went down and always find yourself under the same familiar blanket of stars. That will always be the best definition of home to me.

The October wind whipped in my face as I made my way to the center of one of the fields. The night felt hollow. Come to think of it, the whole of October felt hollow and I've never been able to claim again that October holds the same kind of feeling it used to for me. It's like half of the invincible feeling that used to fill my lungs has been lopped off and replaced by this somber grace trailing through the air. Now October always makes me wonder how hard the world tried to keep that boy in its grip. I wonder if the world twisted and wrenched and manifested rainstorms and hurricanes in places we'll never know about just to get that boy to stay a little longer.

I stood on the mound where I knew Nate had pitched countless games. Just five months earlier, everyone we knew had been there on the outskirts of the field supporting him for his fund-raiser for Relentless Against Cancer—the nonprofit he started even in the midst of cancer. He looked good. I remember that. I think I tried to convince myself that he was getting better. The fields were empty now. I made my way to the bleachers and sat down.

What came next was natural: *Write a love letter for Ronny. Write it on the same stationery you picked out for Nate. Don't be afraid.* Every time I picked my pen up off the page, all I could remember was Ronny laughing at me over the phone, telling me the world probably needed love letters but he never would.

And maybe he didn't need a shred of paper or cursive on a page. He probably didn't need another reminder Nate wasn't here any longer. But who doesn't need to know that while some days will hold darkness, others will bring the most remarkable light? Even though he'd one day reach the point where he didn't feel Nate any longer, Nate would always be sturdy and real inside of him. Nate would come trickling out in every hand he'd ever hold, or cheek he'd ever kissed, or set of arms that took him in for a hug. Whether he felt it or not, his best friend would take up residence in all of those things because that was the way Nate always was. If you gave him just five minutes, he'd dare to change your whole life.

As I kept writing, I could almost feel Nate with me in the moment, the same Nate known to grab you tight and say something like, "Hey, I love them more than anything. My family. My friends. Ronny. And you've got to watch out for him. You need to show up for him. This is the real letter that needs to get delivered."

Nate's funeral was empty and full all at the same time. It's strange how a packed room can feel so empty when the one person you're waiting for doesn't show up. We all wrote messages of good-bye to Nate onto leather baseballs and threw them into the hole in the ground. You could hear them thud against the casket. Nothing about that whole day felt like good-bye to me—you never really get to say good-bye to the shakers of this planet. Someone is always bringing up their names.

When I handed Ronny the letter at the funeral he took me in for a hug without saying anything more. A few days later, he took me in for another as we watched two of our best friends get married. I wore the green dress with the dancing blue tulle. He wore a gold tie. We matched. We sat together at our table, scraping potatoes around the plate and talking with old friends who had no idea we were missing someone that Saturday night. And when one of those typical country songs, about long lives and thick romances and sunsets and all those cliché things, came on, tears started coming down my face. I watched a father dance his daughter around the room.

"It's just unfair," I whispered to Ronny, knowing he would understand what I meant. I pushed my chair in closer to him. "He should have all the stuff in this song."

"No, no," Ronny said to me. "You can't cry right now, you know Nate would call you out if he saw you crying at the table."

Without hesitation, he stood up to pull his key chain from his back pocket and unclipped an extra Relentless Against Cancer bracelet from the chain. He slid the white band onto my wrist.

"Come on," he said, holding out his hand. "We are going to do this for him." And just as the country song faded out and the lights in the venue dimmed, I placed my hand into Ronny's and he led me out onto the dance floor.

This Is a Story About Swimming

I have this real and sturdy belief that one day in the fateful future Don Miller and I will sit down on some sort of wraparound porch with peach shutters and slug sweet tea together. I don't even know if he likes sweet tea. I guess I'm holding out hope he does. And I'll get to say thank-you to him for some of the words he wrote. Specifically, I'll get the chance to tell him how much it meant to me to read these words off the page: *We don't know how much we are capable of loving until the people we love are being taken away, until a beautiful story is ending.*

It opened up my eyes as I threw myself into the love letters harder than ever before after Nate passed away. I think I grew an extra compartment in my heart or something when he was gone, nearly like he tore into me and opened my eyes to people who were seeking answers for the pain. Some had been waiting for years. Some were ready to give up. I never knew I had any real capacity to love those people, to look them in the eye and find some sort of commonality between the two of us. But together, we were in the "Never Club." This secret club they have no idea I initiated them into. The Never Club is the bunch of us who have tried and failed and are still figuring out how to carry the word *never* like a watering jug. It's those of us who are just trying to get over the hump of that word. Never getting back together. Never seeing you again. Never getting to tell you I like the way the color blue looks on you. It's such a pretty word and it sometimes makes me wish it meant something different, like "specks of fallen gold on the windowsill" instead of "No, I won't be seeing you any longer. And that just hurts."

Kate was one of those people. One of the newest members in the Never Club. I met her one week after Nate passed away. She came to me in the form of an e-mail, so someone might read this and just roll their eyes and say I haven't really "met" her, but that's the thing about the Internet—she's a matchmaker in the sense she stitches hearts together when otherwise the elements of miles, and different states, and time zones would keep two similar souls from ever swapping stories like trading cards.

I've just accepted the fact my life will always be one where I meet people over the Internet and I allow them to change me. Even if they have fake profiles, I still give people the benefit of the doubt and I let them walk into my life and see me for who I really am. And I get on planes to see them. And I move to new cities to spend time with them. And I will probably have a Twitter table at my wedding that no one over the age of fifty is going to understand but I'll just keep the secret tucked inside of my cheeks: it is possible to meet best friends, and life partners, and God's children through 140 characters or less.

So when I tell you that I met Kate, I really mean when I read her words, it was as if we were sitting at one of those high-top tables in the middle of Starbucks, tucked over by a big glass window overlooking city streets at lunchtime, and we'd already drowned the rest of the world out.

She wrote to me that her mother had passed away in January of that year. I sat at my desk in my office and spread my fingers out wide to count the months . . . *January, February, March* . . . Tapping each finger down as I counted, I realized it had been ten months since she lost her mother. The culprit, the villain, the thief—whatever you want to call it—was lung cancer.

"It has been a difficult year for me, filled with tears and terrible firsts . . . ," she wrote. "First Valentine's Day without a card from her, first Easter without a silly care package full of Peeps and jelly beans, first summer without her." She could sense her mother being sucked out from the world by the emptiness of her own mailbox.

I wanted to warn Kate it was only going to get worse, probably before it got better. That's just the way the holiday season acts when you miss someone. The leaves fall. The weather chills. And we all start recognizing the pockets of this earth that still keep someone who isn't here anymore. The memories hide, like rail-thin slivers of children, behind Frank Sinatra ballads and slow-moving Christmas carols. It's as if the air gets colder and we start saying things we never thought to say when the sunscreen was out—*I miss you. And I wish you were here. And why can't you just be here? It's not fair. Life is fine. It's good, even. But I don't miss you any less.*

When the sympathy cards first rolled in for Kate, she felt this overwhelming need to thank others for their condolences. Like it would be some form of closure for her. So she bought a box of cards and a pretty sheet of stamps. They sat there. Untouched. Then she bought another box. Again, they went unwritten upon. And so she bought another box—this time with smaller cards. She figured that smaller cards would be less intimidating. Still, the cards went untouched. Finally, one day when she was sitting across from a friend who'd lost her father ten years earlier, nearly maniacal about needing to mail out these cards, her friend stopped her and just said no. She told Kate she didn't need to write a single card. People, naturally, understood. She didn't need to thank people for sending "sorry for your loss" cards in the mail. It was just time to deal with the loss.

Kate wrote that now she had boxes and boxes of cards that no longer fit their intended purpose. *I want to let them go*, she wrote to me. *And now I know how.* She'd already begun taking the boxes of stationery and leaving love letters all throughout the crooks and curves of Washington, DC, in honor of her mother, a woman who would have loved the love letter project and swallowed it whole.

As I read her e-mail, I remembered a verse I'd stumbled onto earlier that week. It was in the 126th Psalm. *Those who sow in tears will reap the songs of joy.* Mind you, I am not a verse giver. I can smother you with pretty words and adjectives all day but dealing out verses is not my jam. "Hannah gave me a really great verse today," said no one, ever. Anyway, I gave Kate the verse.

There was just something so beautiful, to me, about the thought of someone with their hands and knees sunk deep in the dirt, sowing crops with their tears. Their sweet, glistening tears. And the eventual songs of joy that would come storming through the fields to find them. The line threw me off. I guess I'd just gotten into the habit of not looking for beauty in the Bible. After years of looking toward the book for rules, I stopped believing there was anything in there to make my jaw drop.

Sow into tears, I wrote. *Kate, I think that is what you will do when you begin writing these love letters. You will sow into the tears. I can only imagine the way it must pulse and ache to not have your mother anymore . . . but sow into your sorrow and give it to others who need it as well.*

I clicked "send."

From outside the scene, you would have seen me sitting there in my cubicle beside a cactus one of my coworkers got for me because he knew I wasn't capable of keeping much more than that alive (and even though it is nearly impossible to kill a cactus, I knew the thing was dead already). The minutes after I sent that e-mail looked ordinary. And yet I couldn't move. I could not do much more than sit there, amazed to the point of waiting for the goose bumps to fade from my arms. I had no clue my little idea of scattering love letters could mean that much to someone.

Something inside of me shifted. I could feel it. It was some sort of turning point. I looked down at my hands, already knowing how very small they were. I laughed. It was a great, big belly laugh that shocked me when it rose out of me. I was so happy. And then, when the laughter stopped, I just kept staring down at my hands until I let out a whisper that only I and the dead cactus heard: "This is beyond me. This is so far beyond me."

A month later, I was standing in the middle of the locker room of my town's gym. It was five a.m. The moon was still out. I went to plug my earbuds into my phone to start my workout and noticed a message waiting for me on Facebook. It was from a girl in my town named Lauren. Lauren and I knew each other in high school. As with most people from our small town, I would say Nate was a common thread between us. Whether he'll ever know it or not, he still binds us closer in his absence than most people will ever manage to do through their presence.

Lauren—like a lot of young people in our friends' circle—tumbled into a drug addiction when we all went off to college. It felt like this secret we were all keeping, the thing we never talked about, how drugs were swooping in and causing a lot of destruction in our small circle. It was strange because painkillers were a bigger issue than any of the adults ever knew or understood. A lot of beautiful boys and beautiful girls lost the light in their eyes for a really long time. It was strange to watch friends get high, one by one. It was strange to know pills were going around in our circles. It was strange to think some people wanted to be numb and now we had all these options of how numb and how drunk and how high we could be. It was like friends you loved could become strangers in front of your eyes. Sometimes it felt like you were writing letters to people who were standing right beside you. It was like someone was right next to you and yet they never got the message the postman carried away from you that read, *I miss you. I miss the way you used to be before the party started. You were remarkable. You're still remarkable to me. Nothing will ever change the things I want for you. Please come home soon.*

I found out in the Facebook message that Lauren was in Delray Beach, Florida, in a halfway house beside what she called "other beaten down should've, could've, would've women."

She wrote to tell me she was trying. She would show up to meetings on time. She kept her phone in her bag to pay attention. She would listen to the messages in the meetings. I felt like she was sitting beside me, like our shoulders were touching, and I could watch her head fall into her hands when she told me she lived with the insurmountable guilt that she wasn't at Nate's funeral because she couldn't stop trying to kill herself on a daily basis with the needle and the spoon. The real enemy was herself. She couldn't stop fighting herself.

She wrote that this holiday season, two dining room tables would have empty seats at them. Two families would have broken hearts sitting between the turkey and the cranberry sauce. Nate's family—because God chose him. Her family—because for too long she refused to choose God.

At the end of the message, she wrote there was probably a long line of worthy candidates for love letters who should go ahead of her. She didn't think she was worth the stationery or the stamps. But if I could, would I write her a love letter? Would I send it to her at that halfway home?

I never did make it into the gym that day. I grabbed my jacket from the locker. I went home. I lay down on the floor. And I cried hard— really hard—into the IKEA carpet. I ugly-cried the thready guts out of that IKEA carpet. They were the kind of tears you have to get out of you through slow and ugly sobs because keeping them inside of you will make you go crazy. I just remember my mother telling me those kinds of tears will rip you apart if they stay inside of you.

"Sometimes it's not good enough to just cry," she said. "Tears can feel like a wimpy thing. One day it was so bad I went walking in the woods. And when I got to the point where all the trees were surrounding me, I started howling like a wolf. I was standing around all these trees crying out, 'Awooooooooooo, awooooooooooo.'"

Long, slow howling that started and stopped and started all over again. I think my mother is right though; madness like that can't stay inside of you. You have to get it out of you. Whatever this thing was inside of me, I wanted it to release. I just wanted it to go.

I cried for what I could not hide from anymore, what Lauren made me see. I cried because sometimes no matter what you try to hide behind—letters or texts or e-mails or a busy schedule—life still finds a way to barrel through all the distractions. And life still hurts. Even though it's beautiful. Even though there are quiet moments that leave you breathless, wondering if it will be this good again, life still hurts. And people you love still get broken. And maybe Lauren's message was too real for me in that moment, maybe it was tethered too close to my own brother—the one I never really talked about. The one I tried to

ignore because it would just be easier than facing the fact I couldn't fix
him. I couldn't play God to the situation and my prayers weren't working and I was hurt. That doesn't mean you should just walk away. You
can't just choose to only keep people in your orbit if they are perfect
and promise never to hurt you or leave you. If one of us walks away,
that makes it easier for all of us to walk away. And this whole life thing
cannot possibly be about just walking away when it gets hard or when it
doesn't unfold how we want it to.

When I got home from work that night, I noticed a long,
skinny envelope on the kitchen table. It was addressed to me. I'd never
seen the handwriting before but as I looked at the return address, it all
fit right into place. Ronny. He was writing back to me.

Dear Hannah,

*A few months ago you told me of this love letter idea of
yours. Right off the bat, I knew it would be a good idea. I mean,
with all that is wrong in this world, who would not want a love
letter?*

*I didn't think I would ever need a love letter though. From my
perspective, I was sure there were people more deserving than
me. My life was steady, and it was simple enough. Great family.
Great friends. And I got to play baseball. Who had it better than
me? Then I got the call. It was 2 p.m. Monday. March 30, 2009.
It was sunny outside and I was in my car, just got out of class.
What do I tell him? That I am here for him? That I'll be in his
corner? That he is too strong to let this beat him? For the first
time in my life, I remember not having any confidence in talking
to him. All I could do was reassure him, yet I could not reassure
myself.*

*I had no idea what to do. Never have I been so depressed,
angry, upset, miserable in my entire life. The next 30 months I
did whatever I could. I spent weeks in New Jersey at a time. I
went to every event. I always talked to him when he needed it.*

I did everything I could to be there for him. And I wish I could have done more.

When Nate's dad called me that morning, I knew. I had been having these dreams for probably three weeks. Every dream was the same. I always started the dream with Nate. I remember seeing him. By the end of the dream, he was gone. I would call out his name, call him on the phone. The dreams are spacey in my mind but I distinctly remember waking up and thinking Nate was gone, even though he was at home in New Jersey. Maybe that was God telling me his time was going to be soon. I don't know.

I do know that the last weeks have been the worst of my life. I miss him every day. I think about him every day. They say it gets easier as time moves on. I don't think so. I am crying thinking about him right now like the time I cried when Nate's dad called me and told me to get to the hospital, because Nate wasn't going to be OK.

I never thought I would need a love letter. I'm too tough, not emotional, and not a pretty boy. Love letters are for women who need reassuring. You proved me very, very wrong. I read the letter you gave me after I read the eulogy every night before I go to sleep. It has not left my nightstand since the day I got back to school. I read it, and I feel better. I feel like a blanket has been wrapped around me on a cold night. I feel like that moment when you get into a hot shower on a winter morning, most important, I feel love. I can feel you holding my hand as I read it. I can see your smile. And I can hear your voice in my head, narrating the card for me. I look forward to reading it every night. Sometimes, it literally gets me through the day.

I told you it was a good idea, I knew it was. But in no way could I ever think a love letter could make me feel whole again. And now I know how powerful those letters are. This idea may not make you a millionaire, it may take up a lot of your time, and sometimes, I am sure you think you are in over your head. Just know, Hannah, that what you do is important. Because I know there are people *like me who read their letter every night. I guarantee it. Your words give people so much hope and it makes them feel love, in their own unique way. You can't ever stop writing. Your words in the time of misery and despair are too beautiful to go unwritten. People need these letters. I need your letters.*

In all that you've done for others, has anyone written a love letter to you before? They're magical. They pick you up when you are feeling low, or they just put you in a better mood. I got my second letter from you today and I will cherish it like I do my first. Here is my feeble attempt to write you one:

Hannah,

You need to know that you are an amazing person. What you do with your letters is inspirational. You help so many people, I'm sure many more than you will ever know. You are special, funny, kind, and just remarkable in how you approach your day to help others. Whenever you feel down, people are here for you and always will be. Keep writing. Don't ever stop. You have saved me from drowning in my own misery, and I will always be grateful. I will always remember what you did for me.

Love,
Ron

Not the best letter but a pretty good attempt. I hope if you felt anything by reading that, then times it by 1,000,000, and that's how people feel when they read a love letter from you, at least I know that is how I feel.

Thank you for everything you do, Hannah, you've helped me so much. I love you. I miss you. I will see you soon. Keep writing. Ron

P.S. I swim for brighter days, despite the absence of sun. Choking on salt water, I'm not giving in—I swim.

I wrote back to Lauren. Two weeks later, I sent my letter sailing into whatever mailroom caught all the notes meant for the "should've, could've, would've" women Lauren claimed lived there. First, I told her she was wrong. I could not have disagreed with her more when she labeled herself and a slew of other vibrant women as the ones who never stepped out there and did something brave or noble. I told her she was never made for that tiny of a box. The God she wrote about made her for dancing and for words too eloquent to say with more than a whispered voice and for tinsel delicately strewn on the branches of baby evergreens and for Frank Sinatra songs that make you weep at a wedding because love is just beautiful like that. I told her sometimes I don't even like writing the word *God* into letters because I understood when people didn't like reading it. Seeing those three letters there, I understood when they would say they couldn't believe in Him or believe He was good. But, at the very same time, I couldn't sit in any waiting room or stand in any grocery checkout line, or do much of anything in a given day, without admitting I probably need something bigger than my own body to steer my life. Whether people believe in something or not, I think the consensus might be the same for everyone: Something feels uneasy about the world we're living in today. Something feels off center and out of sorts.

You hear about children being trafficked and movie theaters being shot up. Your mind is marred by the thought of what it would feel like to suddenly be forced to the ground, your torso crushing the bag of buttered popcorn beneath it while a masked figure opens fire on you and all the other people who paid $11 that night to block out realities like this one with a big screen.

I look at all the pain, suffering, and fragments of insanity that riddle the nightly news and it just makes me run toward God instead of away from Him. Add an extra layer of heartbreak, dishonesty, and a loneliness that crashes into you on a Friday night and stays curled up at your ankles until morning, and it all feels like a recipe for wanting to do anything but look in the mirror and say, "It's on you, buddy. You get to save the world today."

I know when I get real with myself, and I actually look at the world

I'm growing up in, I want a savior. I'm sure of that. On most days I could not tell you what coffee I want, what train I want to take, or the jacket I want to wear, but I've always ached for a savior. The kind who gets right up close to your face and says, "Babycakes, this ain't your battle. Stand back, I'm here now."

I ended the letter by telling her she needed to swim. Just like Ronny told me, I was passing the message along. It was a reminder to be strong. It was a call to push forward, even when she wanted the weight of things to hold her back.

It was the only message I could think to give back to Lauren. She had to learn to move her arms. She had to learn to kick her feet. She had to learn to hold her breath beneath the water. And then she would be swimming. Swim, swim, swim. It was an anthem. It was a chance to live. I ended the letter with just those words:

Lauren—please swim.

A Pretty Thing Called "Us"

In the months that trailed into the holiday season, there was a lot of work. I'd work for eight to nine hours at my first job, take the train home to New Haven, and then set out to do another four hours of work at night. My friends and I can look back and joke that those were the Valleys of No Social Interaction, but I was in love, more than anything. I was in love with the work placed before me, and that was the best feeling in the world to me.

My routine became seamless. I'd head to the post office in the center of our small town every couple of days and unlock Box 2061. There, waiting for me, would be a long yellow slip of paper that was an indicator that there was too much mail to fit inside.

The postal service worker would emerge from the back room with either a heaping stack of letters, held tight together by elastic bands, or a mail crate. Sometimes two. I collected so many of those mail crates that I challenged my friend once to a mail crate sculpture-building contest. She looked at me for a second, blinked twice, and then said, "We're going out for a drink and some fresh air. Get rid of the crates."

But most nights I'd take those mail crates home with me and I'd sit on the floor and tear through letters, stacking them into piles and getting them ready to be mailed out. I read every single letter, scanning each one to make sure the content of the letter was decent.

Most people just stared at me blankly when I confirmed that yes, I did read every single letter, and then I would proceed to tell them about the influx of letters I would get every week from state penitentiaries. Apparently, somewhere in the Northwest, a rumor must have started that I am not just a girl who leaves love letters across New York City, but that I am actually a really highly regarded matchmaker, and if you were a prisoner, and you mailed me a letter with some of your favorite "pics," I would match you up with a dreamboat of a lady who didn't care if you still had ten years left to your sentence. I've gotten really good at writing the kinds of letters that say, *Dear Joshua, Thanks for the pics. I'm sorry that I am not actually a matchmaker.*

All that to say: Every letter was read. And then bundled up with a note on top that explained how hundreds of people around the world had come together to write and arrange this bundle that was now sitting in the hands of someone who wasn't expecting to get mail beyond bills and coupons that day.

I learned so much about people when I would sit on the floor, cross-legged, with a cup of tea beside me and just read those letters. I learned so much about humanity as I got to read other people's poetic and not-so-poetic scraps of honesty and regret and heartbreak as they tried their best to write a love letter that would carry someone somewhere else.

First off, I learned most of us are good. I know that's always up for debate, but it feels like, at the core, most of us are good. And we want to be better. And we aren't stuck in the mud so much as we think. A lot of us are just a few steps away from a breakthrough. Maybe all of us are just thirty seconds away from being different people today.

We lose. We fight for things. We lose the fight for things. We fail. We forget birthdays (strangely way more than we used to before Facebook) and we forget the names of people we really should have remembered. We get lost. Sometimes we don't show up at all.

We make mistakes. We hurt the people who mean more than the world to us. And we get hurt.

We get rejected and talked about behind our backs. Many of us have been the people others point to and laugh at. We fail tests. We oversleep. We break promises. We break hearts. We keep people for too long, long after they've served a real purpose in our lives. We let go, even when we know we only want to hold on a bit longer. We doubt ourselves. We celebrate. We drink too much. We laugh too little. We fall hard. For boys with sullen blue eyes and girls with rips in their tights. We are cheated on. We cheat. We get left standing in the middle of doorways, and train stations, and restaurants before the appetizers have even come out. We do elaborate and crazy things for people who make our hearts feel like they're coming up through our throats. We are lovers. And we are hopeful.

We are the life of the party and we aren't, all at the same time. We are surrounded by people and we are more alone than we have ever felt. We get older—and we sometimes think that's terrifying and we sometimes think it's beautiful.

It's a lot of "we." A lot of "we" combating all the times I ever closed myself off and said, "I feel so alone in this. I feel like no one knows what I am feeling." It turns out we do, more often than we don't.

Maybe trying to pluck out the differences, the unique things that set us apart, wasn't supposed to be the point. Maybe it's something so much mightier to stand knee-deep in the solidarity of the things that make us not so far off from one another, the things that make us nod our heads in unison and whisper, "Me too . . ."

In February of that year, I was hired by a boutique in SoHo to write love letters for a Valentine's Day campaign in New York City. To be honest, I was shocked to get the call from the public relations company that wanted to hire me because I'd never done an event before and they wanted me to recruit some "professional love letter writers" to sit with me in the storefronts of these high-end boutiques strewn across New York and write letters to customers. I got off the call thinking, *Is there even such a thing as professional love letter writers? What should I even look for?*

I had no clue what to expect as I rallied a team of eight people. It wasn't until I was sitting at the front of the store wearing a white tee with a demented cupid on the front of it (apparently there was an error with the T-shirt printing that day) that I realized how terribly awkward it is for a shopper to come by, fill out a card about their loved one, and have a complete stranger write the letter. They'd sit in the seat across from me and they'd circle attributes like *confident, sexy, handsome, caring,* and my letter writers and I basically had to construct a fill-in-the-blank letter for them to take home with their shopping bags and tuck the bright red envelope into a place where their lover could find it. I can imagine it sparked really normal conversations when women would open up the letters and then ask their husbands and boyfriends, "What other woman wrote me a love letter?" To this day, I think nothing says "I love you passionately and sometimes I want to rip your clothes off" quite like a complete stranger, who has no actual personal attachments to your love life, putting it all out there on pretty, store-branded stationery. Regardless, we had a lot of fun. And I think we all get to qualify as professional love letter writers now.

At the end of our second day of professional letter writing, a woman walked into the store carrying multiple bags. They weren't shopping bags, like the kind that looked like she'd just been swiping her card up and down Madison Avenue. They were bag bags. Like, she looked like a bag lady. She came right up to the table I was sitting at and took two slips of paper.

"I'm coming back for my love letters," she said, and proceeded to walk around the store. I watched her going through the racks of orange monogrammed dresses with Target bags on her arms and I couldn't help but think she didn't really fit the mold of the store. It was high-end. But she proved me wrong when she came back to the table a half hour later with a bag from the store.

"I told you I'd be back," she said, placing her bags down and sitting in the chair across from me. "I need two love letters. One is for my boyfriend and one is for my ex-husband." She slid the two sheets over to me.

For the next ten minutes, she asked me questions as I wrote. Where are you from? How old are you? How did all this happen? Where did the love letters come from? It was like playing twenty questions while trying to focus on what words to give her ex-husband.

"Compassionate?" I asked, lifting up the sheet that described him.

"Hmmm," she answered. "Definitely. Sometimes you can still be best friends even when you know staying with each other would have hurt too much."

She went back to asking me questions and I looked up a minute later to see her on the other side of the table, taking notes on everything I was saying.

The questions continued. I remember her asking me three things I'd learned. I'm pretty certain I told her I learned people are just looking for ways to be good. Really, most of the time. There's a reason why certain videos go viral—the ones of people showing up for one another through random acts of love. There's a reason why we watch them and pass them on. I think we all sort of want what's there, hidden behind the moments on the screen. We want to believe that kind of love and goodness is still out there. We want to hold out hope for the moments that push and whisper, "The world isn't about you. And love still wins."

"One more question," she said, putting the pen down and looking right at me. "Have you always been this way?"

At first I didn't know what she meant—had I always been what way? But she clarified before I could even open my mouth. "I guess the better question is, is it truthful? Is all that you are doing real?"

Before I knew what to really say in response, I just started rambling about growing up but never actually feeling like I fit in. I told her about constantly being sorry for the fact I'm not a small-talker. I don't care about the weather. I'm not one to lead the crowd in movie-quote recitations. I haven't seen nearly enough movies to make me that girl, but if you feel like reciting the United Nations Declaration of the Rights of the Child then maybe, just maybe, I'd somehow be the life of your party (that's a proclamation that gets me a little rowdy). And I just wanted to fit in. As pathetic as it sounds, I just wanted to fit in. Because I think most people want that.

I told her about how for the longest time, I let the voices of other people dictate to me. I just wanted so desperately to be something for someone else—whatever that looked like. At one point, I tried so hard to wedge myself into a box while living in New York after a group of girls from college ripped me apart online for posting this on Facebook: *If I have only one quality for the rest of my life I hope that it is foolish . . . Foolish enough to think that I can make a difference in this world and I can go out there to do the things that cannot be done.* They'd pulled me apart for that statement, declaring that I should shut up about wanting to change the world and just go out there and do it. I'd been friends with the girls the year before. And while it amounts to nothing in the grand scheme of things, I think it pulls at the anxiety that I know I don't carry alone: What will people think of me if I try to stand out? What will people think if I just try to do something?

A lot of us might never reach the point of realizing that by standing out, by actually being the people we say we want to be, we get to set ourselves free. Not in all capacities, but definitely in some.

"I guess I just never understood why they had to do it," I said. "I wasn't angry. And it wasn't like it was the end of the world or something."

"Did it hurt you? Did it sting when they thought you weren't truthful?"

"You know," I said, "it used to. It was like I carried them with me wherever I would go. It made me feel wrong."

"But you did something anyway," she said. Her eyes didn't leave me.

"I guess you keep pushing until you feel invincible," I told her.

Just a few minutes later, she was gone. She picked up her notes and her two love letters—one for her boyfriend and the other for her compassionate ex-husband—and she left the store. I'll never know what she did with those notes. I guess I'll always wonder. On top of that, I'll definitely always wonder if she would have told me what she was going to do with the notes if I had just asked.

As I was riding the train home that night, I couldn't help but think about the woman. How I sat there and wrote her love letters while she asked me questions I probably needed to be asked. But more than anything, I realized every question she asked me was like a confirmation that I'd somehow become a different person without even realizing it.

I was no longer the same girl who used to tell herself the biggest lies: You can't make a difference. The world is too big. Your hands are too small. That isn't true. It really isn't. But that girl would never know that until she stepped out there and learned how to forget about herself and all the things that had ever made her heart break. She needed to learn to sit with herself so much that she could stare strangers in the eyes with hellfire confidence and say, "I know exactly what sits at the root of me. And I'm afraid of it no longer."

She needed to go out there and find out for herself that there is no right or wrong way to do this life thing. There is only knowing what she wants and stopping apologizing for wanting those things in the process. And on that journey—the one with fewer apologies—she needed to pay more attention to the dotted lines, not just the destinations. The dotted lines are the silent, unspoken victories of this lifetime.

All those dotted lines were just the parts of the story where she would get on the ground and get her hands dirty with the mess of it all. The mess and the glory of other people's hearts and heart songs. She would learn it would take grit, and guts, and courage to make a difference. But the world will always need people who care enough to make a difference, so she needed to not miss her casting call.

It would take all of that, and some things I'll probably never talk about, and a bag lady in SoHo to realize the girl who always believed her hands were too small was gone. The girl was gone, and all that was left in her place was other people.

Other people. Like the girl who e-mailed me that she was waiting for a paper to print in her college's library one morning when a boy came up to her. They started talking and she realized they had a class together. They had similar upbringings and a common thread: he was a heroin addict in recovery and her boyfriend had struggled with the same sort of battle.

The boy didn't show up at the next class. She didn't see the boy for a while. One day before class, she was walking through the hallways and she came across a love letter on the floor. She picked it up to read it. The letter was about God and how He felt about her. She already knew these sorts of things and wished the letter could have been spared for someone who actually needed the words.

The boy showed up in class that day. She asked him where he'd been. He told her it was bad. He didn't really want to talk about it. With trembling hands at the end of the class, she handed the boy the letter, saying, "Here, maybe you need this right now." She told him to look up a song called "Hello, My Name Is" by Matthew West. Her boyfriend would listen to it when he was doing badly as well.

A week or so later, somehow the boy got her number and he sent her a message. He told her he believed she was meant to give him that letter that day. It was meant for him. He'd been second-guessing his strength and getting weaker. He read the letter. He broke down to the song she recommended on the ride home. "You completely changed everything," he told her. "I have been doing well ever since."

In the girl's e-mail, she told me she'd believed in God for fourteen years. But in those fourteen years, and with one love letter, this was the first time she actually saw Him.

And then there was this one man whom we found out about because his friend approached us and told us he had tried to commit suicide. He posted a Facebook status as a way to say good-bye to friends and family. I have to believe that was some sort of cry for help but I don't really know. All I do know is that we got a sorority to rally together and write him notes and cards and send him all sorts of glittered, lovely things that feel delicate when your fingertips touch them. We didn't hear back about the man for a really long time. The woman who requested the love letters reached back out six months later to tell me the man who got the letters sleeps with them beneath his pillow every single night.

But maybe my favorite was Luke. Luke's daughter got a rush of surprise when she came home to her mailbox and saw a package waiting for her. She tore the thing open, wondering what it could be, and found all the cards and letters. She knew instantly. Love letters were arriving for her father. Her father was in his last round of chemotherapy and was having a rough morning when the bundle arrived. Together they sat for hours upon hours and read every last one.

Luke's daughter wrote, *We laughed, we cried, we reminisced, we cherished the moment. He was filled with so much energy after reading those letters—he's even decided to make a collage out of them, a project he's begun. He plans to frame the collage and hang it proudly on the walls of his office.*

And when Luke wrote to us—all on his own—he told us the truth: that even on days where the illness got so bad that he just wanted God to take him, he knew he couldn't go. Because now there were people all across the world who were praying when he was praying, hurting when he was hurting, and crying when he was crying.

Luke's story always makes me think of a soldier and his sister. The soldier had the dirt of both Afghanistan and Iraq deep in the grooves of his boots. PTSD hung on his shoulders like a cloak when he finally came home. We mailed him a big bundle of love letters. We didn't hear much for a while. And then one day he called his sister crying—sitting on the floor and unable to speak—over the letters strangers had sent, cheering for him. His sister told me in an e-mail that one small act renewed her faith in humanity.

And then there was Mary—a woman who was the queen of baking bread and making homemade doilies. She lost her best friend and her soul mate after sixty-nine years. And even when she tried to fill up her mind with busyness and the laughter of her grandchildren, there were still those days where it didn't matter how many rows she crocheted, she just wanted him back. Plain and simple. It hurt and she wanted him back.

And her granddaughter—young and fiery with ambition—could not bear to see her grandma Mary living in so much desperation and sadness. There was one time where she drove the forty-five minutes to see Mary just to sit at her kitchen table and hear her grandma say that she thought she wanted to let go now. She wanted to let go.

"The rain will stop." That's what the girl told her grandmother. Eventually, the rain would stop. It's all she could think to say at the time. That same girl wrote to us and collected letters for her grandma. She got to give them to her for Christmas. Mary read every single letter in her favorite chair that day. She gathered up her strength and wheeled her walker into the kitchen and made an announcement to the entire room that she was going to stick around now. She was going to read the letters over and over again and stick around.

And then there was Helen. Helen e-mailed me to tell me she'd grown up just a small country girl. She had a college degree but was forced to stop working because of a disability. She was fifty-one years old. She'd met her husband a little over four years ago. She wrote in the e-mail that the two only ever wanted to find unconditional love. They had each other now. They found what they both needed.

She was sitting in a doctor's office, waiting on another appointment, when she came across a story about the love letters. She took it home and she showed her husband the article. With financial issues and medical bills and so much on their shoulders, they couldn't possibly give back in the form of money. But when she read the article, she realized they had love. They could give love. So in the past few weeks they had begun writing love letters together and leaving them throughout the town as they would go about their days. They would leave them in the courthouse, in the park, and in the grocery store. Sometimes in odd places, like under a rock at the lake.

She told me she had one small wish for her life. She wanted to know the impact she made. She wanted to see someone touched and moved by her existence. One morning, after leaving a letter in the courthouse, she noticed someone pick up the letter. She watched the person share the letter with two other people. They cried as they read. *You gave me my wish*, she wrote. *I will never stop doing this as long as my old hands let me.*

Strangely, though, ever since this couple began leaving letters, people had started showing up randomly at their home and delivering food and clothes. They hadn't put it out there that they needed those sorts of things; people just started showing up. There had been several strange instances. She wrote that she didn't know what she believed in. She didn't know if it was God. She wasn't really sure what to call it. She just knew she believed in unconditional love. And that was really all that mattered.

When I wrote back to Helen, I stopped after I wrote down one paragraph. *I think whatever you choose to believe in, whenever you choose to believe in it, will reveal and unfold itself in time. It will give itself a name. It will make itself known to you, roaring on the inside like some sort of lion. And whatever that is, I truly hope it is tangled in love and not fear. That it is laced with dignity and nothing short of that. Because you deserve dignity, beyond anything else in this world. You deserve a God, and a faith, and a belief that finds you dignified at the core.*

That's what I was learning of God and of humanity in those days—this whole thing was about dignity. And restoring it where it had been lost. And victory and all the better things that were always there before we learned to give our little lives away to weaknesses and lies. All of it is a process. Love, especially, is a process. Whether that's loving God or another sticky human, it's hard. It's doors unlocking. It's windows breaking. It's the discovery of new rooms inside of yourself. It's the dark. And it's the light. And it's dark and light all scrambled into one. At the root of it, it's a slow, trusting, building process that starts with letting someone in.

I want to believe it all comes down to truth. And if you've ever loved someone in a way where it seems the oxygen is rushing out of the room when they walk in, then you know certain truths. Certain unchangeable truths about love: You want to give them everything in your world. And you want to give them everything outside of your orbit. And if they need the morning to come, you want to be that morning for them. And if they need the stars, you want to be those fragments of light too. And you just want to sit by them. And you just want to know they're doing well. And you just want to witness their greatness, the moment they're finally shining out. You want to be right there next to them for that. And you want that honor of being in their life.

It's crazy because I feel this way about people who have broken me and given up on me, but I used to think it was just too wild to believe in a God who might feel that same way, that very same way, about a little thing like me.

I know I'll change in the next few years, and I'll grow up more as I go, but for right now I believe in that sort of love. And I believe in a religion that doesn't sit pretty in the church so much as it rages beautifully when it's out on the sidewalks. In the hands of people who know how to love on others right. I believe in people who use every shred of their composure to go out of their way to tell someone else how very striking they are. No matter where you've been or what you've done, someone should have told you that before. I believe in whatever it is, whatever uncommon kind of love, that causes us to stop—square in the middle of our busiest days—and show up for someone else. To take someone's hand, whether it is a familiar one or not, and say, "There is something more waiting for you. You have much bigger work to do. That work is so big, so wide, so far, that it laughs at all those weaknesses that tried to hold you back before.

"So take my hand and don't look back. You were made to carry bigger things than the small stories you tell of yourself. So say it as we go: Bigger than this. Bigger than this."

The stories kept coming. They keep coming every day. And with each one I read, there is less urgency to tie the thing up with a white bow or look for the happy ending. I'm learning that most stories don't get those pretty white bows. And that's for a lot of reasons, but the few I know are these: Sometimes the story becomes too big, too beyond you, to tie every little micro-shred of it together in one place. There are always going to be a few you'll miss. And sometimes, you are crazy and you are foolish to think you get to end the story. That's the one I'm going with. I'm going with that and a line from T. S. Eliot I heard the other day over a banana-and-chocolate crepe: "You are the music while the music lasts." Those words fell out of the mouth of a friend of mine and I think they are just so perfect. So perfect for this, these moments when the white bows and the endings won't do.

"You are the music while the music lasts." The point is not to search throughout the symphony and figure out how it works. It isn't to figure out where it ends and another form of music begins. That would ruin the reason life floods the music all around us: So we can just stand rich and amazed in the center of it and get swallowed up by something so much bigger than ourselves. Cling to the notes of others from time to time. Find good dance partners. Take off our shoes and just practice dancing barefoot, inside of the stories that will outlive us all. Inside of the music, while it lasts.

I think that's all there is. That's the ending I have to a thing I was crazy to think I could end on my own: for right now, we are the music. We've been given this space. I want to get better at dancing barefoot on the ground.

When I sit down in coffee shops in the years to come and wrap my fingers around massive porcelain mugs—the kind that are perfect for sipping cappuccino—and tell people this story from start to finish, I know there will be those details I always include. Every story has them. My friend Preston calls them the tent-pole moments—the parts of the story where you evidently grew and changed and developed. The stand-alone moments of any good story where you become a different person than the one you were the day before.

And then there will be the details I don't always share with everyone. They'll come in quietly when the moment in the conversation is just right. Like the day I realized that while sending letters is great, and calling someone from time to time is good, you really should just show up, if you can. If you are able to show up, then show up.

I didn't learn that lesson until the day I showed up at Lauren's door, several months after I'd sent the letter to her halfway home in Delray Beach, Florida. She had come home. Sober. And my heart felt like it was going to burst straight through my chest when she took me to tour a workshop she'd made for herself in her basement. A place where she concocted all these crazy combinations of wax and pasty goops to make soap. She'd come home and she'd started a soap-making company. And she was actually really gifted at it. I could see in her eyes and in the confident way she showed me every part of the process that she was happy. Really happy. She handed me a business card as a way to tell me she had decided to swim. She'd kicked her arms and her legs and decided to swim. We sat at her kitchen table that day while the Keurig machine hissed in the background and inched our way into talking about everything we never really talked about before, or maybe it was just that we didn't have the words for those sorts of things back then. We talked about my brother. We talked about why it was good to be home. I asked her if I could ever share her story with people. I knew it was her story and I wanted to respect that it was personal.

"Yes," she told me without a second thought.

"Are you sure? I don't want to cause you any kind of pain."

"Of course you can share this story. I am proud of it. There's a part you didn't see," she told me, sitting back in her chair as she spoke. "What you didn't see is that asking you for a love letter was me admitting I needed help. That I didn't have anyone else to turn to. I needed help and I am really proud I finally stopped trying to do it all on my own. I will always be proud of that moment."

Just hearing that meant everything to me. More than love letters. More than however big the organization would grow. I got into the car that night and I remember whispering to the steering wheel, as if it were a microphone to God, "More of this. Please, just more of this."

It's days like that one I know I will remember, or the day Ronny and I sat side by side on two bar stools with margaritas the size of our heads before us. There'd been some time since Nate passed. We still wrote letters back and forth. Sitting there, my finger circling the rim of the glass for any last shreds of salt, I got real quiet.

"Do you believe in God?" I asked him.

"I'm not really sure," he told me. "But if I do, I don't know how He could let a thing like this happen."

I didn't know that either—why He allowed heartbreak, and death, and grief to sweep in. I still haven't found the answers for that. I doubt I ever will.

I know I could have said something more. But I also knew nothing I said would ease his hurt. That would have to fade in time. And the hurt was so small—just a tiny moment in that meeting space—compared to the ways I could just look at Ronny and be proud. He was back at law school. He was looking more and more like Nate every time I saw him in a way that would make you laugh if you knew the two. So I didn't say anything else.

It was just a moment in a world where it's hard to imagine there used to be a time when moments were just moments. It was just him and me and this space of time. From the next bar stool over, he shot me a grin that was just for me to pocket. I remember being so content in that moment that I didn't want to capture it and I didn't want to filter it. I just wanted to learn to live inside of it.

But above all stories within this story, I will always try to find a way to weave Matt from Ohio into the conversation. Truthfully, that's all I really know about him: His name is Matt. He is from Ohio. He e-mailed me one night about two years ago. I was coming off the train in New York City and I stopped at the top of the subway station stairs to read the message. Only four lines long, it still feels like the heaviest thing I've ever read.

Matt told me he was getting older. His family and he were all pretty disconnected, sort of like stars that go on shining for too long on their own—never pausing to see they could make constellations together this whole time. He didn't have very many friends. He was starting to believe he would never make an impact and he'd never leave anything behind. He'd be forgotten. It was this secret, seeping fear that he would live and die and never make any noise.

At the end of his e-mail, he wrote these words, and I am still waiting for the day when they will stop giving me goose bumps: *Please keep doing what you are doing. Everyone is so afraid of what will happen when the screen shuts off.*

Funny thing about Matt from Ohio: he never left an actual e-mail address. The message was sent through a contact form with reply address attached. There was no way to write back to him. I looked. I hunted. I searched. But you can't do much with just a four-line e-mail written by someone with one of the most popular boy names in the history of boy names who happens to live in the state of Ohio.

What Matt from Ohio doesn't know is that he was the confirmation to my heart, and anything inside of me that's ever wanted to matter, that I would write this book. If anything at all, I would write this book just to hang on to the hope that he would maybe pick it up somewhere, like one of those first unsigned letters in New York City, and find this final letter waiting for him on the very last page.

Matt—wherever you are, thank you for this.

Dear Matt from Ohio,

"One true thing," my mother used to say to me. "Just start off by telling me one true thing, and then another true thing, and then another. And soon enough, you'll have said everything you needed to say."

So I guess it only makes sense to start this letter to you, the one I've been scripting in my head for years, by telling you one true thing about myself.

So here it is. Here it goes: I am afraid I will miss life. I am afraid I will miss the very thing we're always dissecting so adamantly in deep conversations and blog posts. I am afraid to look up suddenly and realize I missed the stitching of this lifetime, that I wanted so desperately to make a quilt and yet I never slowed enough to learn how to make a sturdy stitch.

That fear is just a culmination of little things: That I won't become who I've always wanted to be. That I won't remember to call when I know I should. That I will miss the things—little and big—that make other people stop in the middle of what they are doing to say, "That . . . that was absolutely everything. That made everything worth it." I want things like that. The things that make everything undeniably and unexplainably worth it.

I think you've probably been there too. And while I am only twenty-six, and I hate half the things I say after I say them, I think this whole thing isn't about being big or known or remembered. The world tries to prove that to us daily but it isn't. I think it's just about showing up. I think it's about choosing people when people are just so hard to choose. I think it's about saying things we know we will regret if we don't say them sooner. Fighting hard for the people who make us feel like they've swept all the oxygen out of the room. I think it's about remembering to commit to the small things. And remembering that love still wins. No matter how much we try to say that something else matters more than it, love still wins. We still want it most. It still keeps this broken world spinning. Somehow, somehow, it does.

I have a friend who tells me that you can either go through life with fistfuls of joy or you can survive it by the skin of your teeth, never once looking down at the blessings in your hands. I think maybe the brave ones ask themselves that question: Do I just want survival this week or do I want to become a part of someone else's history?

Do you want to become a part of someone else's history this week?

I don't think I imagined I would ever plant such a corny line right here. But yet you sent me a very short e-mail—probably a small task on your to-do list, two years ago, that you've long forgotten about—and that one e-mail shifted my entire history. For good. And I've carried your story into conversations with me. And I've talked about you in crowded rooms. And if you are out there, I just want you to know: You were wrong. You were wrong to think you'd be forgotten. And I was wrong to think people couldn't walk into our lives and shift our histories in an instant. Because you did that for me.

So I can't say it doesn't happen that way. I only get to say believing it could happen that way—that we actually play that deep of a role for every person we meet—might change everything: The postures we hold. The e-mails we send. Our morning interactions. The ways we bustle through the checkout line in Target. How we take care of the company we keep. All the little shreds of the day that never reach the to-do list but ultimately will prove whether you and I standing here—with gifted oxygen in our lungs—actually meant something.

Do small things. On repeat. And think about other people. I guess that's all that is left to say. Imagine what it might be like to live in a world full of people who often stop in the middle of a crowd and say, "I didn't know that person for long . . . I don't even know their whole name . . . but they are a piece of my history."

Do small things. On repeat. And think about others. I think that's it. That's all. I don't even worry anymore about becoming a piece of someone's history because (a) knowing isn't the point and (b) sometimes our greatest points of impact will be the kind we never come to know about.

And maybe that's the one true thing that drives every other true thing forward.

Sending light and love,
A girl just trying to find her way.

PS: Matt, I'm also afraid of what will happen when the screen shuts off. I think maybe we should go there anyway.

Acknowledgments

I decided to write these book acknowledgments from 10,000 feet up in the air. It's a Delta flight, I have a bag of pretzels to keep me going, and it feels symbolic to be so high up and looking down below. I mean, the world seems so small from up here when all you can see is specks. In that same vein, this book was written for all the people who have always reminded me that this was always about something so much bigger than me—I was always just the speck. Thank you for keeping me grounded and making me fly, all at the same time.

I give thanks especially to:

God. I owe you for all the beautiful things. I'm indecisive and I cry too much and I fall too hard and you paved a road for me anyway. May I never breathe in without thanking you first.

My incredible editors. Beth Adams and Amanda Demastus, thank you for helping me stop hiding behind pretty words and just let the truth speak for itself. You taught me how to search for victory in my words. Thank you also to everyone at Howard Books, for giving my book a home.

My fierce literary agent. Mackenzie Brady, I don't know what means more to me: how you found me and fought for me or that I know I can call you—before first dates and after hard wake-up calls—and I know you'll always pick up. Let's write lots of books together. Forever. Okay?

My first cheerleaders. Mom and Dad, thank you for teaching me not to settle for less than I was made for. You supported my individuality and my cowboy boots. It made all the difference. To my family and the Belvedere Heights, thank you for being my first readers. We've come a long way together. To my grandmother Baccu, I do this for you. Always.

My unofficial team of soundboards and editors. Heather Kirkpatrick, thank for waking me up to write at 5 a.m. every single morning and loving me regardless of my crankiness. Kelly Towart, thank you for going along with my plan to wear headlamps and sit in the middle of sketchy baseball fields at night while I read pieces of this manuscript to you. Jenna Bednarsky, thank you for letting me know this all was real and sweet and worth it.

The More Love Letters Team. You ladies are the glue and the goodness behind it all. Thank you for wearing all the hats and being my soundboards, writers, grammar checkers, movers, shakers, coordinators, and dreamers. You make me feel like a cool kid—a sappy and thankful, cool kid.

Most of this book was written in an office with black sheets tied up over the windows to keep out the daylight (I am super dramatic, I know) but I am thankful for the hospitality of the LaCoilles, the Samuelsons, and the Towarts for their couches and their desks and their kitchen tables. Carol, without you, this book would not exist.

To City Church in New Haven, Connecticut, thank you for just loving me. And letting me go. And teaching me that this life is not about holding on too tightly, it's about sending people out to where they need to be. You taught me miles mean nothing.

To Celia, Carleigh, Corey, Tammy, Lauren, Lindsey, Eryn, Jill, Tiffany, Leanna, and too many other girlfriends to list—I don't think enough words exist in the world to thank you for how you've made me feel invincible along this road. You are the gold and the laughter.

Nate, Ronny, and the Shatsoff Family, here's to just this—staying relentless for as long as we are down here dancing on the ground.

My communities. A big thank-you to all who gathered around me during the year in New York, before, and after—especially the women at the UPK, UN, Assumption College, Save the Children, She's the First, The Dancer's Studio, and Plywood. I was always afraid I wouldn't belong in this world. Thank you for kicking that fear in the face for me.

I can't resist thanking the coffee shops that let me be the mysterious writer girl in the bright, red cap throughout this writing process. Starbucks in North Haven and Taproom Coffee in Atlanta, I am indebted to you for your writing spaces, caffeine, and good strangers.

To the readers who've stayed with me this far, you helped me carve out a home and a voice on the Internet. I can only hope the future holds hundreds of coffee dates for us.

There are too many additional people to name who played a part in my becoming through countless tears, prayers, letters, 2 a.m. diner trips, sing-scream sessions to Taylor Swift ballads, yellow sweaters, lattes, old photographs, corsages, pancakes, sunflowers, and conversations that normally ended with "you're okay." You each deserve a life that never grows tired with blessing you. You know who you are.

The World Needs More Love Letters is a global community using the power behind social media to lift, empower, and mobilize individuals through tangible acts of love.

Started in 2011, the More Love Letters community leaves notes of support where people will find them and writes letters to people in need around the globe. Every month, bundles of letters are mailed to chosen recipients who've been nominated by family and friends.

More Love Letters is always looking for the people out there who are brave, passionate, and looking to do good in the world. Head over to MoreLoveLetters.com to the join the community of movers and shakers today.